Explorations

ALSO BY GILBERT HIGHET:

*The Classical Tradition: Greek and Roman Influences on
    Western Literature* (Oxford University Press, 1949)
The Art of Teaching (Knopf, 1950)
People, Places, and Books (Oxford University Press, 1953)
Man's Unconquerable Mind (Columbia University Press, 1954)
The Migration of Ideas (Oxford University Press, 1954)
Juvenal the Satirist (Oxford University Press, 1954)
A Clerk of Oxenford (Oxford University Press, 1954)
Poets in a Landscape (Knopf, 1957)
Talents and Geniuses (Oxford University Press, 1957)
The Powers of Poetry (Oxford University Press, 1960)
The Anatomy of Satire (Princeton University Press, 1962)

EXPLORATIONS

GILBERT HIGHET

NEW YORK · OXFORD UNIVERSITY PRESS · 1971

For HELEN

Voici des fruits, des fleurs, des feuilles et des branches,
Et puis voici mon coeur, qui ne bat que pour vous.

Acknowledgments

————————————————

MY WARM THANKS to those who have helped me in solving
questions and tracing references: notably my former pupil
Miss Doris Borrup (who gave me the story about the Shakespeare First Folio on p. 361), Professor Arthur E. Gordon, Mr.
Colin Roberts, F.B.A., Dr. William J. Ronan, Professor
William York Tindall, Mr. Eugene P. Sheehy (head of the
Reference Department of Butler Library in Columbia University) together with his courteous and efficient staff, the members of the Music Division of the New York Public Library,
and the researchers of *Horizon*.

Preface

———————————————

THIS IS a collection of essays on unusual books and odd people and the life of language and the art of writing.

They have never appeared in book form. Some of them were given as talks on the radio between 1952 and 1959 under the sponsorship of the Oxford University Press, New York, and were published as pamphlets by the Book-of-the-Month Club; several were printed in *Horizon* and other periodicals, whose editors I thank for permission to republish them here. All have been revised, many have been considerably expanded, some have been largely rewritten.

East Hampton, N. Y.   G.H.
January 1971

Contents

Forgotten Books

An Unwritten Book

ONE OF THE MOST painful things that can happen to an intelligent man is to think of an idea for a great book, to plan it, and then to be prevented from finishing it. Imagine discovering an important truth; imagine doing years of research and collecting vast quantities of information, making mistakes and correcting them, detecting mistakes in the work of others and avoiding them; imagine seeing the book as though it were completed, floating in your mind during a sleepless night— as Mozart said he had an opera finished, when he only had to put the notes down on paper; and then imagine realizing that, for some reason, the book could not be written and would never be written. It is like being full of music, and being banned from composing and playing and even singing. It is like being able to talk well and teach others, and then being thrown into solitary confinement. It is almost like being cast up on a desert island.

Something like this happened to an eminent man during the last thirty years of the nineteenth century. His book was to be *The History of Liberty*. Hundreds of people awaited it eagerly. Some of them had heard parts of it delivered as lectures. One of them at least—that great scholar Lord Bryce—said that he could never forget the tremendous experience of hearing the author sketch the outline of his unwritten book. But it was never completed: in fact, he never published any book whatever. Yet he was a learned and brilliant historian, and we must bitterly regret the loss of the masterpiece which perished with him. His name was John Emerich Edward Dalberg Acton, Lord Acton, and he died in 1902 after a lifetime of profound historical thinking.

His name sounds English. He was an English peer. But he had a Central European background and education, and was in fact half-German. He was rich: his income was something like £5,000 a year, which might correspond nowadays to about $50,000 after taxes. Yet he worked hard all his life, very hard, too hard: he seems to have died at least partly from overwork as professor of modern history at Cambridge University. There he helped to initiate a large project which he did not live to see completed: *The Cambridge Modern History,* a twelve-volume series covering the last four hundred years. He did not invent the idea, but he laid out the outlines, organized the production, and suggested the names of many of the experts who were called in to write its chapters. He did not live to see even a single volume published.

Personally he was a fascinating character: handsome, winning, a marvelous talker. Also he was very scholarly and very wise. It is possible for historians to know a great deal and put together thousands of facts, without having much wisdom or even common sense. It is possible to be deeply thoughtful without knowing the mass of facts which help to compose historical truth. Few men are capable of both. Acton was.

The most famous utterance of his wisdom is a saying which has more meaning for us today than it had for his own time.

Power tends to corrupt, and absolute power corrupts absolutely.

Is that a cynical saying? Americans have no reason to think so. It is the essence of the Constitution, which was drawn up in order to prevent the misuse of power (so common in old

Europe) and which was firmly based on the system of checks and balances. Interests must be balanced against one another. Excesses of emotion and excesses of force must be braked. The republic is designed to last for a long time, for much longer than any single crisis in its history, or the ambitions of any one of its parts. Only a well-balanced state, in which power, like a huge engine, is surrounded by as many safety devices as possible, can survive for long without frequent shattering upheavals, of which any one may be fatal, and—mark this—permanently fatal. Some of us do understand that power corrupts. For several generations we have been taking strong measures against the inevitable corruption fostered by financial power; and now we are becoming wary of the inevitable corruption fostered by organizational power.

The epigram about power is only one of many deep sayings uttered by Lord Acton. He was a Whig, not a Conservative; he was a liberal, not a radical of either extreme; and he opposed Conservatism just as he would have opposed the dictatorship of the working class called Communism, saying

> The danger is not that a particular class is unfit to govern. Every class is unfit to govern.

Commenting on one of our present dangers, the centralization of governmental power, he either coined or adapted the epigram that centralization means

> apoplexy at the center and paralysis at the circumference.

Restated, although less crisply, this becomes:

> State absolutism . . . is the modern danger against which neither representative government nor democracy can defend us. . . . If we do not bear this in mind, we shall be led constantly astray by forms to overlook the substance, to confound freedom of speech with freedom of action, to think that right is safer against majorities than against tyrants.

He was very good at analyzing historical processes, which are more important and more elusive than static and isolated historical facts. In May 1861 he published a thoughtful essay

called 'Political Causes of the American Revolution.' By this
term he meant not the comparatively brief struggle that won
independence for the American colonies of Britain, but the
long development that started with the formation of the
United States in 1776 and appeared likely to end by destroying
it in the Civil War. The article is full of quotations from the
writings and speeches of eminent American statesmen from
Hamilton to Seward. Many of them will be new to most readers
except specialists. They are striking in themselves, but they
gain more force because Acton groups them around one central
idea: the conflict—within democracy—between abiding law
and arbitrary power. Recently we have seen many political
activists calling out 'Power to the people!'—usually with the
implication that the American political and legal system is
designed to restrain them from doing whatever they want to
do, regardless of future retaliation by opponents in the ensuing
social strife. Our system *was* designed to restrain them. If it is
destroyed, they and most of us and the whole country will be
destroyed. Extreme democracy produces a situation in which
(as Acton puts it) 'the majority have no duties and the minority
no rights.' To prevent such situations from arising, or from
lasting if they do arise, a system of checks and balances and
delays was devised by the men who founded our country.

Acton starts his article not with an up-to-date report of the
opening of the Civil War, but with something clinically rele-
vant although far earlier. It needs a little explanation nowadays. When the war between Athens and Sparta was dragging
toward its end, and Athens was ruled by violent demagogues,
the Athenian navy won a great victory, the battle of Arginusae
(406 B.C.). Many ships were damaged. Rough weather grew
into a storm, too violent to allow the Athenian commanders
to rescue the survivors on the hulls still afloat. The casualty
list was long. The commanding officers were impeached for
criminal negligence. The Athenian legislature proposed that
a single ballot taken in an assembly of the entire people should
decide their guilt or innocence without individual trials. The
proposal was passed, Socrates dissenting. The ballot was taken.

They were found guilty, and those of them who had not fled into exile were executed—including the son of Pericles, the founder of democratic Athens.

With an allusion to this act of monumental ingratitude and injustice Acton begins his study of the 'American Revolution.'

At the time of the utmost degradation of the Athenian democracy, when the commanders at Arginusae were condemned by an unconstitutional decree, and Socrates alone upheld the sanctity of the law, the people, says Xenophon [the historian], cried out that it was monstrous to prevent them from doing whatever they pleased. A few years later the archonship of Euclides witnessed the restoration of the old constitution, by which the liberty, though not the power, of Athens was revived and prolonged for ages; and the palladium of the new settlement was the provision that no decree of the council or of the people should be permitted to overrule any existing law.

The fate of every democracy, of every government based on the sovereignty of the people, depends on the choice it makes between these opposite principles, absolute power on the one hand, and on the other the restraints of legality and the authority of tradition. It must stand or fall according to its choice, whether to give the supremacy to law or to the will of the people; whether to constitute a moral association maintained by duty, or a physical one kept together by force.

Yet even the wisest of Acton's verdicts, such as these, never got into a book. 'Power tends to corrupt' was thrown out in a letter to a friend. The others are usually to be found in magazine articles, or in his private notes. His wisdom failed to assume a durable form.

It was not laziness. He studied constantly and methodically. He knew eight or ten languages. He collected a large library, nearly sixty thousand volumes.* There he read, and thought,

---

* That library was the object of a charming act of philanthropy. Toward the end of his life Acton got into financial difficulties, and thought of selling his library. Before it could be auctioned off, Andrew Carnegie bought it, and made Acton trustee of it for the rest of his life. This was all done through friends and third parties, so that Acton would never be embarrassed by knowing his benefactor and having to thank him personally.

and took notes. There are still in existence at Cambridge University many hundreds of files, packed with his neat handwritten summaries of trains of thought: enough to be expanded into several shelves of books, if they had ever been assembled and composed and printed.

But the books—or rather the great book—never appeared. *The History of Liberty* remained unwritten.

It will not explain this to say that Acton knew too much. There have been other scholars who knew a great deal and wrote copiously: Acton's own master Ranke, the German classicist Mommsen, and the tireless Eduard Meyer.

It may have had something to do with his attitude to authority. Although he was a devout Catholic—or rather (as he would have said) *because* he was a devout Catholic—he spent much time and effort criticizing certain aspects of the activity of the Roman Catholic church. He strongly opposed Pope Pius IX's proposal to declare the infallibility of the Pope; he wrote a number of articles unfavorably analyzing such institutions as the temporal power of the Popes and the Holy Inquisition. For a long time he expected to be excommunicated; and his teacher, the German priest and scholar Döllinger, actually was excommunicated. But Acton's attitude to Döllinger showed something of the same combative, oppositional character. At first he was devoted to Döllinger; he remained close to him during his disputes with the Vatican; then he began to criticize him; and finally he dropped him. A man who spends much energy on criticism and opposition is not often able to write a large positive work.

Also, Acton was lonely. He had no certain reliable audience close to his mind and voice. He said himself that he 'had never had any contemporaries.' Books must be written for someone, aimed at a person or a group, real or ideal. It was only toward the end of his life, when he became a professor, that he came to understand whom he should address and what he ought to tell them. It is touching to see him beginning his inaugural lecture, not with the conventional 'Gentlemen,' but with the more modest and friendly 'Fellow students.'

The chief hindrance which prevented *The History of Liberty* from coming to birth was Acton's difficulty in defining the scope and function of history. He lived in the nineteenth century, when it was believed that history could be a science, purely objective, like crystallography. It was held that history should deal with pure facts: Ranke said it was meant to explain 'how things really happened.' But a history of liberty could not be written in such a way. Acton had a prejudice in favor of freedom: he could not write a 'scientific' history of liberty any more than we could be dispassionate watching a man fighting a shark. He half realized that he had chosen the wrong field, and that he ought to have embarked on a work of moral and political philosophy, illustrated by historical examples. There is a point where history passes into ethics, and even into metaphysics.

The nineteenth century was an age full of great men in many different fields. Acton was one of them; but unlike many of them, he was a realist. If some of the forces now abroad in the world can impose their will on the rest of us, the history of liberty never will be written. In resisting these forces it is good to remember one more of Acton's wise dicta:

> Do not overlook the strength of the bad cause, or the weakness of the good.

Lord Acton, *Essays on Church and State, edited and introduced by D. Woodruff* (Viking Press, New York, 1953).

The Adventurous Traveler

I COULDN'T do it now. Probably I could never have done it: I doubt if I ever did possess the resilient muscles, the iron constitution, and the gay self-confidence which are necessary for such an adventure. Still, I must say I love reading about it, even though it often appalls my imagination and occasionally turns my stomach.

The adventure was a tour of the Middle East, through much of what was then the Ottoman (or Turkish) Empire—not by airplane, for the airplane had yet to be invented; nor by car, for the same reason; nor by train, for the railway train was scarcely a generation old; but on horseback, on camelback, in small and rickety sailing boats, and not infrequently on foot. The traveler started from Belgrade and reached Istanbul; then he went on to place after place which we should dearly love to visit—although, as they were then, perhaps they might have repelled us: Troy, Smyrna, Cyprus, Lebanon, Galilee, Jerusalem, Gaza, Cairo, and Damascus. When he got home he published a book about it, as so many travelers do; but his was far better than most: it made him famous at once, and went into edition after edition for many years. His name was

Alexander William Kinglake. His book succeeded in spite of having an awkward and obscure title: *Eothen.* (*Eothen* is ancient Greek; in fact it means *At Dawn,* but Kinglake thought it meant *Out of the East.*) It was first published in 1844, and is still delightfully readable.

There is usually some danger to be met in the Middle East. If your timing is unfortunate, you can be shot in Jerusalem, blown up in Cyprus, or torn to pieces by a mob in Cairo. But Kinglake throughout his journey faced another special danger which has almost disappeared. You meet it on the first page of *Eothen,* and its silent menace haunts you through almost every chapter. It is the most terrible of all diseases: plague. In those days it was endemic in the entire Middle East, and there were frequent catastrophic outbreaks in cities a thousand miles apart from each other. Therefore death might strike the traveler down on any day of his journey. Except when he was riding across the remote and sun-cleansed desert, he was in as precarious a situation as though he were moving, eating, and sleeping in an isolation hospital for dangerous diseases.

This was made perfectly clear to Kinglake on the day his travels began. In those times, Hungary was part of the Austro-Hungarian Empire, while the Balkan peoples were still controlled by Turkish garrisons. He crossed the frontier between the two realms by sailing across the river Sava; but he was explicitly warned by the Austrian frontier guards that if he once came into contact with any creature or thing belonging to the Turkish Empire, he could not be permitted to return into Austrian territory without undergoing an imprisonment of two weeks in quarantine. (This was designed to see whether he was carrying the infection of plague within him, and to give him time, if he were, to fall sick and die without polluting the clean air and water and earth of Europe.) Kinglake agreed to all this. His friends came down to the river bank to say good-bye. As he stood waiting for his baggage to be loaded onto the ferry, they asked him again and again if he had wound up all his affairs in Christendom, and had forgotten nothing. Like a man making his will before undergoing surgery, he assured them that he had forgotten nothing whatever. They shook hands with him for the last time, and backed away. Then the single Austrian frontier official who was 'compromised' by passing between plague-ridden Turkey and healthy Hungary advanced, and extended the hand which no other European would touch. (A good theme for a short story by Franz Kafka.) Kinglake shook the hand, and entered the boat, and sailed over to Belgrade. Above the walls of the city, a single vulture was wheeling in slow circles.

And all these precautions were not mere idle imaginings. When Kinglake reached Cairo, he found the entire city terrorized by a desperate attack of plague. There were 200,000 people in Cairo then; and 500 were dying of the disease every day. Kinglake says he was the only European traveler in the city. His banker (although he had imprisoned himself in a quarantined house to avoid contagion) died; his landlord, a Scotsman converted to Islam, died; one of his donkey-boys died; and when Kinglake consulted a doctor about a sore throat, his sore throat was cured, but the doctor died. At last, after a long ride in the blazing hot wind called the khamsin, Kinglake himself fell ill. He stayed in his room but refused to go to bed. When he was served dinner, he could not eat it, but he would not send it back untouched. So he filled his plates, even adding salt in the usual way; then he tucked all the food away in an old newspaper and hid it, as though he had really been able to eat it. An hour or two passed—uncomfortably. At the usual time he ordered his hot tea. The moment he drank it, he broke out into a delightful health-restoring sweat. His mind was relieved and refreshed, he slept soundly (still sweating), and—in his own words—'when the morning came, and I asked myself how I was, I answered "Perfectly well." '

One of the terrifying things about bubonic plague was that no one knew how it was transmitted—by the air? by water? by body contact? We know now. It is a disease of rats and other rodents, which can be passed to human beings through bacilli carried by fleas. But then they could only guess. And their guess—at least the guess of the Europeans, because the Moslems, true fatalists, did not care—was part way to the truth.

> It is the firm faith of almost all the Europeans living in the East, that plague is conveyed by the touch of infected substances, and that the deadly atoms especially lurk in all kinds of clothes and furs: it is held safer to breathe the same air with a man sick of the plague, and even to come in contact with his skin, than to be touched by the smallest particle of woollen, or of thread which may have been within the reach of possible infection. If this be a right notion, the spread of the malady must be materially aided by the observance of a custom prevailing among the people of Stamboul. It is this: when an Osmanlee dies, one of his dresses is cut up, and a small piece of it is sent to each of his friends, as a memorial of the departed—a fatal present, according to the opinion of the Franks [= Europeans], for it too often forces the living not merely to remember the dead man, but to follow and bear him company.

In fact the infection was not carried by the clothes, but by the vermin which might lurk in the clothes; and a tiny flea hidden in the seam of a silk jacket could be as powerful as the Angel of Death. Kinglake was in contact with many people when the plague was raging, and was even accidentally touched by the foot of a corpse on its way to burial; but either he was never bitten, or he was never bitten by a carrier flea, or he was lucky.

As well as facing the perils of the plague, Kinglake was often in a type of danger which is building up again nowadays: the hatred of Moslems for Christians and of Arabs for non-Arabs. He visited Nablus, a city in Jordan noted for its xenophobia. Only a few months before his visit (he remarks) it would have been madly rash for anyone wearing European clothes even to walk through the streets; but there had been an insurrection against the governor, which had been so savagely repressed that now the inhabitants were quiescent. Still, he says, 'it was quite plain that the effort with which the men of the old school refrained from expressing their opinion of a hat and a coat was horribly painful to them. As I walked through the streets and bazaars, a dead silence prevailed. Every man suspended his employment, and gazed on me with a fixed glassy look, which seemed to say, "God is good, but how marvellous and inscrutable are His ways that thus He permits this white-faced dog of a Christian to hunt through the paths of the faithful!" '

The city of Damascus had for long been equally hostile. Until a year or two before Kinglake visited it, 'it had kept up so much of the old bigot zeal against Christians, or rather against Europeans, that no one dressed as a Frank could have dared to show himself in the streets.' But that had been changed, not by chastisement from Turkish officials, but by the firmness of a recently posted British consul-general. This was just at the beginning of the Victorian era. British soldiers and British sailors turned up all over the world. British diplomats and British travelers, believing themselves to be the salt of the earth, demanded for their flag and themselves privileges which no other nation would presume to expect (except the Chinese). The new British consul in Damascus made it clear that he expected all British residents and visitors to be treated as equal to the Syrian Moslem inhabitants of the city. For instance, in the principal streets of Damascus there were sidewalks for pedestrians, a foot or two higher than the main road where the donkeys and camels trod. Until the arrival of the British consul, none but a Moslem had been permitted to use the sidewalk. He stopped that: how, we are not told. Kinglake says, 'I always walked upon the raised path as free and unmolested as if I had been in Pall Mall. The old usage was, however, maintained with as much strictness as ever against the Christian Rayahs [= subjects of the Sultan] and Jews. Not one of them could have set his foot upon the privileged path without endangering his life.'

He was so rich and self-confident, and many of the Arabs were so poor and downtrodden, that he naturally treated them with good-humored contempt. And they accepted it.

From their Turkish overlords they got treatment far worse, because it was deliberately intimidating and cruel. When he set out from Gaza to cross the desert to Cairo, he hired four Bedouin nomads to give him both guidance and safe-conduct: he and his servants and baggage were to use their four camels while the Bedouin walked. All right: this was the usual procedure. But at the end of the second day out, the four Arabs told Kinglake's servant that they had brought no food with them and had to be supplied out of his stores. Kinglake had only enough for himself and his own people; but he was ready to put the entire party on half-rations and make do. His Greek servant, who knew Arabic and the Arabs, dissuaded him, telling him that the men had thoroughly understood, before they started the journey, that they were to provision themselves. So he hardened his mind. The Arabs begged earnestly for food. He refused.

'Then we die!'
'God's will be done.'

Gloomily they moved off. Ten minutes later they had a fire going and were busy cooking their bread. They had of course brought a bag of meal with them, hiding it under the baggage. 'In Europe,' says Kinglake with unconscious haughtiness, 'the detection of a scheme like this would have occasioned a disagreeable feeling between the master and the delinquent, but you would no more recoil from an Oriental on account of a matter of this sort than in England you would reject a horse that had tried and failed to throw you.' In fact the Arabs respected him more and liked him better.

In spite of such incidents, Kinglake was cheerful and enjoyed himself through most of his travels. He must have been fairly strong; he was young, only twenty-six when he made the trip; he had plenty of money (*not* in cash but in letters of credit); and he had that arrogant self-confidence which well-bred, well-to-do young Englishmen used to carry all over the world. This is one of the few features of the book which will irritate some modern readers, the assumption that anyone whom he addresses is (or ought to be) an Englishman of the same type, with the same sympathies and a similar education. Yet usually this is not offensive, but droll. For example, he was crossing the desert from Gaza to Egypt. In the solitary waste he saw a moving speck on the horizon. In an hour or so it drew close enough for him to see what it was: a small party traveling in the opposite direction: two Arabs on foot, one baggage camel, and two riding camels, one of which was carrying an Englishman and the other his body-servant. King-lake wondered whether he ought to speak to the approaching Englishman. He did not (as you might expect) think that it might be improper because they had not been introduced; but he did consider that they had nothing particular to talk about. So he touched his cap, and even went so far as to wave his hand; so did the other; and thus, among the lone and level sands, the two passed in silence. That is very English, and perfectly comprehensible. If Kinglake had wanted to chat with other Englishmen, he would have stayed at home and gone to his club every day. Since he was traveling in the lonely desert, it was obvious that he did not. Besides, he had nothing particular to talk about.

(Lawrence Durrell surprised Henry Miller by doing exactly the same thing, although he accounted for it more eloquently and bitterly. Miller records the incident on p. 218 of *The Colossus of Maroussi*.*

On the way back [from Mistra to Sparta] we passed a friend of Durrell's—without stopping. The greeting impressed me as most nonchalant and casual. 'What's the matter,' I enquired, 'are you on the outs with him?' Durrell seemed surprised by my remark. No, he wasn't on the outs with the fellow—what made me think so? 'Well, isn't it a bit unusual to run into an old friend in an odd corner of the world like this?' I asked. I don't remember the exact words he used in answer to this but substantially they were these: 'What would we do with an Englishman here?

* New Directions, Norfolk, Conn., 1941.

They're bad enough at home! Do you want to spoil our holiday?')

There was another characteristic episode in Cairo, where Kinglake hired a professional wizard to do some feats of magic. The wizard offered to conjure up the phantasm of any of Kinglake's friends. To do this he brought in a boy, wrote mysterious figures on the boy's hand, and told him to gaze into his palm, where the phantasm would appear. Asked which of his acquaintances he would like to call up, Kinglake named John Keate. Not John Keats, but John Keate, the formidable little schoolmaster who helped (mainly by flogging) to make Eton into a great school—a furious termagant with shaggy red eyebrows, who used to wear 'a fancy dress partly resembling the costume of Napoleon and partly that of a widow woman.' John Keate, Kinglake's old headmaster, who had often beaten him. 'Say what you see,' said the wizard to the boy. The boy answered what would have been right for most Englishmen, but not for a quizzical Etonian: 'I see a fair girl, with golden hair, blue eyes, and rosy lips.' The experiment was a failure, but it did not have time to damage the wizard's reputation. A few days later he died of the plague.

One of the minor torments of traveling in 'underdeveloped' countries is the prevalence of body-vermin. (When told that we intended to visit Troy and sleep overnight in a small local inn, a Turkish friend in Istanbul shook his head ominously and advised us to take our own bedsheets.) Kinglake usually ignores this problem, but once in a sudden flow of eloquence he warns his readers about fleas: in particular the fleas of Palestine, which are imported by travelers from all over the world. He remembers one specially bad night.

> The fleas of all nations were there. The smug, steady, importunate flea from Holywell Street [London]; the pert, jumping 'puce' from hungry France; the wary, watchful 'pulce' [from Italy] with his poisoned stiletto; the vengeful 'pulga' of Castile

with his ugly knife; the German 'Floh' with his knife and fork
—insatiate—not rising from table; whole swarms from all the
Russias, and Asiatic hordes unnumbered;—all these were there
and all rejoiced in one great international feast. . . . After
passing a night like this, you are glad to pick up the wretched
remains of your body long, long before morning dawns. Your
skin is scorched, your temples throb, your lips feel withered
and dried, your burning eyeballs are screwed inwards against
the brain. You have no hope but only in the saddle, and the
freshness of the morning air.

Although *Eothen* is carefully written, it is quite informal,
as though Kinglake were talking to you and you were one of
his friends. It opens with Kinglake crossing the frontier into
the Ottoman Empire; it closes with Kinglake and another man
bluffing their way through quarantine on the way back; but
it tells us little or nothing about his travel plans, it has no
proper conclusion, and it sometimes looks as though it were
put together out of a series of letters not originally meant for
publication. When you read it, therefore, you need not expect
a systematic study of 'social conditions' and full explanations
of geographical and historical facts. On the other hand, you
will be spared the atrocious triviality and slovenliness of
many modern travel writers, who think it is enough merely
to transcribe their diaries, without troubling to edit them or
to excise superfluities. (*July 27th. Woke early with a stiff neck:
there must be a concealed draught in the cabin somewhere.
This is Mother's birthday, I must send her a cable if I can find
a telegraph office. At breakfast, one of the three remaining
eggs was bad. . . .*) Instead, you will get some brilliantly vivid
descriptions, much deadpan humor, some strongly individual-
ized psychological episodes; and many pages of the last thing
you might expect from a young amateur's book: superb prose
style. Here is Kinglake's description of the sun in the desert.

You look to the sun, for he is your taskmaster, and by him you
know the measure of the work that you have done, and the
measure of the work that remains for you to do. He comes
when you strike your tent in the early morning, and then, for

the first hour of the day, as you move forward on your camel, he stands at your near side, and makes you know that the whole day's toil is before you; then for a while, and a long while, you see him no more, for you are veiled and shrouded, and dare not look upon the greatness of his glory, but you know where he strides overhead by the touch of his flaming sword. No words are spoken, but your Arabs moan, your camels sigh, your skin glows, your shoulders ache, and for sights you see the pattern and the web of the silk that veils your eyes, and the glare of the outer light. Time labours on—your skin glows, your shoulders ache, your Arabs moan, your camels sigh, and you see the same pattern in the silk, and the same glare of light beyond; but conquering time marches on, and by-and-by the descending sun has compassed the heaven, and now softly touches your right arm, and throws your lank shadow over the sand right along on the way for Persia. Then again you look upon his face, for his power is all veiled in his beauty, and the redness of flames has become the redness of roses; the fair, wavy cloud that fled in the morning now comes to his side once more—comes blushing, yet still comes on—comes burning with blushes, yet comes and clings to his side.

No, I could never make such a journey; but, in such noble imaginative prose, I love reading about it.

One Man's Scotland

BORN very close to poverty in a small town in eastern Scotland, James Barrie became rich, famous, and (within limits) beloved. He is still famous in Britain, although he died more than thirty years ago: for *Peter Pan* still delights many young hearts. It is a very upper-middle-class English play, *Peter Pan*, with its children ensconced in a cosy nursery, and a big dog, and an atmosphere of effortless unearned comfort. You would scarcely guess that Barrie himself was brought up in almost the exact opposite of such a world. Yet what might be stuffy or self-satisfied in *Peter Pan* is lightened by Barrie's own special gift. The patronizing word *whimsy* does it less than justice. It is something finer: playful fantasy, idealistic daydreaming. Again and again Barrie's romantic dramas leave the ground to frolic through the air on invisible wings.

But he started by writing bitterly realistic tales. They were not about the Never-Never Land. They dealt with a region which existed during his and his parents' lifetime. It was small and isolated, and its population would scarcely amount to six hundred souls; but he knew them well. He described them and their hard resolute ways, their quarrels and their rivalries and their deeply felt religion, and the harsh penury of their lives, in cold grey and black tones and sharply etched outlines, with phrases as direct as those of Balzac and Maupassant, and sometimes almost as cruel.

These stories were among the very first things he published. They were refused by numerous magazines both in Scotland and in England, but at last printed by the *St. James's Gazette.* He collected a group of them into a little book. It was rejected again and again. It was rejected even when he offered to forgo all royalties. At last a good firm (Hodder & Stoughton) took it and brought it out: so that Barrie became not merely a hack journalist but a real 'book author.' A year later he produced a second volume. The two collections are little read nowadays. They are quite thin and light as books go today. There is a great deal of Scottish dialect in them, which is sometimes almost unintelligible even to a native Scotsman of the present time, and which is rarely attractive.* Also, their titles are among the least felicitous names ever invented: *Auld Licht Idylls* (1888) and *A Window in Thrums* (1889). Still, they are good regional stories, and they give a wonderfully clear picture of a society which has virtually disappeared.

They are studies of the people of a little town in eastern Scotland. Barrie called the place Thrums, because its chief industry was handloom-weaving, and thrums are the threads at the ends of a weaver's web; but it was the real town of Kirriemuir in Forfarshire, where he was born and is buried. The name of the first book, *Auld Licht Idylls,* puzzled me when I first read it as a boy, and still repels me: it means 'idylls,' or short half-poetic sketches, about the Auld Lichts [= Old Lights], a hyper-orthodox sect of Scots Protestants, whose offi-

* It was very old-fashioned. The English word *knife* is spelt with an initial *k* (from the Old English *cnif*), which nobody has pronounced in English for hundreds of years, although it can still be heard in the French *canif.* The folk of Barrie's town called it, with an echo of the original sound, a *t'nife.* Their name for the game of checkers was *dambrod,* from *brod = board* and the French *jeu de dames.* Instead of *I suppose* they said *I sepad.* To indicate someone of very refined tastes they had a dandy word: *kyowowie.* None of these words or pronunciations is in Burns, who came from the west of Scotland.

cial title was the Original Seceders. The two books deal with a period which is not, after all, so far away from us, only two or three generations; and yet the pace of change has been so intoxicatingly rapid in these years that the books seem to describe a world almost as remote as the Middle Ages. (For instance, rereading them the other day, I was astounded to learn that when the men of that region put on their best clothes they wore, not the kilt, for they were not Highlanders, but velvet knee-breeches.)

It was a desperately hard world. The people were poor, crushingly poor; yet they refused to permit themselves to be crushed. (The velvet knee-breeches were for the best days, and would last a lifetime and maybe more.) Against poverty they struggled all their lives, day after day, making and mending and saving and never relaxing, seldom allowing themselves the smallest pleasure that had to be purchased with money, always thinking of the terrible emergencies of illness and accident, and—some of them at least—living in lifelong horror of being destitute when they could work no longer, and of being taken to the paupers' home. After reading Barrie's two books about Thrums, it is very hard to make jokes on Scottish thrift, for you see how tightly the teeth of the trap of poverty were set about these men and women. One of the cobblers in Thrums lived in a two-room house (a *but and ben,* an outer room and an inner room), worked from early morning until nearly midnight, and contrived to make six or eight shillings a week. I suppose this might be equal to two or three dollars. When that is your weekly income, you have to count every cent, and stretch it as far as it will go. Even more pathetic than the cobbler was the knife-grinder, Cree Queery, who walked over three neighboring counties, wheeling his heavy grindstone, and sharpening knives and scissors for a penny or two apiece. He was the only support of his widowed mother. She walked with him wherever he went: for obviously they could not afford to keep up two separate establishments. But she grew old. Her limbs failed. She became almost blind. Cree was told she would have to be sent to the poorhouse. He would not have it. Instead, he still took her with him on his endless journeys. He would wheel the grindstone a few hundred yards along the highroad, then hide it in a ditch, and then walk back for his mother, and lead her—sometimes almost carry her—to the place where the grindstone lay; and so, by doubling each of his journeys, he kept her with him: poor, desperately poor, but loved, and at home, and not a pauper in an institution.

Some of Barrie's tales about the poverty and closeness of his people make you wonder whether to laugh or cry. In one sketch a man returns to his village after having been away for forty years. He has done well and is prosperous. But the villagers remember how he left his home. 'Ye mind his father had been lickin' 'im, an' he ran awa in a passion, cryin' oot 'at he would never come back? Ay, then, he had a pair o' boots on at the time, an' his father ran after 'im an' took them aff 'im.' Boots, you see, cost money. If the boy was leaving home without permission, he could not be permitted to take part of the family capital with him on his rebellious little feet.

What kept these people going? What gave them such willpower and such a strong sense of duty, such conviction and such dogged courage? It was religion. Like the poor Jews of the ghettos and the shtetls, they were upheld all week by the blessed thought of the coming Sabbath—although I must say these Scots made the Sabbath less of a festival and more of an intellectual and even social competition. There were not less than six kirks in the little town—all in dogged rivalry with one another, for attendance even in the deepest snowstorms, and for virtue even in the most exacting circumstances. The standards of all the kirks were high. From their ministers they demanded long sermons, accurate knowledge of the Book, closely reasoned argument, and, above all, direct inspiration. Once, and once only, a minister who was preaching to the Auld Lichts on probation was conducting an outdoor service on a fine calm evening. He had the Book open in front of him. His sermon was going well, and apparently it sprang directly from his own heart as a vehicle for the Divine. But suddenly an inexplicable gust of wind crossed the common, and made the leaves of the Bible shiver. Out from among them leapt twenty closely written pages of the sermon. The minister had not been preaching. He had been reading; and he had not scrupled to disguise his crime by fastening his pages into the Holy Book itself. Before they had stopped fluttering in the air, his career was ended; and the congregation, growling bitterly in their hard throats, had turned their backs on him for ever.

They were scant of mercy, these folk, even to ministers whom they trusted and admired. Mr. Dishart himself, best of all their shepherds, had his shortcomings. Once during an epidemic three of his children died in one week. On the following Sabbath Mr. Dishart preached as usual, although once or twice he stopped and gazed strangely round the kirk. It was raining outside. He spoke of the rain, and said it was the tears of the angels for three little girls. The Auld Lichts let that pass; but they discussed it a great deal after the service was over. The precentor [= hymn-leader] Lang Tammas summed up their feelings by saying, 'If you materialize angels in that way, where are you going to stop?'

Combine poverty and moral uprightness, and what have you? Sometimes you get asceticism, noble or crazy. Sometimes you get peering censoriousness and envious spite. These emotions inspired one of Barrie's strangest stories about his townsfolk. It was important among the Auld Lichts to have a baby baptized as soon as possible after it was born; and of course no baby born to an Auld Licht could be baptized on any day except the Sabbath. If the child were to miss one Sabbath, it was in danger of hell-fire during the days when its young life was frail, for it was born under the burden of original sin, and the true Calvinist doctrine is that 'Hell is paved with infants' skulls.' Furthermore, its parents would be laughed at as lazy and irreligious. In his effort to avoid all this, the chief elder of the kirk, Sandy Whamond, involved his family in an unforgettable disaster. His daughter Eppie was born at a quarter to ten on Saturday evening. How could she possibly be made ready for christening on Sunday morning? Yet, small, pink, and wretched, christened she was. She screamed so hard that the congregation became suspicious; and her father looked more miserable than most fathers in such a situation. Surely there was something wrong. And there was. Another member of the congregation betrayed it. She had crept round behind the Whamond house during the night when the baby was born; and now she attested that the Sabbath had been broken. The light was still lit, and six eggs had been cooked and eaten *after midnight*—evidently to help the exhausted mother to recover in time for the ceremony. How did she know? She had counted the eggshells that were thrown out next morning. The following Sabbath, the minister preached in the morning from the text *Be sure your sin will find you out* (Numbers xxxii. 23) and in the afternoon from *Pride goeth before destruction, and an haughty spirit before a fall* (Prov. xvi. 18). Soon thereafter the chief elder resigned, and another sat in his place. So was a man humbled by six eggshells and two sharp pitiless eyes.

Poverty. Religion. What of the third powerful impulse, sex? Sex is scarcely mentioned in Barrie's books, except as a comic subject. Awkward and inarticulate, the young men of Thrums found it almost impossible to propose marriage. At best, after a long silence, they said, 'Will ye hae's [= have us], Bell?' and Bell, with her thumb in her mouth, answered, 'Ay,' and then they both said, 'Guid nicht to ye.' They were incapable of speaking words of love. 'The only really tender thing I ever heard an Auld Licht lover say to his sweetheart was when a young man looked softly into his girl's eyes and whispered, "Do you sweat?" Even then the effect' (says Barrie) 'was produced more by the loving cast [= squint] in his eye than by the tenderness of the words themselves.'

Yet this is another proof that no artist tells the whole truth about his subject, however well he knows it. How virtuous and somber was the Kirriemuir drawn by Barrie, with its tight moral and social framework! Would you ever imagine that there existed another Kirriemuir, with radically different emotions? Barrie's picture is so complete that you might think it impossible. True, he does have one or two strange tales about savage feuds between Kirriemuir and the neighboring township of Tilliedrum, one of which begins with a man spitting on a coffin and ends with the mourners smashing one another's heads with their poles. But sex? No.

Nevertheless, Kirriemuir is known more widely in Scotland for a single warm song than for all Barrie's cold hard stories. The song is called *The Fair at Kirriemuir*. It describes a village fair, which—as the afternoon wears into the evening, and the whisky gets a little more authority and the dancing a little more frenetic (like the witches' reel in *Tam o'Shanter*) —comes to resemble a pagan fertility rite. It is a great song, with a great refrain: it has forty stanzas. Now, this is a song of Dionysian ecstasy about the same town which Barrie described, and about the same people whom he made predominantly glum, taciturn, and inhibited. Both the song and the stories are true but incomplete. In every group of people, however small, there are many conflicting forces; and only a great artist can give account of them all. Remembering his native town, Barrie ventured to speak about only a few aspects of its life. It took a greater man to record both the puritanical quality of Scottish life (in *The Cotter's Saturday Night*) and the Scottish enthusiasm for drinking and lovemaking (in *Tam o'Shanter*): Robert Burns. Although Barrie began as a realist, he carried realism just to the point where it would not offend the little mother whom he adored. There he emasculated it, and fitted little transparent wings on it, and set it soaring off high above humanity, determined never to come down to earth and grow up.

Denis Mackail, *Barrie* (Scribner's, New York, 1941).

A Young Man's Fantasy

———————————

IN 1855 a young English author published his first story. Like most young authors, he had no money: later he said that he wrote it 'with duns [= debt collectors] at the door.' Nevertheless it is quite obvious that he did not intend the book to be a quick easy best seller. It was wildly eccentric, extravagantly fantastic, frequently incredible, and sometimes all but unintelligible. The setting was a remote Oriental country. The period was an undefined epoch of the distant past. The hero was a barber, the heroine a witch, the villain a powerful demon. The plot made the destinies of mighty kingdoms and vast populations depend, literally, upon a single hair.

I think it is one of the most entrancing books I have ever read. So did many reviewers. George Eliot (of all people) hailed it as 'a work of genius, and of poetic genius'; other critics were equally enthusiastic. The publisher, Chapman, always believed in it, telling his family it was 'the finest Eastern story outside *The Arabian Nights*.' But it did not sell. In 1855 Dickens had recently published *Hard Times* and Thackeray *The Newcomes*: people were not ready to accept a prose fantasy which demanded the complete suspension of disbelief.

The book was remaindered, and finished up on cheap stalls and book-barrows—like Fitzgerald's *Omar Khayyam* a few years later. Subsequently, when the author had become famous, the book was reprinted; but it has never been really popular and never will be. It is very emphatically a work for special tastes: you must, perhaps, be slightly daft to enjoy it.

It is called *The Shaving of Shagpat*. Its author, who later became distinguished as a graceful satirist of contemporary society, was George Meredith. At first sight the book appears to have nothing to do with his later novels of proud English fops and enchanting English beauties. It all takes place in Persia, and is set at least a thousand years ago. Yet if we look at it more closely, we can see that it is inspired by the same conviction that made Meredith into a brilliant novelist of manners. This is (putting it bluntly) the conviction that most people are funny, even when they are being heroic or alluring; that the best way to enter into life and enjoy it is through laughter; that our days are wasted and our souls are burdened not so much by sins as by shams and follies, and that comedy —far more than tragedy or religious fervor—can sweep them all away and restore us to health. This is a fine idea. Meredith shares it with a few, only a few distinguished authors who have simply refused to be serious even about serious things: Aristophanes, Rabelais, and (in some of his work) Cervantes. They at least would have thoroughly appreciated *The Shaving of Shagpat*.

The plot of the romance is weird and phantasmagoric. Without Meredith's sparkling prose style to embellish and support it, it might simply sound insane. But it is not. It is carefully planned. Although it looks like a wild improvisation, it is actually a complex work of deeply meditated art. To appreciate it, you must think yourself out of the present and out of your home; leave Here and Today far behind; let the flying carpet carry you aloft and away; with your inward ear call up the suave melodies and pulsing rhythms of

Scheherazade; and then, after a long flight to the Orient, you can watch the gradual approach of that momentous event, the Shaving of Shagpat.

The scene is Persia (which in 1935 was renamed Iran). The hero is a young barber called Shibli Bagarag: there is destitution in his very name, for Shibli is like *cheaply* and Bagarag like a *bag o' rags.** He has no shop of his own, no property except his razors and the rest of his shaving tackle. Desperately poor, on the verge of starvation, Shibli Bagarag is tramping from place to place in search of work. As he approaches the gates of a city, he is accosted by a hideous old woman. She tells him that he is destined to become rich and famous. This, he replies, he always knew: at his birth the astrologers foretold that he would become a mighty hero if he only stood steadfastly by his craft as a barber; and yet in his errantry he has found that, because of some malevolent influence, his profession has become disreputable, so that sometimes he has been hunted like a criminal, and is now starving. Shaving and haircutting have quite fallen out of fashion; barbers are reduced to beggars.

Here then (replies the hideous hag) is a wonderful opportunity for advancement. In this city lives the famous tailor SHAGPAT, the son of Shimpoor, the son of Shoolpi, the son of Shullum. Shagpat has the most wonderfully rich beard and the most majestic head of hair in the world. No one needs a barber more than Shagpat. The exploit of shaving him would, for a knight of the razor, be one of pure delight and sure glory. Convinced and excited by this encouragement, Shibli Bagarag enters the city and offers to shave Shagpat.

'Shave Shagpat! *Shave* Shagpat? Shave *Shagpat!*'

The citizens who have been admiring Shagpat's miraculous wealth of hair turn on Shibli Bagarag, and hunt him, and thrash him when caught, and throw him out of the city like

* In 1855 the splendor of Burt Bacharach's fame was still asleep in the womb of Time.

garbage. Treason it was, treason and blasphemy, even to mention shaving in the city inspired and indwelt by Shagpat; and the barber has paid dearly for it.

But the hag finds him again and gives him shelter in her father's home. There she reveals the secret to him. It is a supernatural secret, which she knows because she is a sorceress long trained in magic. She is not old, though she looks ancient and deformed. She is young, a princess: she was once beautiful, and may be beautiful again, if she can break an evil spell placed on her by an enemy. And the secret? The secret is a thing of power: a magical hair, called the Identical.* Once it grew in the head of a demon, Karaz. Through it he had mighty power over men, for it commands their souls and forces them to do reverence to anyone who possesses it. But the princess stole it from him and fled; he pursued her, roaring with fury. The hair twisted and writhed in her hand and grew fiery hot. As she sped through the air ahead of the frantic fiend, she saw a city beneath her. Diving down like a hawk, she planted the hair in the head of the tailor Shagpat; and there it grew, surrounding him with homage and worship, while the genie Karaz became the rebellious slave of the princess.

That is only a small fraction of this wonderful fantasy. Meredith decorates it with a richly poetic style. He inserts many little poems within it, following the manner of *The*

---

* This name I have always found difficult to accept. Meredith wanted to give the magical hair a special name, like the Palladium or the Talisman, implying that it was unique. Why then did he choose the word Identical, which implies that the hair was not unique but closely resembled at least one other? If I write identical letters to two men, they do not differ even in a comma. Perhaps he meant simply that normally the magical hair *looked* like all other hairs, and was indistinguishable from them until its particular powers were evoked: if so, the name is at best a weak choice. Or perhaps Meredith (who went to school in Germany) was parodying the mystical phraseology of the followers of Hegel. The Neo-Hegelian A. E. Taylor builds much of his *Elements of Metaphysics* (London, 1903) on a concept he calls 'the Absolute,' i.e. the one non-dependent non-contingent entity: which turns out to be God. This is of course much later than *The Shaving of Shagpat,* but many Hegelian philosophers wrote like that.

Thousand and One Nights, for heroic men and delightful women in those distant times showed their wit and charm by repeating aptly chosen verses in conversation, or even inventing them on the spur of the moment. He also interrupts the flow of his tale twice, to insert extraneous narratives, a short one satirically humorous, and a grisly nightmare about the Queen of the Snakes. Although broken from time to time, his main story is never incoherent. Improbable, certainly; extravagant, without a doubt; still it moves on, not with the steady rhythm of a river but with the excited and capricious flight of a bird in springtime.

With the Identical rooted in his capacious scalp, the tailor Shagpat is revered; he has become a political power; charisma oozes out of him; all the folk of his city and of neighboring cities honor and adore him. But for what? They cannot tell. They feel the power of the Identical; they are in the grip of an illusion. Before they can be liberated from that illusion, Shagpat must be shaved until not a single hair remains upon his head. But (the princess tells the young barber) no ordinary razor will shave him. The Identical will turn the edge of any blade made by mortal man. The current of power that flows out of it will repel any workaday barber, send him flying, paralyze his operating arm. A magical blade is needed: the sword of Aklis, which will not only slice through the Identical but destroy the innumerable reflections and phantoms and doublets of Shagpat which his evil protectors create whenever he is threatened. Only a gallant and resolute hero can penetrate to the place where that sword is kept in readiness for such an Event. The journey itself will be his training for the final exploit, the Shaving of Shagpat.

Off then goes the young barber to find the sword. His adventures are boldly imaginative, among the best parts of the book. There is a voyage across an enchanted sea.

They sped between the rocks, and came upon a purple sea, dark-blue overhead, with large stars leaning to the waves. There was a soft whisperingness in the breath of the breezes that swung there, and many sails of charmed ships were seen in momentary gleams, flapping the mast idly far away. Warm as new milk from the full udders were the waters of that sea, and figures of fair women stretched lengthwise with the current, and lifted a head as they rushed rolling by. . . . Long paths of starlight rippled into the distant gloom, and the reflection of the moon opposite was as a wide nuptial sheet of silver on the waters: islands, green and white, and with soft music floating from their foliage, sailed slowly to and fro.

There is an enchanted lily, whose root is not a lily bulb but a crimson human heart, soft, warm, palpitating. There is a dangerous queen who keeps a sackful of human eyes to be her looking-glass: when she shows her beauty to them, they sparkle. All temptations and all dangers the barber manages to overcome—just, but only just.

His hardest trial comes in the palace of Aklis, where he is greeted by twenty-seven beautiful girls. They caress him and flatter him and offer him their love. Calling him their king, they propose to crown him. They show him a golden throne and a diadem glittering with gems. Although he has not yet obtained the sword, far less accomplished his mission, the shaving of Shagpat, he is foolish enough to accept their cozening homage. He takes his seat upon the throne. He accepts the crown upon his head. At once his throne grips him fast and slides backward into a dark cell. He can neither rise nor free himself. Duped, he has been duped by one of the many illusions which victimize mankind: the flattery which convinces us that, even before we have done anything outstanding, the world ought to recognize our innate worth. Poor Shibli Bagarag! In desperation, he shakes his fist. At once the door of his prison bursts open. All around the hall similar doors open up. Within them he sees other adventurers who preceded him on the same quest and were similarly befooled. They are crowned as he is crowned, helpless as he is helpless. . . . And then suddenly, in a mirror, he sees his own crown. It is made of bejeweled asses' ears and the grinning skulls of monkeys. At this he falls into a healthy convulsion of laughter, so violent that it sets him free from the throne; and although he must still wear the silly crown for a time, the gust of merriment has restored him to normal sense and life, and he can pursue his quest.

The sword of Aklis is given to him and he is taught how to use it. Through further adventures, he returns to the city of Shagpat. The climax of the tale is a battle in mid-air between the evil demon Karaz and the dangerous queen Rabesqurat on one side, and the young sorceress and the young barber on the other. The conflict is desperate, bewildering, superhuman.

> While the heavens raged, Shibli Bagarag prepared a rapid lather, and dashed it over Shagpat, and commenced shearing him with lightning sweeps of the blade. 'Twas as a racing wheel of fire to see him! Suddenly he desisted, and wiped the sweat from his face. Then calling on the name of Allah, he gave a last keen cunning sweep with the blade, and following that, the earth awfully quaked and groaned, as if speaking in the abysmal tongue the Mastery of the Event to all men. . . . Shibli Bagarag had smitten clean through the Identical! . . . Day was on the baldness of Shagpat.

It is a very unusual imagination that can create a world crisis out of a single hair, and, for the climax of a brilliant book of visions, show us a half-unconscious tailor with his bald head gleaming in the sunlight. Meredith gave his book the significant subtitle *An Arabian Entertainment.** Like many highly intelligent people, he had been impressed by the extraordinary inventiveness of *The Thousand and One Nights,* and by the power which many of those stories have of stating the absolutely impossible in such a way that, while you read, you must believe. He determined to outdo them all. In my view, he succeeded. In *The Arabian Nights* there are many miracles; but they are sometimes crudely materialistic, and reflect the wishful dream of becoming rich without brains

---

* The first English version of *The Thousand and One Nights* (published early in the eighteenth century and taken from Galland's French translation) was entitled *Arabian Nights Entertainments.*

or hard work, by finding a hidden treasure, and living happily ever after. Supernatural beings serve sumptuous banquets at a moment's notice, produce bowlfuls of gems, or build a palace overnight. The sorcery is usually confined to simple transformations by which, with a few mystic words and a sprinkle of water, a man is changed into a dog: that sort of thing. But *The Shaving of Shagpat* creates a world in which magical powers can dominate and dwarf ordinary life like a violent earthquake or an erupting volcano. The final chapter, called 'The Flashes of the Blade,' describes a battle waged by Shibli Bagarag and his supporters against demons and witches, vultures, scorpions, and flying serpents—a wilder and more poetic phantasmagoria than anything in *The Thousand and One Nights.*

Meredith also felt that some of the *Arabian Nights* tales, although exciting, are rather pointless. Sindbad the Sailor, for instance, undergoes a number of appalling shipwrecks and outrageous perils, but they all end simply with Sindbad returning home so many thousands of gold pieces richer. What Meredith added to *The Arabian Nights* was deeper meaning and higher purpose. He is said to have denied that *The Shaving of Shagpat* should be interpreted as an allegory; but I believe he did that simply in order to keep his readers' enjoyment of the fantasy from being spoilt by the search for inner significance. The story does have a valuable meaning, which is far from being platitudinous. It tells us that most men prefer illusion to reality; that illusion is always ridiculous and often dangerous; and that it must be extirpated by the keen blade of criticism and the cleansing deluge of laughter.

It was a remarkable book for a young man of twenty-seven to write. Meredith may have been stimulated by the conversation of his father-in-law, the brilliant fantast Thomas Love Peacock; but in a curious way it was also a comment on his own origins and an announcement of his own mission. Meredith's father, like Shagpat, was a tailor. A tailor's aim in life is to cover people up, and to create an illusion of dignity and elegance. Meredith's hero was a barber. A barber's job is to scrape off the superfluous, to cut through the extraneous, to make a clean sweep. What Meredith was to do in the rest of his work as a writer was to slice away pretenses with the keen edge of hearty laughter.

L. Stevenson, *The Ordeal of George Meredith* (Scribner's, New York, 1953).

Peer Gynt

NEARLY everyone knows the fine incidental music that Edvard Grieg wrote for Henrik Ibsen's fantastic drama *Peer Gynt*. Grieg did not much want to accept the commission, for he did not find the play sympathetic; but he needed the money, and Ibsen was a famous playwright, so he consented. And now his *Peer Gynt* music is better known than the play itself.

Very few of us read *Peer Gynt* unless we are specializing in the history of the theater; and fewer still have ever seen it performed. The drama is of course acted in Norway and Denmark, occasionally also in France; for some time it was in the repertory of the Old Vic in London, where that versatile actor Ralph Richardson played the star part (and it is truly a star part, with magnificent opportunities for both comic and pathetic acting); but I have never heard of a complete performance in the United States, and I never expect to see one.

It is not that *Peer Gynt* is a bore—a mechanical product indistinguishable from a thousand other plays. No. One of the essential things about drama is that it shall be full of the unpredictable, vibrating with that sense of the unexpected which means adventure and revelation; and *Peer Gynt* is full of startling surprises. No human being, reading or seeing it for the first time, could possibly guess from one scene what would be the material, or even the place and the emotional tone, of the next. There are several big episodes which appeal to every spectator as wildly exciting: a storm at sea, with a shipwreck; a rape at a wedding ceremony; a wild revel in a Norse hell with earth-dwelling half-animal devils. In the very first scene of all, Peer Gynt, the hero, describes how he rode a wild reindeer along a narrow ridge at the top of a lofty mountain, half a mile high above the deep fjords on either side, until—

> Suddenly, on the precipice's edge, from the hole where it lay hidden almost at the reindeer's feet, up a ptarmigan rose, cackling, flapping with its wings in terror. Then the reindeer, madly swerving, gave a bound sky-high that sent us plunging o'er the edge and downwards. Gloomy precipice behind us! Fathomless abyss below us! First through clouds of mist we hurtled; then a flock of gulls we scattered, wheeling through the air and screaming. Downwards still and ever downwards! But beneath us something glistened, whitish like a reindeer's belly. 'Twas our own reflection mirrored in the lake beneath us, rushing up, it seemed, to meet us, just as swiftly and as madly as we downwards rushed towards it. Buck from air and buck from water met with mighty splash together, scattering the foam around us!

The whole monologue is a colossal lie; but it is one of the finest dramatic narratives in the whole modern theater.

It is not because *Peer Gynt* is boring, or conventional, or out of date, that it is so seldom performed. The main difficulty is that it is *too* imaginative, *too* fantastic. It contains many effects which can scarcely be put on the stage of a theater, and many scenes which would be ruinously expensive to produce. Just think of showing an armed camp in Morocco, with a squadron of cavalry bivouacked, alerted, and galloping off— for a single scene which lasts no more than three minutes. The entire drama was meant to be out of this world, or at least far removed from the narrowly realistic theater where nearly all Ibsen's other plays were performed. I have sometimes thought that when he conceived and wrote it, Ibsen knew it would be almost impossible to produce, and was working for a new medium which had not yet been invented. Like Goethe in writing *Faust,* like Hardy in writing *The Dynasts,* like Shelley in writing *Prometheus Unbound,* he was dreaming of something like the modern motion-picture screen, where it is relatively easy to show impossible fantasies and to make the real almost superhumanly intense and beautiful.

Eccentric enough for a fantasy movie are the rapid succession of scenes and the phantasmagoric variety of backgrounds against which the life of Peer Gynt is set. But the plot is more fanciful than all but our wildest surrealist pictures. It is the life of a single man, in three almost wholly disparate sections.

In the first we see Peer Gynt, a young ne'er-do-well living on a farm in a poor region of Norway with his widowed mother. He will do no work, but lives only for excitement and the play of his wild imagination. (His father was a drunkard. Peer drinks too, but he can become more thoroughly intoxicated without alcohol, on his own dreams.) He fights all the toughest men in the neighborhood. He carries off the richest girl in the place, and deserts her after one night. He becomes an outlaw. Finally, when he meets the trolls, the foul spirits of earth and rocks and animalism, he thinks of abandoning humanity and joining them. He is saved only by the sound of church bells in the distance, and by the prayers of his mother together with those of a good young girl who loves him.

Now off he goes to America, where he makes a fortune by importing slaves from Africa and exporting pagan idols to China. When we next see him, he is a middle-aged tycoon without principles, without relatives, without loyalties, and indeed without roots: he is a bag of money labeled simply Peer Gynt. He owns a private yacht. But it is hijacked, and he is cast ashore. At this point occurs one of the best comic effects in the play. From the desert shore of Africa, where he has been marooned, Peer watches his yacht sailing away, and prays heaven for justice. There is a distant flash, followed by a cloud of smoke and a dull boom. After thanking his Maker, Peer remarks to himself, 'God takes a fatherly interest in me; but he is not economical!' Next Peer becomes chief of a tribe of Arabs; he acquires a lovely Arabian mistress, who robs him; all is meaningless, and he finishes up in a Cairo asylum as the chief of the lunatics.

In his final appearance, Peer Gynt is a man of sixty or seventy, dead poor, but hard and resourceful. He comes back to Norway, and enters—not his home, which is wrecked and empty, but a sort of purgatorial testing-ground, where supernatural figures meet him and question him about what he has done with his life. They ask him who he is. He cannot answer, for he has never really been anybody. He is pursued by withered leaves and broken straws and other symbols of futility, which cry out to him that they are the acts and thoughts he should have produced, but did not. At last he is arrested by a spirit which is very like to Death: but not the mystical religious incarnation of Death as the crowned skeleton and king of terrors. This is a Button-Molder, who explains that, since Peer has proved to be nothing all through his long life, he must be melted down. After his substance has been mingled with that of all the other useless un-persons, it will serve to make a real human being. And with that the play is about to end: when, just on the verge of complete dissolution and disappearance, Peer is temporarily saved. He reaches the house where the girl who truly loved him, Solveig, has waited for more than half a century. She is old, and almost blind; but, as 'mother and wife,' she accepts him. In her at last he finds some identity, a meaning for the meaningless life he has led until then.

I have tried to do justice to the plot in summarizing it, although it means leaving out some macabre episodes such as Peer Gynt's murder of his fellow-sailors on the sinking ship, and some fine symbols such as the invisible spirit of inertia, the Great Boyg. Still it cannot be called a good plot, even as a fantasy. It is difficult to believe that the ignorant, useless, rebellious boy whom we first meet in Norway could ever settle down to hard trading in a foreign country, and stick at it until he had amassed a fortune. No, that is possible, you might say, citing the lives of many European immigrants to the United States. Granted; but then it is difficult to believe that such a man, after attaining a fortune and growing to middle age, would let it all slip through his fingers again and become the plaything of circumstance, ending in a lunatic asylum. If he did, surely he would never get out, and certainly never return to Norway, where his whole youth was broken and buried under the snows of fifty years? And the climax, the redemption scene, in which a woman who has waited for Peer Gynt throughout that long time saves him from annihilation—surely that is rubbish? Surely such a man could not be loved, could not be saved, and was not worth either loving or saving? H. L. Mencken, in his preface to the Modern Library edition of some of Ibsen's dramas, points out that Ibsen, when planning his realistic plays, wrote down ideas of the utmost simplicity and then surprised his audiences by dramatizing them. And so it seems that in *Peer Gynt* Ibsen started with a platitude—that a man without principles may gain money or power but will never become an individual—and ended with a piece of saccharine sentiment—that a good woman's love will redeem even the unredeemable. Perhaps that is not so sentimental if we apply it to normal husbands and wives, or mothers and sons; but it is impossible to believe in Solveig waiting in her little hut, clutching her prayer book, for fifty years, and then welcoming her gray-haired gray-bearded 'boy' back from his play to sleep in her lap.

It is a distinguished failure, *Peer Gynt*. I wonder why it did not succeed. Perhaps it was because Ibsen, who usually worked on original notions, was hampered and haunted by two prototypes: a legend, and a model. Peer Gynt was a real man, who had lived in Norway some generations before Ibsen and around whom there gathered many legends of prodigious lying and roistering and challenging fate. Evidently Ibsen started with him. The first three acts, which show young Peer blustering and fighting, are powerful and consistent. But then Ibsen could not really decide what such a man would become in later life. He made him a colorless millionaire, successful but boring, and finally brought him back home to realize that his life was meaningless—whereas the real Peer Gynt would have continued to lie and fight and dissipate like Munchausen or Casanova or Tyl Eulenspiegel.

The model is obviously Goethe's *Faust*, whose second part was published in 1832, when Ibsen was a little boy. But apparently Ibsen could not make up his mind whether he wanted to emulate it or to make fun of it. In a rapturous love scene with his beautiful Arabian slave-girl, Peer Gynt actually parodies the final sentence of *Faust* (in German, too); and I imagine that Peer in love with Anitra and singing to her on the Arabian lute might be a parody of Goethe himself writing the *West-Östlicher Diwan* at the age of seventy for a girl half a century younger. On the other hand, the serious aspect of *Peer Gynt* is like the central idea of *Faust*: an individualist, selfish and versatile, searching for a meaning throughout human existence and failing to find it until the end. The symbolic scenes are sometimes parallel, although Ibsen's are less powerful and more provincial—the trolls are like Goethe's Brocken witches, and the Stranger and the Button-Molder are a little like Mephistopheles; and the final resolution of both dramas is almost one and the same. The redemption scene at the end of *Faust,* although almost jejune from a religious point of view, has a certain emotional strength: Faust is saved by Gretchen, whom he once dearly loved. But Peer Gynt is saved by a woman whom he ignored even when she was a girl, who has no genuine reason to love him, and who is in fact not real: she is merely a projection of his mother. While *Faust* ends in fake religious sentiment (since Goethe himself was not a Christian), *Peer Gynt* ends in fake domestic sentiment: wander as far as you like, my dear extravagant boy, but you will find your way home to mother at last. This leading idea is unacceptable as the basis of a serious imaginative drama; and it is a tribute to the power of music, the kindest of the arts, that Grieg in *The Death of Aase* and *Solveig's Song* was able to transmute it into a truth which cannot be denied or even questioned.

Father and Son

ONE OF MY favorite books went out of print not long after its
author died, and for years remained completely unknown in
the United States. Yet it is a good book. It is written in a beautifully clear, light, sensitive style; it deals with a difficult but
important theme; and it is a fine example of a fairly rare species
of literature. It is still unobtainable in hard-cover format; but
now several intelligent publishers have issued it in paperback;
and I have reread it with delight.

It is called *Father and Son*; its author is Edmund Gosse.

Edmund Gosse was a distinguished literary critic who died,
after a career full of achievements and honors, in 1928. He
was a stylist, a linguist, an aesthetic aristocrat; he had a gift
for making important literary friendships and keeping them
warm; his large splendid house was usually full of rising
authors and their established elders, whom he introduced to
one another—sometimes with a genuine desire to encourage
the young through contact with the old, sometimes with
amused zest at observing the not always friendly interplay of
competitive characters. He was remarkably successful in intro-
ducing to the English-speaking world some difficult European

writers, such as Ibsen and Björnson and José-Maria de
Heredia. Had we met him, we should have been charmed and
a little overawed by his wide reading, his vast acquaintance,
his finely polished taste, and his keen gift for enjoyment. A
man, we should have said, of the world.

Such was Edmund Gosse at the height of his career. But his
childhood was almost the exact reverse of this worldly, accomplished, satisfying life. It is of his childhood that he tells in
Father and Son; and in particular—since his mother died early
—of his long companionship with his father, which turned at
last into a curious blend of love and opposition, and after a
spiritual crisis ended in a permanent, an unbridgeable break
between the two.

Surely this is one of the great themes: the relation of a
father to his son, of a son to his father. The relation molds
the character of the son. But it also tends to remold the character of the father. It has been dealt with in drama and fiction,
it appears constantly in history and myth, and it is not yet
nearly exhausted. David and Absalom; Prince Hamlet and
King Hamlet; old Karamazov and his sons; Odysseus and
Telemachus; Prince Hal and Henry IV; Abraham and Isaac;
Aeneas and Anchises, whom he carries out of the flaming ruins
of Troy and later meets in the realm of immortality—scores
of these couples flood into our minds. Edmund Gosse and his
father are less impressive than most of the famous father-and-
son pairs; their fate was less tragic, less inspiring. Yet in its
own gentle and sensitive way Gosse's book epitomizes some
of the essential conflicts and tensions of fatherhood and son-
ship.

It is an extraordinary story. Gosse's father and mother were
intellectuals. She had been a governess and was something of
a poet. He was a zoologist, writing books on nature with his
own exquisite illustrations, giving lectures on the new worlds
revealed by science, and managing (although with difficulty)
to support his wife and child. But what they thought most
important was that they were both devout Christians, spend-

ing hours every day in prayer, and in close examination and discussion of Holy Scripture. They both belonged to a tiny sect of highly eccentric Protestant Christians known as the Plymouth Brethren. At that time few of its members living near them were educated people like themselves, so that they were forced to inhabit a strange little world of their own. They took a particular interest in interpreting the Book of Revelation as a literal forecast of events which were happening, or were about to happen, in their own day. In their son's words,

> When they read of seals broken and vials poured forth, of the star which was called Wormwood that fell from Heaven, and of men whose hair was as the hair of women and their teeth as the teeth of lions,* they did not admit for a moment that these vivid mental pictures were of a poetic character, but they regarded them as positive statements, in guarded language, describing events which were to happen, and could be recognized when they did happen. . . . They were helped by [like-minded interpreters of Scripture] to recognize in wild Oriental visions direct statements concerning Napoleon III and Pope Pius IX and the King of Piedmont, historic figures which they conceived as foreshadowed, in language which admitted of plain interpretation, under the names of Denizens of Babylon and companions of the Wild Beast.

One result of this, for the little boy, was an upbringing so rigid and so limited that it appears to us to have been almost mad. The parents of Edmund Gosse (who was to become an eminent critic of literature) believed that all fiction was equivalent to lies, since it was invented; and lies were sinful. Therefore they never read a novel or a romance; they never allowed their son to read a story; and, what is worse, they

---

* Gosse got it wrong, doubtless because he recalled his father's preaching but was unwilling to verify his remembrance in Scripture. It was worse than he remembered. The hair and the teeth belonged to a multitude of locusts with crowns and breastplates and scorpion-stings, who served the angel of the bottomless pit and tormented those men which had not the seal of God in their foreheads (Rev. ix. 1–11).

never told him any stories. They described missionaries to
him, but not pirates; he was (through his father's work)
familiar with hummingbirds, but he had never heard of fairies
or giants. This strikes me as particularly pathetic, for two
reasons. One is that telling a story to one's own child is a
unique delight, both for oneself and for the child. (My wife
and I enjoyed it so much that we took turns at it on alternate
evenings. She could invent wonderful tales, and still does. I
could never invent a good story, but I remember stories, and
so in several years I got through the adventures of Odysseus,
and King Arthur and his knights, and Sindbad the Sailor, and
Hercules, and Grettir the Strong, and such great names as
these.) The other reason is that Gosse's mother was a gifted
storyteller with a splendidly fertile imagination. As a little
girl she used to tell wonderful fantasies to her brothers, until
at the age of nine she was informed by a Calvinist governess
that it was sinful to tell stories. Twenty years later (she wrote
in her diary) she was still hotly tempted to use her God-given
faculty of imagination and make up fictitious tales; but at
last she overcame the temptation, denied her son and herself
much innocent delight, and perhaps cheated the world of a
good romancer.

The little boy grew up solitary, thoughtful, and melancholy.
He never played with any other children. Nor did he go to
school—at least until his mother died. He might perhaps have
become an idiot; but two things saved him. One was that he
learned to read before he was four. Although he was limited
to books of travel, and astronomy, and theology, and an
encyclopaedia (which he read and reread with fascination),
he got enough mental pabulum to keep his intellect working
and growing. The other was that his parents had active
though narrow minds, and talked freely to him.

They talked chiefly about religion, but this started the
youngster on primitive philosophical speculation, and even
theological experiment. Once, for instance, he heard his

mother say that no concern in the world was too small, too insignificant, to be brought to the notice of God; and he often heard both father and mother declare that he should ask God for anything he needed, and it would be granted if it were God's will. Into his nightly prayer he therefore inserted a special request for a large humming-top which he had seen in a shop window, carefully adding the saving clause 'if it is Thy will.' This produced some concern in the family. The father told the boy that he should not pray for 'things like that.' To which young Gosse answered that we were told to pray for things we needed, and that he needed the humming-top much more than he needed the conversion of the heathen or the restitution of Jerusalem to the Jews, which he prayed for regularly every night. He won the argument, but he lost the contest: his father peremptorily forbade him to pray for trifles like humming-tops, and there the matter ended. But the boy was not quite convinced.

Edmund Gosse's mother died when he was eight. For a time after that, his upbringing became even more strict, and even more devoid of pleasures. Yet the need for poetry and imaginative exercise was strong in his soul; and he tells how, through quite unexpected channels, it began to be fulfilled. When he reached nine, his father started him on Latin, by the very worst possible method—handing him an out-of-date Latin grammar book and making him learn it by heart, a page at a time. He did it. He was schooled in obedience, and he did not expect the world to be easy. But one evening, after listening to him repeat his dry lists of conjugations and declensions, his father took down his own copy of Vergil, which had been with him on his zoological expeditions, and read out the exquisite opening of Vergil's first bucolic poem. The little boy stopped and listened in amazement. The sweet spirit of poetry invaded his life for the first time, through a language which he could scarcely understand and in a convention which was utterly incomprehensible to him. Yet the mere melody and rhythm of the words

> tu, Tityre, lentus in umbra
> formosam resonare doces Amaryllida siluas

haunted him. He persuaded his father to repeat them again and again, until at last, though scarcely knowing what they signified, he knew them by heart, and could voice them for his own pleasure like a piece of music.

A year or two later his father married again: a gentle, cheerful, loving lady who suffered from only one almost fatal defect. She was a pedobaptist. (This defect was removed by total immersion.) Among the books she brought with her was a set of Walter Scott's fine romantic poems, and, quite unexpectedly, the elder Gosse began, as a sort of aftermath of courtship, to read them aloud in the evenings. Now poetry, stirring, gallant, boldly rhythmical, wildly adventurous poetry flooded into the little boy. He shuddered with excitement as his father read the passages containing weird Gaelic names and superstitions:

> A sharp and shrieking echo gave,
> Coir-Uriskin, thy goblin cave!
> And the grey pass where birches wave,
> On Beala-nam-bo.*

He had now been introduced to poetry in his native language, enlivened by the intrusion of Highland and Lowland Scots. Shortly afterward, his new stepmother asked whether he might not be permitted to read Scott's novels. His father said No; but then suddenly decided that the boy might read Dickens. 'My stepmother,' says Gosse 'showed some surprise at this, and . . . my Father explained to her that Dickens "exposes the passion of love in a ridiculous light." She did not seem to follow his recommendation, which indeed tends to the ultra-subtle, but she procured for me a copy of *The Pickwick*

---

* The names, with a few minor variations, are in Scott's *Lady of the Lake*, Canto Third, stanzas 25 and 27; but I cannot find this stanza, nor indeed a stanza of this shape. Perhaps Gosse had once again trusted his memory.

Papers, by which I was instantly and gloriously enslaved. My shouts of laughing at the richer passages were almost scandalous, and led to my being reproved for disturbing my Father while engaged, in an upper room, in the study of God's Word.'

Not long after this the boy was allowed to read some poetry all by himself. Since he was forbidden to play on Sundays, or to go for a walk, or to read ordinary books such as narratives of scientific discovery, he was hungry for reading matter. By accident he came upon a volume containing four heavy religious poems written in the eighteenth century: Blair's *The Grave,* Boyse's *The Deity,* Porteus's *Death,* and Young's *The Last Day.* Although stiffly formal, the poetry was vigorous enough and the ideas suited the young theologian. The boy read on and on with avidity, and soon memorized some of the luridest passages.

After some months he was invited to a boys' and girls' party. As part of the entertainment, the youngsters repeated poems which they knew: 'The boy stood on the burning deck,' 'We are seven,' and other delectable lyrics which are still sought for in the correspondence columns of literary magazines. In time, the hostess called on young Gosse. He came forward boldly, and started with a passage from Blair's *The Grave* on the relation between sin and immortality.

> If death were nothing, and nought after death,—
> If when men died at once they ceased to be,—
> Returning to the barren Womb of Nothing
> Whence first they sprung, then might the debauchee. . . .

At this point the hostess stepped in. 'Thank you, dear, that is quite enough, we won't ask you to repeat any more.' More astonished than hurt, the boy withdrew into a corner, his mind still buzzing with the potentialities which, in an Epicurean universe, would confront the debauchee.

It is a short book, Gosse's *Father and Son,* perhaps 150 pages of the contemporary novel size. But it is a full book, and a charming book, humorous and pathetic. Even though times and religious attitudes have changed so profoundly, much of it is still valid, still moving, still (in the best sense) instructive. I recommend it strongly, both to perplexed fathers and to their bewildered sons.

On First Looking into

The Arabian Nights

———————

SOMETHING over fifty years ago, in an industrial city in Scotland, a small boy was looking at a large book. In Scotland half a century or so ago, children were not expected to have any fun on Sundays. They spent the entire morning at Sunday school, followed by church. In the afternoon they might be taken for a nice slow family walk, but they were sternly discouraged from playing games out of doors. Indoor games also were viewed with disapproval unless they were very silent and static. Of course there was no radio, far less TV; and as for the movies, any 'picture palace' which ventured to open its doors on the Sabbath would have lost its license swiftly and inevitably. Therefore there was very little for children to do on Sundays; and they often passed the afternoon and evening wrapped in a fog of melancholy which made them positively welcome the arrival of Monday morning, even when it brought with it school and the customary downpour of rain.

On Sundays the boy was often taken to see his aunts and his grandmother. Since he could not join in the family conversation and must not make any noise, the only things he could do were (*a*) to look out of the window and divert himself by writing down the numbers of the passing trolley cars, and (*b*) to read. Fortunately his grandmother possessed (among others) three extremely interesting books: fine large ones, weighing about six pounds and containing about six hundred pages each, a good foot and a half in height, printed on rich solid paper with hundreds of pictures. They could be read only when they were lying on a broad stout table, not held in the hand or laid on the floor; and the boy usually had to prop himself up on a series of cushions to reach the correct reading height; but when he was ensconced, he soon forgot even the pervasive, glutinous gloom of a Scottish Sabbath.

One of these books was a bound volume of a picture magazine, an early predecessor of *Life* and *Look*. (It is amusing to notice that student attendants in a big university library, surrounded by all the wealth of literature, often prefer to spend their time on duty glancing through back numbers of *Life* and *Look*.) Another was *Don Quixote,* with the spirited illustrations of Gustave Doré.

In the picture magazine there was nothing much to read except the captions. The boy could read some of *Don Quixote,* but the story was too rambling for him to follow. Also, after long exposure to the tales of King Arthur and the Round Table, he could never see what was so funny about a man wearing armor and claiming to be a gallant knight. *The Arabian Nights,* though—that was a book the small boy never tired of, even when he did not fully understand it. It fed his imagination; it populated his dreams with heroes and princesses and sorcerers and ghouls and sultans; it took him far away to distant places—the Magnetic Rock, the Mountains of Ispahan, Baghdad and Khorasan and Kashmir; it told him about curious people and religions—Persians and Kurds, Moslems and Fire-Worshippers; it gave him the beginnings of a sense of style, because the original was often gracefully written and the translation was good standard English; and, best of all, it had practically no moral lesson to teach—except that it was good to be faithful to one's wife (which scarcely concerned the small boy at that time) and imperative to keep out of the way of demons and ghouls (a principle with which he heartily agreed).

The Arabian Nights. The Thousand and One Nights. Evocative, the very titles; the very phrases stirred the boy's blood. Not that he knew where Arabia was, except vaguely; nor did he know when all those astonishing adventures happened: yesterday, last year, or a thousand years before. No, what made the book precious to him was that it was the exact reverse of his own surroundings. The streets of the city where he lived, and the routine of his own life, were featurelessly monotonous. The people all looked pretty much the same, with pale gray faces above dark gray clothes; they moved in straight lines along the streets of a largely rectilinear city, like robots in a cheap game; the sky was always gray. *The Arabian Nights* was not even one continuous story, which might have grown monotonous through pursuing the same subject too long; it was an ingenious maze of separate tales skillfully interwoven with one another to produce successive surprises, or switching tempo and level from low to high, noble to vulgar, grim to gay. Some were long and intricate, like the famous fiction of Aladdin and his wonderful lamp; some were series of adventures, like the seven voyages of the Sailor; some were groups of convergent narratives told by different people, like the biographies of the One-Eyed Kalandars [= beggar monks]; some were short anecdotes hardly more than a page long. The small boy was sometimes bedazzled and bewildered by *The Arabian Nights,* but he was never for an instant bored.

In his own personal life there were few novelties. He lived in the same house year after year and went to the same school with the same children and had his summer vacation in the same part of the country year after year. The only novel adventure which might happen to him was to see a runaway horse in the street, or a falling-down drunk. But *The Arabian Nights* was crammed with unimaginably exciting events, told so convincingly and illustrated with such clear and detailed pictures that they had to be believed even when they were incredible. Nothing was what it seemed to be. A dog turned out to be a prince under enchantment. A tree was the dwelling of dangerous spirits. An old pot fished out of the sea contained a powerful demon. A forest was a palace transformed by magic, and the animals in it were the courtiers waiting for the spell which would release them. A worthless old lamp could give its possessor inestimable wealth and illimitable power. A single word uttered by chance might release forces of incalculable energy. The beggar at the corner might be a malevolent magician waiting for his chance to seize the combination which would make him powerful; the rich man in his carriage might be a beggar, tricked out and disguised for the pleasure of a capricious Jinni. Time and distance could be annihilated. A dream could tell the truth.

From between the covers of this magical book there emerged —like the demon out of the pot uncorked by the poor fisherman—a rich world of fantasy which was . . . I shall not say more real, but certainly more intense and more convincing, and ultimately (even with all its fearful dangers) more desirable than the life of the cold wet northern city where the boy lived. Some time later, when he actually saw that fantastic world brought into visible moving life, with Douglas Fairbanks as its gallant hero, in *The Thief of Bagdad,* he was overpowered with delight; and not many years after that, standing among the half-price people at the back of a concert hall, he heaved with happiness to hear the waves surging round the vessel of Sindbad in Rimsky-Korsakov's *Scheherazade.*

It would be mistaken to call this other world simply an escape from the boy's own life. It is an easy word to use, 'escape,' but it is incorrect to apply it to the spiritual wanderings of boys and girls. Grownups often escape through literature and plays on the stage or screen into stories which they know to be unreal, impossible. Young people are not sure *which* of the many worlds they simultaneously inhabit is real, or how many of them might be real at the same time. For the small boy in Scotland, the Caliph Harun al-Rashid was a good deal

more real than the Lord Provost of his own native city. He
could describe the Caliph, the Commander of the Faithful
(may his days be lengthened and his shadow never dimin-
ished!). He knew Harun with his habit of going out at night
in disguise; he knew his chief adviser, the Wazir Ja'afar, his
bodyguard the swordsman Masrur, and the names of several of
his chief concubines. (Harun possessed many concubines of
surpassing beauty.) But at the age of eight or nine, the boy
did not even know the name of the Lord Provost, far less the
names of *his* Wazir or *his* swordsman, and he would have been
puzzled to tell you what they did all day and all night. One
thing was certain, he found out a little later. They did not go
out at night in disguise to seek adventures and right wrongs;
they attended the annual dinner of the Hydraulic Engineers'
and Valve-Fitters' Protective Association, made a speech, and
went home to bed at eleven p.m.

The real difficulty in the boy's mind was to distinguish between several eccentric and vivid worlds which he knew from
books, and the quiet everyday worlds which he knew from
routine and experience. (Remember that for youngsters, school
and the home are two different universes.) He spent many
Sunday afternoons reading *The Arabian Nights.* He spent
every single Sunday morning reading the Holy Bible, receiving instruction in the Bible, and hearing the Bible read aloud.
During the sermons for adults in the church (which were beyond his understanding) he used to read the Bible, and try to
comprehend the marvelous adventures and the astounding
stories which it related. There were proud and domineering
kings—one of them threw a spear at his son during dinner,
just for asking a question. There were giants, one of them
with six fingers on each hand and six toes on each foot. There
was a donkey that talked to its rider in human speech. There
was a beast with seven heads and ten horns, which looked like
a leopard but had feet like the feet of a bear, and the mouth
of a lion. There were creatures which looked human but had
four faces, man, lion, ox, and eagle, and sparkled like brass.
The names were just as strange as those in *The Arabian*

Nights: Gilgal, Taanach, Chimham. There were dreams, and visions, and deep sayings, and strange prophecies. Of course the boy knew that the Bible was a sacred book, whereas *The Arabian Nights*, however impressive, was not sacred. And yet they both had a kind of authority, an urgent spiritual energy, which drew them together in his mind and set them apart from the ordinary life of his own daily worlds. Sometimes, at the age of nine, he even confused the two. The names sometimes sounded much the same: Harun reminded him of Aaron, Ibrahim was like Abraham, and King Solomon appeared in both books. In both there were complex rituals of prayer and sacrifice which resembled nothing the boy had ever seen in his own life. Each of the two books was filled with miraculous events recounted with sober conviction as though they had truly happened. Both contained an ómnipotent deity whose decrees dominated every moment of the life of every human being: Allah, the Compassionate, the Compassionating; and the LORD. Nothing of importance was done in these books without reference to the deity, and his name was often in the mouths of their characters. When the most fearsome fiend appeared in *The Arabian Nights* and threatened to kill a traveler, the traveler would console and strengthen himself by saying, 'There is no majesty and no might except in Allah'; and in the Bible there were suffering men, wise and brave, who would say, 'Though he slay me, yet will I trust in him.' Yet in the Bible people were constantly challenging the LORD and disobeying his direct commands and doing evil in his sight; in *The Arabian Nights* only a few villains ever forgot to pray and to perform their religious duties, while as for directly disobeying Allah, it was unthinkable, even for the Jinn.

That is all fifty years ago and more. The boy is still reading both the Bible and *The Arabian Nights*. In both of them he finds, as he did long ago, an almost overpowering violence of emotion and fertility of imagination. Nowadays he reads Sir Richard Burton's 'plain and literal translation of *The Arabian*

Nights' Entertainments, entituled *The Book of the Thousand Nights and a Night'* (plain and literal!), in which the tales seem far more brutal and crudely sexual, far more sentimentally romantic and coarsely realistic at once, than he had remembered. The Bible now seems much more like history in its early stage when it is mixed with myth or indistinguishable from myth; more like discipline than fantasy; more like prayer than adventure. And even now, from time to time, he recalls the gray wet Sundays of long ago, rereading the two books which helped him to enter other worlds. One is fantasy, told as gravely and urgently as truth; the other is truth told in terms which are sometimes fantastic. For sober northerners, both represent spiritual universes which are distant and difficult; yet perhaps both are necessary.

Language

Secret Languages

———————————

ONCE UPON A TIME, and a very good time it was, an American tourist was strolling on a beach in Wales. He was talking to an English professor—not the ordinary unadventurous conventional professor, but a truly extraordinary man, an Orientalist who knew many recondite languages and who, only five years later, was to be ambushed and murdered by Bedouin in the Egyptian desert. They were discussing the peculiar lives led by exiled people such as gipsies, and their complex characters and their secretive natures. Suddenly an alarm was sounded. Blasting was going on, a huge explosive charge was to be set off, and the beach had to be cleared. Everyone ran for safety. The American and the Englishman set off down the beach out of range. As they ran, they passed a miserable little man in ragged clothes, crouching in a sheltering overhang.

The professor saw him first. He wanted to point him out, but he did not wish to hurt the poor fellow's feelings, so he spoke in a secret tongue. He said 'Dikk o dovo mush adoi a'gavverin' lester kokero,' which means 'Look at that man hiding himself.' The American replied 'Yuv's atrash of i baria,' which means 'He's afraid of the rocks.' And they were passing on, when the little man smiled and said 'I know what you're saying, gentlemen. That's Romany!' And so it was. It was Romany, the language of the gipsies.

Gipsy language is ultimately an Indian dialect—not Red Indian, but East Indian: a kinsman, or a descendant, of Sanskrit. Both the language itself and the people who speak it are so fascinating that they have often attracted people who are both scholars and adventurers: men like the English evangelist George Borrow, or the Irish musician and linguist Walter Starkie, who are willing to live with the gipsies, and share their irregular meals and their regular vermin, in order to appreciate their life and learn their tongue. Such men were the American tourist, whose name was Charles Godfrey Leland (1824–1903: he wrote *Hans Breitmann's Ballads* and was an expert in witchcraft), and the English professor, E. H. Palmer (1840–82). Although the lonely little fellow on the beach was so grotesque that most people would have turned away from him without a moment's thought, they saw in him a man who could speak the ancient speech of the gipsies, and they invited him to sit down out of range of the blasting, and talk. They expected he would talk Romany. But they were bewildered by his first words. Leland asked, 'What do you do for a living?' The man answered, 'Shelkin' gallopas, just now.' 'What's that?' said Leland. 'Selling ferns,' said the man, and went on, 'I thought you'd know that. That is tinkers' language; I thought because you understood the gipsies you might know the tinkers' language. The right name for the tinkers' language is Shelta.'

Leland was astonished. About a year earlier he had been walking in the south of England; near Bath he had picked up a hobo, bought him a beer, and talked with him about Romany. The hobo told him that Romany was now not secret enough, and that back slang and rhyming slang had been 'blown';* but he said there *was* a language which was really

* Back slang is still used by Cockney traders. It is made by inverting the words: penny becomes *yenep*, look (out for) the police becomes *cool the esclop*, and a boy is a *yob* (now general slang). Rhyming slang, a

secret and was very hard to talk: it was called 'Shelter.' And
now at last Leland had met a man who understood Shelta.
Not only did the little fellow talk it, but he had a theory
about its origin. 'I believe it's mostly Gaelic,' he said, 'but it's
mixed up with Romany and with thieves' slang, or Kennick.
Once it was the common language of all the old tinkers, but
of late years, since the railways were made, the old tinkers'
families are mostly broken up, and the language is perishing.'
(Tinkers are traveling tinsmiths, menders of pots and pans.
I used to see them drifting through Scotland in small groups,
and the last time I was in Florence I met three families en-
camped outside the city, feeding their broken-down horses on
the roadside grass; but I have never seen any in the United
States.) Leland knew nothing until then about the Shelta
language, except its name; but he took out his notebook and
talked to the little man, and in an hour or so he had written
out the first dictionary of the Shelta speech ever put on paper.

Time passed. Leland went back home to Philadelphia,
where he had a house on Broad Street. It was a garden spot
in those days, nearly a century ago. One morning Leland was
walking out among the honeysuckle and the grape vines when
he heard the tap tap of a tinker's hammer. He went up to the
tinker, an elderly Irishman, and talked to him in Romany for
a while. Suddenly he asked, 'Can you thari Shelta, soobli?'
The tinker sized him up slowly, took him for a friend, and
replied yes, he could talk Shelta. Quite soon, much to the
amazement of Leland's colored servants, the two worked out a
vocabulary of eight or ten pages in the Shelta language—
strange words, utterly incomprehensible to us: *yiesk* = fish;
guop = cold; *medthel* = black.

Leland published his vocabularies; and then other people
who were interested in gipsies and tinkers began to contribute

linguistic joke and a speciality of Cockneys, may be used before outsiders
to mystify them. In a pub a Cockney might ask for a *Walter Scott* (pot)
of *pig's ear* (beer): he won't get *elephant's* (+ *trunk* = drunk) because it's
half *fisherman's daughter* (water); but if he does, his *trouble and strife*
(wife) will pick him up off the *Rory O'More* (floor) and get him safe into
Uncle Ned. (J. Franklyn, *The Cockney*, p. 293.)

their own discoveries. In Scotland, several people had heard tinkers talking in an unknown tongue, and had written down some of what they heard. For instance, a lady living on the remote western island of Tiree copied out some curious words used by a little girl from a family of wandering tinkers. The mother of the girl came up afterward and assured the lady that the words were all nonsense, invented by the child for pure fun. She wanted to preserve the secret of Shelta.

Finally an experienced linguist set out to rediscover and reconstruct the entire language. This could not be done by academic research. To hear Shelta from people who habitually talked it, he had to go down to the lower depths. His name was Sampson, and he was a brave man. He got a great deal of information from a tinker nearly eighty years old, who lived in one of the Irish slums in Liverpool, in a street which was normally safe only for the doctor and the priest. His most exciting adventure came after he had spent some time with two knife-grinders and an umbrella-mender, memorizing and later copying down their words. 'Three more uncleanly and evil-looking men,' he wrote later, 'I never saw. One, an Irish tinker, passed under the name of "Manni" Connor; another was known as the Re-Meather, or "King-Devil"; and the third was a tall cadaverous man called "The Shah." ' After Sampson had met them a number of times in taverns of the Liverpool slums, they began to look askance at him: he was not a regular tinker; he asked too many questions; he had too good a memory; perhaps he was a nark, a police spy. At one meeting Sampson was chatting away over the beer, when he saw the three men glance meaningfully at one another. 'Manni' Connor rose to get between him and the door, while the Re-Meather quietly took off his heavy brass-buckled belt. Sampson instantly decided that this particular phase of his investigations could be pursued no further. He grabbed the table with both hands, and turned it up on edge so that it jammed the three in their seats for a moment, with the blue and white pots of beer sliding down into their laps. He had just a moment to make a getaway. Glancing back as he left, he saw the three Shelta specialists framed against the wall in a triptych, and wished for more time to admire their astonished faces.

After some years there was enough of the Shelta speech on record to allow the philologists to get to work analyzing it. They discovered that it was a hybrid of two different languages, working on two different systems. One was Irish Gaelic; the other was modern English. The words of Shelta are mostly Irish Gaelic, and so are the sounds; but the arrangement of the words is English, as are some of the auxiliary words, and many important details of grammar. (For instance, there are no masculine and feminine nouns, as there are in Gaelic.) Furthermore, many of the Irish words are distorted —not simply twisted by hard usage among illiterates, but deliberately altered so as to be difficult even for Gaelic-speaking people to understand. The result is that Shelta is a language which can be spoken both in England and in Ireland, and will still remain opaque both to the people who speak English and to those who speak Irish Gaelic. It is, or was, the language of the traveling tinkers, at home nowhere, but, like the gipsies, holding themselves aloof from the people who live in static houses, stick to sedentary trades, and speak a public tongue.

There have been many such languages. In that admirable historical romance *The Cloister and the Hearth,* by Charles Reade, the hero falls in with a professional cripple—a beggar who, although perfectly fit and strong, can disguise himself as a pitifully diseased hunchback and who sells saints' relics on the side. This crook talks a curious language which sounds part French and part German. As he gets to like the young stranger, he advises him to join the fraternity. 'Come with me to the rotboss, and I'll show thee all our folk and their lays, and especially the lossners, the gickisses, the genscherers, the veranerins, patricos, swadders, and walking morts. . . .' Gerard was wise enough to resist the temptation; but another youth of the same period was neither so wise nor so lucky. François Villon, banished from Paris after being denounced as a thief, spent four years drifting through France without a home. Two of his friends belonged to wandering gangs of thieves. Whether Villon himself did or not, he left an astonishing collection of poems called *The Jargon,* composed in the secret language of the French underworld, and now very difficult to interpret.

In eighteenth-century London, whole sections of the city were inhabited by paupers, prostitutes, vagabonds, and criminals. There is an excellent picture of that hideous society in Gerald Howson's life of Jonathan Wild, *Thief-Taker General* (St. Martin's Press, New York, 1971). Mr. Howson gives a list of the cant names for different types of criminal specialists and specialities. The crooks included Millkens (burglars), Anglers (thieves who used rods and fishing-lines), Wild Rogues (who snatched hats and other portables out of coaches), Badgers (water-thieves and corpse-disposers), Vulcans (picklocks), Autem Divers (pickpockets who worked in churches), Rufflers (muggers), Buffers (who killed horses almost undetectably by thrusting sharp wires into their hearts), Abraham Men (fake lunatics), Confek Cranks (fake epileptics), Faytors (forgers), and Ripping Coves (burglars who broke into houses by tearing up the roof). Among the highly developed rackets were Flying the Basket (putting a boy into the baggage section of a coach so that he could throw out the bags), the Hook-Pole Lay (pulling a traveler off his horse with a hook on the end of a long pole), Sweating (shaking gold coins in a bag and collecting the dust to make a new coin), and the Lodging Lay (renting an apartment and then removing everything but the kitchen sink). Mr. Howson observes that this last racket is still practiced in motels.

There is also a language of signs which is spread all over Europe from Scotland to Rumania. It is the code by which tramps tell one another whether or not to approach a particular house or village: no more than a collection of simple signs made with chalk or pencil, which might almost be a child's scribble or a random doodle. There are two types of these signs, soft and hard. A soft sign means 'this is a good place.' The simplest is a tick of approval: ✓. Another soft sign, a circle with a cross inside it, ⊕ , might represent a coin, or even Christian charity; while an oval with crossbars, ⬭, is a stylized loaf, meaning 'free food here.' Among the hard signs, a line of sharp angles ⋀⋁⋀⋁ means 'beware of the dog' and looks like teeth ready to bite; and a design of horizontal and vertical lines clearly signifies prison bars: ▦ .

The most widespread secret language in the United States continually changes, and is split into dozens of local and specialized dialects. It is, like the language of Villon and Jonathan Wild, the language of the underworld. Like Shelta, it is meant chiefly to identify members of an in-group and protect them, while bewildering and misleading members of out-groups. Some of it is recorded in *Carnival,* by Arthur H. Lewis (Trident Press, New York, 1970); and there is a complete lexicon of it, *The Dictionary of American Underworld Lingo,* edited by Hyman E. Goldin, Frank O'Leary, and Morris Lipsius (Twayne Publishers, New York, 1950). This lexicon was entirely written, its editors assure us, within one of the chief American prisons. It is a most instructive, though frequently disgusting and sometimes terrifying book. Suppose you were in a gambling house. If you were playing but not losing very much, you might hear someone say, 'Lug the mark, he's a TB.' This would mean an order to get rid of you, not because you had tuberculosis but because you were a Total Blank. If you still hung around until the police charged in and broke up the game, you might hear someone shout, 'Zex! Cop a mope!' If you did not zex (or look out) and cop a mope (or escape), you might meet the bulls, and then have to take a rap, perhaps get hit with a deuce: in which case you would soon learn more secret language than most people have ever heard in all their lives.

Julian Franklyn, *The Cockney* (Deutsch, London, revised edition, 1953).

Mario Pei, *The Story of Language* (Lippincott, Philadelphia and New York, revised edition, 1965), Part Two, Chapter Ten ('Cant and Jargon').

R. A. Stewart Macalister, *The Secret Languages of Ireland* (Cambridge University Press, 1937).

Changing Words

LANGUAGE is a living thing. We can feel it changing. Parts of it become old: they drop off and are forgotten. New pieces bud out, spread into leaves, and become big branches, proliferating.

There is one thing which we often forget about language. This is that essentially it lives long, but peripherally it alters, often very fast.

The language which we speak today is the same language as that of Shakespeare and his friends, the language which was spoken and written four hundred years ago. Agreed, it is not the same in all ways. The pronunciation has changed a good deal, some of Shakespeare's words have fallen away, and many new ones have been invented. But it is the same in what matters. If we met a man of Shakespeare's time, or one of the Pilgrim Fathers, and talked with him, we could understand him and he could understand us after the first ten minutes. We can hear a play of Shakespeare acted, and understand ninety per cent of it. But the paradox of language is this. Shakespeare used many of the same words as we use; but he used some of them with a different meaning, a meaning which has now been forgotten and may even seem absurd. Words live long; but their meaning often alters from one generation to another. And often the meaning of a word which we use today is so far from the meaning it had a few generations ago that we can scarcely believe the change which must have taken place. It is like meeting someone whom you knew in school as a timid, underfed, awkward, dreamy hobbledehoy, and finding that he has become a tall, strong, resolute, aggressive man.

What is a *Whig,* and what is a *Tory?* What is a *snob?* What is a *prig?* What is a *vamp,* and what does a pianist do when he *vamps* an accompaniment? Suppose you describe someone as *nice*—are you praising him or disparaging him? Do you admire a man for being *eager* and dislike him for being *silly?* And what is a *glamour* girl?

Originally a glamour girl was any girl who could read and write. A silly man was innocent, to the point of being helpless. An eager man was cruel and bitter. Anyone who was nice was either effeminate or foolish. A vamp was a living corpse. A prig was a drunken tinker, a snob was a poor shoemaker, a Tory was a fierce Irish outlaw, and a Whig was a Scottish countryman.

Glamour is merely a mispronunciation and miswriting of *grammar.* In the Dark Ages, a grammar meant the knowledge of how to read and write. Most people then could not read or write: therefore anyone who knew grammar must possess an uncanny range of knowledge: therefore he might be a magician. Grammar or glamour was therefore a special kind of spiritual power which could not be understood or resisted by ordinary folk.* In eighteenth-century Scottish songs 'casting the glamour' on someone does not mean throwing a book at him, but enchanting him with a magic spell. It was Scott who brought the word *glamour* back into general circulation by

---

* In particular, grammar meant the power to read and write Latin, at a time when there were very few learned books in any other language. There is a variant, which also means magic, and is used by Sir Walter Scott, *gramarye;* and the French word for a book full of occult or unintelligible language is *grimoire.*

using it to mean magic; and perhaps he did not know what it originally signified—for he said that glamour was a speciality of the gipsies, who have never been overfond of book-learning. Not long afterward Tennyson used it simply to mean sorcery, when he wrote of

> that maiden in the tale
> Whom Gwydion made by glamour out of flowers. (*Enid* 743)

Then about fifty years ago it was discovered by advertising men, who debased its significance like advertising men can: until now it means little more than sex-appeal, or allure.

Among the Canterbury pilgrims whom Chaucer described there was a canon, very poorly dressed. His attendant yeoman said that he was a great scientist, but that as far as clothes went he was 'lewed and nyce' (*Canon's Yeoman's Prologue* 648). Nowadays this would mean that he was sexy and elegant, like a young male film star. But then *lewed* or *lewd* meant unable to read, stupid: in the King James version of the Bible, the riotous Jews who expelled St. Paul from Salonica were helped by 'certain lewd fellows of the baser sort' (Acts xii. 5). As for *nice,* it comes from the Latin *nescius* [*ne-scius* = not knowing] and originally meant ignorant. (In modern Spanish *necio* still means 'fool.') Later, perhaps, it came to mean shrinking from the world; then fastidious, and then neat and elegant and agreeable.

Eager is the same as the Latin *acer,* 'sharp' or 'keen.' Waiting for the appearance of the ghost of his dead father, Hamlet feels the Arctic wind (with the chill of death in it) and says

> The wind bites shrewdly; it is bitter cold.

As he often does, Horatio restates and confirms the prince's remark:

> It is a nipping and an eager air.

In the same act (*Hamlet* 1.5.66–70) Hamlet's father describes the action of the poison that killed him, working on his blood like vinegar in milk:

Swift as quicksilver it courses through
The natural gates and alleys of the body,
And with a sudden vigour it doth posset [= thicken]
And curd, like eager droppings into milk,
The thin and wholesome blood.

Silly is even more peculiar. In German *selig* means happy
and blessed. In Wagner's *Mastersingers* young Walter after his
triumph in the singing contest is offered membership in the
order of the Masters. He refuses in two aggressive tenor phrases,
saying

> Nicht Meister, nein!
> Will ohne Meister selig sein!

'I will be happy without the title of Master.' Touches of this
meaning survived until recently in England: the county of
Sussex was known as 'seely Sussex,' a happy, a specially blessed
region. But usually it means 'foolish,' perhaps because so many
saintly people were unworldly and could not cope with hard
practical things; perhaps also because thinking men felt that
no one who thought hard could really be happy.

Whig and *Tory* are contemptuous names created by politicians in opposing parties, and they have a rowdy and even violent background. The Tories are the more rebellious. The first
Tories were the Irish who were driven out of their homes
when the English determined to take over Ireland in the
seventeenth century, resettling it with Protestant incomers.
The Irish moved into the wild parts of the country, living by
their wits, and harrying those who had uprooted them, like the
Greek *klephtai* under the Turkish occupation. In English they
were called bog-trotters, and in Irish Gaelic, tories. (The exact
Gaelic word is not known, but it is conjectured to be *toraidhe,*
'pursuer,' from the existing word *toraidheachd,* 'pursuit.' A
*star before a word means that its existence has been inferred
but that it has not actually been found in a text.) When the
word entered English it came to be used for outlaws anywhere:
for the Scottish Highlanders whom the English found so difficult to tame, and for the Rajput marauders in India. But it

really became popular in 1679–80, when a serious crisis divided Britain. The people of the country were almost entirely Protestant. The king, Charles II, was suspected of being a Roman Catholic in secret, and of being in the pay of Louis XIV of France. (Both suspicions were correct.) Since Charles had no sons—or rather, no legitimate sons—when he died the throne would go to his brother, James, Duke of York, who was known to be a fervent Roman Catholic. A large number of the British people had no wish to see a Roman Catholic ruling them. Their leaders therefore introduced into Parliament a bill proposing to exclude James from the throne for ever. Those who opposed this bill they nicknamed, after the Catholic Irish bandits, Tories. And yet ten years later the origin of the name was all but forgotten. James had become king, had ruled very badly for three years, and had been thrown out in the Bloodless Revolution. Under his successor William of Orange, the political party devoted to supporting the crown, and in general to conservative principles, inherited the name of Tory and wore it proudly. In the American War of Independence it was used for the 'loyalists' who chose to retain their allegiance to the British crown; and so, within just a hundred years, it had changed its meaning from 'rebel' to 'opponent of rebellion,' from revolutionary to counterrevolutionary.

Whig goes back a little further. In the first half of the seventeenth century it was a dialect word meaning 'country bumpkin.' Then the Scottish Covenanters refused to accept, at the bidding of Charles I, the Church of England prayer book and liturgy. They marched to Edinburgh in a demonstration which their enemies contemptuously called the *whiggamore* ride. (*More* or *mhor* is Scots Gaelic for 'big,' so *whiggamore* meant 'big country oaf.') Since that demonstration meant resistance to the crown, to the Church of England, and to the Establishment, the name was extended to the opponents of the Tories and kept that meaning until well within living memory.

How about *snob* and *prig?* Snob is an English dialect word, first used for a shoemaker, parallel to *snip* for a tailor. Then it was taken into the slang of Cambridge University, and was used to mean any townsman—a shopkeeper or such—who was not of the same social class as a member of Cambridge University. The *Oxford English Dictionary* quotes a splendid sentence from a mid-Victorian periodical, which was written in 1865 and has now almost exactly the opposite of its original meaning: 'Happily the annals of Oxford present no instance of a "snob" murdered in the streets.' From the University world it spread into general usage, and was employed to mean anyone who did not claim social eminence, an ordinary man in the street, a commoner. A reporter who described the colonization of Australia in 1852 wrote, 'Most of the Australian colonists are essentially snobs, and they are justly proud of the distinction.' (Try telling that to an Australian today, and watch the effect.) Next, in a period when people were beginning to think more and more about social differentiations, the word came to mean anyone who behaved crudely and vulgarly. In 1846 the English satirist Thackeray (who had himself been at Cambridge and had there written for a little magazine called *The Snob*) published a very successful and amusing series of studies of vulgar people who were *trying* to behave like gentlemen: it was called the *Snob Papers,* republished as *The Book of Snobs.* Gradually the original meaning was forgotten, and a snob came to mean anyone who showed great anxiety to attain, or to preserve, social distinction. And now it means exclusive, ritzy, even, in a limited way, aristocratic. I have seen in the window of a smart shop in Paris a pair of suede shoes marked 'Très Snob.' From snob to snob in six generations.

As for *prig,* it first appears in Shakespeare's lifetime, to mean a drunken tinker. Shakespeare himself uses it once or twice for a petty thief, for instance the pickpocket Autolycus. 'Out upon him! Prig, for my life, prig. He haunts wakes, fairs, and bear-baitings.' (*Winter's Tale* 4.3.109.) In that sense it hung on until last century at least, when to prig meant to steal, usually by a trick rather than by violence. Watching innocent

Oliver Twist cleaning his boots for him, the Artful Dodger remarks thoughtfully, 'What a pity it is he isn't a prig!' But in the seventeenth century it acquired another meaning too. Perhaps because sneak thieves have to be very brisk and smooth and quick, it came to mean a dandy. People in Restoration comedy will point to a fop and ask, 'What spruce prig is that?' Next it became still narrower. It came to mean anyone who was exceedingly or ostentatiously neat and precise in his appearance, or his speech, or his writing, or his ethical standards. Dr. Johnson said that the philologist James Harris was 'a prig, and a bad prig' (Boswell, 7th April 1778), by which he meant the man was a pedant. Others used the word for nonconformist ministers, because they tended to stick to the letter of the Bible and make public displays of ostentatious piety. The same sense of pettiness appears in Emerson's delightful 'Fable':

> The mountain and the squirrel
> Had a quarrel;
> And the former called the latter 'Little Prig.'

The word has moved all the way from the bottom of the social scale to somewhere near the top, but one thing it has always kept—the feeling of dislike and contempt which it inspires, and perhaps that is due to its disagreeable sound.

Some other words which were once neutral but low in the social scale have sunk much lower because they acquired moral and even aesthetic connotations. You would have to be bitterly angry nowadays to call a man a boor, a churl, and a villain; and he would resent it if you did. But, going by the original meaning of the words, you would only be saying that he was a farmer. A *boor* is the same as the German *Bauer* and the Dutch *Boer*. A *churl* is a plain man, a member of the lowest class of free men in Anglo-Saxon England, a peasant drifting gradually into servitude: Carl and Charles mean no more than *man*. A *villain* was a man attached to a villa, which in the Dark Age was a country estate; later it began to mean somebody who was virtually a serf tied to his lord's land. And then, since the Middle Ages and the Renaissance were predominantly aristocratic, and one of the worst fates that could befall anyone was to be born a peasant, *villain* and *churl* and *boor* became words of bitter contempt. Hamlet applies one of them to his treacherous uncle:

O villain, villain, smiling damned villain!

with the same violence as he later upbraids himself:

O, what a rogue and peasant slave am I! *

One of the most curious of these mutating words is *vamp*. It is shortened from vampire, which is Hungarian. (Cognates appear in the Slavonic languages, for instance *vapir* in Bulgarian; it may originally come from the Turkish *uber,* 'witch.') It means a person who is dead but still unnaturally alive, because he or she comes out of the grave at night and sucks the blood of the living. If a vampire's grave is opened, the body is found to be fresh and unputrefied, with color in the cheeks and the lips bright red. To be killed, the vampire must be pierced with a wooden stake (at which fresh blood always spurts out) and if possible burnt to ashes. It is a horrible superstition, peculiar to eastern Europe and the Balkans. The name was naturally enough transferred to the bloodsucking bats of South America; and then, by some genius of publicity, to some of the early motion picture actresses who portrayed *femmes fatales,* mysterious women who dominated and destroyed their loves. Some of them, such as Nazimova and Theda Bara, cultivated an other-worldly look, with great dark eyes fixed in a pallid face, and a cruel sensual mouth. The public soon shortened the name to vamp, which satisfactorily obscured its original bloodthirsty meaning. The other word vamp has nothing to do with that. It means the upper front part of a shoe (from

* *Hamlet* 1.5.106 and 2.5.521. The account above is simplified. For a complex analysis see **F. M. Stenton's** *Anglo-Saxon England* (Oxford, 1947 ²), chapter 14.

the French *avant-pied*). From that, to vamp came to mean to
patch up. When a pianist puts in a simple recurrent figure to
patch over a gap until the singer is ready, he vamps it.

One word is changing its meaning and being degraded at
the present moment, chiefly because people do not know what
it really signifies. This is *cohort*.

A cohort is a body of soldiers: a battalion, or something of
that sort. It was one of the subdivisions of the Roman army.
It has been in English, with that meaning, for hundreds of
years. In Milton's *Paradise Lost* God sends the archangel
Michael to expel Adam and Eve from the garden, and

> with him the cohort bright
> Of watchful Cherubim.   (*Paradise Lost* 11.127–28)

Some time during the nineteenth century the word got into
general usage from Byron's splendid poem 'The Destruction
of Sennacherib.' The facts are in the Bible: Second Chronicles,
chapter 32. Byron's poem begins, in galloping anapests:

> The Assyrian came down like a wolf on the fold,
> And his cohorts were gleaming in purple and gold.

That is, his regiments wore splendid uniforms, to overawe the
poor Jews.

It became a favorite school recitation, and was often reprinted in such books as McGuffey's Readers. Taken from it,
the word *cohort* spread into journalism. Some reporter remembered the beginning of the poem on Sennacherib and inserted
a concealed quotation from it into a newspaper story. Who he
was, and what his subject, are lost in the history of journalism;
but what he wrote was something like this:

> At today's parade in honor of St. Patrick and the ideals of old
> Ireland, none stepped out more bravely than Police Captain
> Francis X. McGeoghegan, followed by his splendid blue-clad
> cohorts.

Now, reporters may not read books; but they read each
other's writings in newspapers, and borrow from them. The

word *cohorts* stuck in the mind of another reporter, who did not quite know what it meant, except that it signified men who were subordinate to a commander. He in his turn wrote something like this:

> The budget meeting at City Hall this morning was attended by Borough President Mario Attilio Squarciafico, with all his cohorts.

He was followed by half-educated writers who did not understand that a cohort was a collective noun, and thought it was something between an escort and a co-worker. They started writing like this:

> One of the principal cohorts of Mayor James J. Walker during his first term of office was. . . .

And by now the process is almost complete. Few people know that a cohort is an armed unit, a squadron, a corps—as it has been until recently throughout English and American literature. Most people think it means a single man, what journalists call an 'aide.' J. D. Salinger has brought the mistake into the contemporary novel. In *Raise High the Roof Beam, Carpenters* one of the sensitive Glass family finds himself walking through the East Seventies of New York with a little deaf-mute, nice situation, dressed for a wedding, keen farce. He writes, 'A silk hat materialized in the air beside me, and my special, only technically unassigned cohort grinned up at me.' To anyone who knows what the word really signifies, this means that fifty or sixty men were smiling at the narrator, while acting as his bodyguard.

There are a hundred such strange histories in our language. *Humor* means 'moisture'; *gentle* means 'noble,' and it has three brothers, *Gentile, genteel,* and *jaunty;* a *toilet* is a cloth cover for a dressing table; and *kind* simply means 'natural.' No wonder Dr. Johnson said that languages were the pedigrees of nations.

NOT MANY years ago (as history runs nowadays) Japanese businessmen started to visit the United States, in order to set up industrial and commercial agreements affecting both countries. They were good at negotiating; but they found that the hardest thing to understand was not the American factory system or American financial conventions or American trade practices, but American social manners. Even when they could speak the language fairly well, they were often baffled. They were never quite sure how they themselves ought to behave, and they could not comprehend why Americans behaved as they did. One of these early Japanese explorers of the United States is said, about sixty years ago, to have written a book to help his compatriots.

He began by explaining that the life of Americans was a complicated mass of ceremonies—ceremonies so intricate that no foreigner could ever hope to understand them fully. It sounds ridiculous. Americans governed by an abstruse system of ceremonial behavior! We, who think of ourselves as the least formal, the most spontaneous and open-hearted of nations, we who have always surprised and occasionally shocked

visitors from other countries by our disdain for artificial restraints, how could our life possibly be said to be dictated by
ceremonious rules?

The Japanese investigator gave an example. He told his
readers about the ceremony that occurs when two American
businessmen meet each other. In Japan, of course, it would
be perfectly simple, with both sides smiling and bowing and
uttering gracefully turned conventional remarks about health
and happiness, polished by many years of custom. But in the
United States, the author implied, it was almost incomprehensible. First there was a lot of noise and shouting on both
sides. Then the two men slapped each other on the back or
poked each other in the ribs. Then, at a given moment—
although no signal could be observed—each man reached into
his pocket for a cigar, and offered it to the other; both men
laughed and refused; and then, after another interval, the
inferior man accepted the cigar offered by the *superior* man.
This terminated the ceremony.

It might almost be a caricature; and yet it has a basic truth
in it. That particular pattern, centering on back-slapping and
cigars, went out with Babbitt and is now obsolete. It has been
replaced by other ceremonies which are likewise meant to
demonstrate friendship, sincerity, and informality. I shall not
soon forget a day in a hotel in Beverly Hills some years ago,
where I watched two Hollywood types, gray-haired, pouchy,
sun-tanned, and bejeweled, two *men* in their middle years,
who greeted each other by embracing, and kissing, and calling
each other 'Sweetheart!' Ritual does not necessarily mean stiff-
ness and elaboration. As you can tell by watching teen-agers,
it needs a good deal of training in specific patterns of behavior
simply to be informal in the right way.

The story about the Japanese businessman's guide to America comes from an admirable book called *The Silent Language*
by an anthropologist named Edward T. Hall. Dr. Hall wrote
it to explain some of the unsuspected difficulties that nations
have in understanding one another. It is common to hear
well-meaning optimists declare that there need be very few

barriers to world understanding. We are all human beings, after all. The color of our skin, or the spot on the earth's surface where we happened to be born, is external and unimportant. If we can only pierce the barrier of language, we shall find that you and I and they and everyone are all just Folks. It might be delightful if this were true; but it is not. Many thousands of Americans who have tried living and working abroad, especially since the second world war, have found that the externals like skin color and place of birth usually cover much deeper differences between nations; and that what really divides various groups all over the world is that they *think differently* about such fundamental matters as sex, happiness, the will of God, the use of the earth, the structure of society, and the purpose of life. Furthermore, they have found that the thinking of any one group about these subjects forms a fairly closely woven pattern, in which the questions and answers are interconnected, so that outsiders cannot simply come in and point to one single belief or custom, and say, 'That is wrong. Correct that, and then you'll be all right.' This is the main theme of Dr. Hall's book. He calls it a primer in the theory of culture. It contains many good examples and some clear forceful writing. The only thing that keeps me from praising it more highly is its author's insistence on putting in a lot of technical words which he and a colleague have worked out to explain a new theory of the patterns of culture. Still, it says many things which need to be said, and illustrates them with real-life experience.

It is a valuable introduction to a set of very difficult problems which confront every traveler nowadays. Every American going abroad, every foreigner coming to America, will be pleased and interested by some things and shocked and disgusted by others; and every day, sometimes every hour, he will be puzzled. When an American lands on foreign soil (say at Istanbul or Manila or Buenos Aires), he finds that

at first things in the cities look pretty much [like America]. There are taxis, hotels with hot and cold running water, theaters, neon lights, even tall buildings with elevators and a few people who speak English. But pretty soon the American discovers that underneath the familiar exterior there are vast differences. When someone says 'yes' it often doesn't mean yes at all, and when people smile it doesn't always mean that they are pleased. People tell him they will do things, and don't. The longer he stays, the more enigmatic the new country looks, until finally he begins to learn to observe new cues that reinforce or negate the words people are saying with their mouths.

And far beneath the differences in methods of expression, there are differences in systems of thought. Consider the case of the American farming expert who went to Egypt to try to help the Egyptian farmers to increase their yield. I need hardly say that he did not know Egyptian Arabic and had to use an interpreter. But he found that he needed an interpreter, not only for language, but for thought. The fellaheen had been farming for many centuries, but their attitude to their farms was apparently incomprehensible and irrational. He asked one farmer what size of crop he expected at the coming harvest. Instead of giving him a rough estimate, the farmer became furiously angry and broke out into a long tirade of abuse. The interpreter translated his reply (obviously leaving nine-tenths of it out) as 'He says he does not know.' In the mind of the Islamic peoples, only God knows the future. It is presumptuous even to talk about it. It is insane to try to predict it. Therefore, when the American asked the Egyptian what size of crop he expected, his question implied that the Egyptian was both impious and crazy. That was not the eccentric notion of a single man. It was part of a widespread pattern of thought which covers much of the Middle East: a fabric of feeling and imagination and religious and social ideology which has woven into it both its own strengths and its own weaknesses, and which cannot possibly be torn apart by any individual or radically altered in less than several centuries. The very word Islam means 'submission' to the will of God. The emotions of the Egyptian farmer could be supported by texts from his sacred book, the glorious Koran; and the passivity verging on pessimism which they imply is the prevailing spiritual attitude of nearly a hundred million people. In the same book Dr. Hall quotes a Lebanese-American sociologist who found some Arab villagers absolutely refusing to let outsiders clean up their water source, although it was contaminated with typhoid. They had three reasons: first, they like water to have a strong individual taste; second, water is almost sacred, and must not be tampered with; and third, they perceived no connection between the filth of the water and the death of their children. Children did not die because they drank dirty water, but because it was the will of Allah; and it was apparently useless to push this theological argument further back and ask whether Allah willed them to drink clean water or dirty water. I wonder if there was not a fourth reason: namely, that these poor villagers had for so many hundred years been victimized by government representatives that they could not possibly believe *any* official would do *anything* to benefit them, free, gratis, and for nothing.

In dealing with foreigners we must treat their cultures as organic wholes: each is a living structure which includes almost every individual man and woman and child within it, and molds him or her, whether he or she can explain it or not. It seems silly for the Japanese to describe a cheery informal American greeting as a complex ceremony. Americans, living inside the American structure of feeling and communication, do such things because they seem to be quite natural; and, conversely, we are apt to regard foreign ways of meeting and greeting as unnatural and affected. But in fact no culture is natural. All systems of social behavior are elaborate organizations many years old, which must be learned through a long apprenticeship in childhood and youth. Every culture seems natural to those who are inside looking out. Every culture seems artificial to those who are outside looking in.

Furthermore, many of the most important things in a culture are taken for granted. Some are assumed to be so obvious that they need not be explained, even to outsiders. Last time I was in Paris I saw a filthy beatnik, half stoned, lounging in a café with his bare feet cocked up on a chair, displaying to the world a revolting horny surface thickly covered with scars and the engrained dirt of the streets. At once I remembered how Lyndon Baines Johnson had given great (though unconscious) offense to a dignitary in the Far East, because he sat beside him at a public ceremony with one leg cocked over his knee—thus thrusting the sole of his foot on the gaze of His Highness. The foot was shod, of course; but any foot, bare or shod, which walks twenty paces in certain parts of the Far East is liable to pick up unmentionable filth. Or again, in many parts of the East the left hand is used to cleanse the body after evacuation. Everyone who belongs to such a culture knows this, and never eats with the left hand; and no one offers anything to anyone else with the left hand—except as a calculated insult. They all know this; but incomers to their cultural area sometimes do not.

There are other patterns which cannot be explained even inside a culture. Dr. Hall used to ask Americans who were going to take up a post abroad to explain what the rules were for using a person's first name in the United States. They always tried to define them, and then gave up, saying 'It's hard to pin these things down.' I can comment on this as an immigrant from Britain. When I lived there, we had four stages of naming: first and commonest, Mr. Jones; then—for quite a long time, sometimes for life—Jones, which is not formal, but does not indicate any degree of affection or intimacy; then, after the barrier had been breached, William; and finally Bill. But in the United States I am still occasionally puzzled. After you stop calling a man Mr. Jones you do not start calling him Jones. You might try Jonesy; or else call him nothing much, for quite a long time, and then move straight on to Bill.

In social matters, there are no absolutes. Surely Time, with the steady march of the hours through day and night, is a fundamental concept? Yet people throughout the world differ enormously in interpreting it. How late (Dr. Hall asks) is 'late'? In the eastern United States it is anything from five minutes to an hour—depending on the importance and the formality of the occasion: a business meeting, a dinner party, a cocktail gathering. But in Latin America you do not even begin to be late until an hour after the arranged time has passed. Among some American Indian people there is no word for 'late,' because the concept does not exist. Time is not thought of by such people as an external standard imposed on the rhythms of life and compelling them to conform to it. Rather they believe that time, like life, flows like a river or drifts like the moving air.

There are no human absolutes. All cultural patterns are different. Are they all equally valuable? Is there no objective standard by which they can be compared with one another? Is it either impossible, or wrong, to convert anyone? Could we not demonstrate, slowly and patiently and working within the closed cultural pattern, that if children were given water not flavored by sewage they might—under the will of Allah— have a better chance of living than if they drank from the drains? Dr. Hall implies that we might; and he even suggests that we should: provided only that we do it very gradually, and very sympathetically, with the tenderness of a nurse taking off a thickly clotted bandage from a wound. What we must not do is to echo Dr. Johnson, who once listened to a group of aliens chattering away about trifles at the top of their voices, and said, 'Does this not confirm old Meynell's observation— *For any thing I see, foreigners are fools*?' We may think it; but we must not say it.

R. Benedict, *Patterns of Culture* (Houghton Mifflin, Boston, 1934).

E. T. Hall, *The Silent Language* (Doubleday, Garden City, N.Y., 1959).

E. T. Hall, *The Hidden Dimension* (Doubleday, Garden City, N.Y., 1966).

Lifetime Labels

POSSIBLY in the future we shall all be known by numbers; or by combinations of digits and symbols—our blood group plus our Social Security number; or by special patterns of slots in IBM cards, identifying us by fingerprints and other unique data. But meanwhile we are known by spoken and written labels, which are our names. They are important. They are usually loved by those who love us. Our friends think of us first by these labels, and only secondly by our changing outward appearance. Yet neither our friends nor we usually know what the labels mean. There are thousands of couples called John and Mary, Bill and Betty: they know each other intimately, they would think it a shame not to remember whether the one they loved had blue or brown eyes, black hair or yellow; yet the name, the beloved name spoken twenty times a day, is usually only a sound without significance.

Surely this is unfortunate. Anything so intimate as a name ought to be more than a collection of agreeable or striking noises. And in fact many people who choose names for their children have a faint conception of the meaning, or at least the general tone, of the words which they use. It is faint, no more. But it would often be well worth their while to learn the true meaning of the name. Even groups of numbers and symbols would be better than syllables without sense.

In the United States and through most of the western world people usually have two names. Many of us have extras; but if we are held to the essentials, we have two names: the family name, which we inherit, and the given name, by which we are known, first to our parents and then to our friends and finally to our husband or wife. The family name represents our legal personality. Whether our family and friends call us Bill or Bind-their-kings-in-chains-and-their-nobles-in-links-of-iron, the law cares little. It is chiefly interested in our family name, the label of the kinship group to which we belong and which shares the responsibility for our existence, Smith or Settiducatti, Cohen or Gomez, Murphy or Margon. The given name is the one which carries emotion. One of the less sympathetic things about the men and women of the nineteenth century is that husbands and wives sometimes addressed each other as though they were strangers: Judge Thompson, or Mrs. Harcourt. Nowadays Americans try to find out the given name as soon as possible, and to use it rather than the legal and external label.

Surnames were not needed until the world became complicated and crowded. At most it was enough to describe a man by his own name and the name of his father, Joseph the son of Jacob, Achilles the son of Peleus. Some ancient Greek families had the excellent practice of giving the boy his grandfather's name, so that two names alternated, each skipping a generation. But now we are packed together upon the surface of the groaning world, and we must try to distinguish one another.

Surnames are inherited from the first 'man of distinction' who founded the family. And they are nearly always based on the four main questions which people ask about an individual: *descent* (who are his folks?), *occupation* (what does he do?), *residence* (where does he live?), and *appearance* (what does he look like?).

Very many people still bear names derived from the given name of the first man who distinguished himself enough to found their family. If he was John, they are called Johnson, because the name passed on and on. Among the Presidents of the United States, most seem to bear simple family names of that type: Jefferson, Jackson, Johnson, Wilson, Madison, Adams (probably from Adamson), Pierce (descended from Peter), and McKinley. Nixon is the son of a Nicholas far back. All the Joneses are sons of Johns. The Macs and the Os are sons of whatever clan or family leader they descended from, be it Brian (which makes them O'Brian), or David (which makes them MacTavish), or the Norse invader Olaf (which makes them Macaulay).

The next most popular kind of family name is the trade name. It never occurs to us, when we meet a man called Miller or a girl called Taylor, to think that he or she comes from craftsmen who worked at milling grain or plied the needle and thread. Yet the trade names are so common that they ought to remind us of the busy rise of crafts in the Middle Ages. In particular, the blackSmiths and the grainMillers must have had enormous families and taken care of them very well. The surname of the late President Eisenhower reminds us that one of his ancestors was an 'iron hewer,' or iron-miner. It is an old trade: the minstrel who walked in front of the invading Norman army as it entered Saxon England, singing the Song of Roland and throwing his sword into the air, was called Taillefer, 'iron cutter.' Among U.S. Presidents there have been descendants of a tailor and a tiler; there almost was a weaver, or webster, but his thread ran out.

Then again, people are often described by the place in which their family lived when it first had to be given a legal name. A remote ancestor was called John at the Bridge or

Henry at the Ford, William Wood, Joseph Thorndike. The descendants of this man, with his fixed and known dwelling, took these names. The two commonest surnames in France come from the man who lived by the bridge and the man who lived near the wood, Dupont and Dubois. (Curious to think that now, in another country, the Bridge family has become very distinguished as the du Ponts.) Several American Presidents bore place-names with which their families were once connected. Buchanan's family came from the parish of Buchanan in Stirlingshire, Scotland. Lincoln's preserves the name of a Roman settlement in northern England, Lindum Colony. Roosevelt means either 'red field,' because the ancestral farm was made of red clay, or 'rose field,' because an ancestor managed to cultivate roses in cold wet Holland. Washington's people took their name from a town, or ton, or farm, homesteaded by the family of Wess.

Finally, many people were named for the personal characteristics of a long-dead forefather. General Grant was not especially tall, but he had someone far back in his family who was sufficiently big to be called Grant or Grand or Tall. The Browns and Whites, Blacks and Grays, all come from men who had something noteworthy in their coloring; but the Greens stem from villagers who had a cottage by the village green. Many surnames more complex than these have grown out of nicknames. Some point to resemblances between men and animals or birds. The mild Wilbur was once a Wild Boar; Poe was a Peacock; and Wolf was more than merely greedy and dangerous, he was highly intelligent, brave, and loyal to his own pack. President Truman descended from a true man, who was absolutely faithful to his friends and was judged honest; and who shall say that his name did not help the American public to judge him, and did not reflect his character?

With a little thought and a little experience of the way words are made and used, most family names can be understood. Given names are more difficult to interpret. There are several reasons for this.

The chief reason is that many given names in America and in Christian Europe are taken either from the Bible—so that they are originally Hebrew—or from the calendar of Christian saints—so that they are, if not Hebrew, Greek or Latin in origin. Take the two best known of all. Who understands them? John, like so many Hebrew names with the syllable Jah in them, is a theophoric name, containing one of the names of God. In all its forms (John, Jean, Juan, Giovanni, Johannes, Ivan, Ian, Evan) it means 'God is gracious.' It is popular because it is the name of the best loved of the disciples of Jesus. And Mary, the name we associate with mildness and gentleness? It comes from the name of Moses' sister, Miriam, and means 'bitterness' or 'rebellion.' The meaning has long been forgotten, and the tradition of holiness remains. Another very common Hebrew name for girls is Elizabeth, with its variants: Betty, Isobel, Elsie, Lisa, and so forth. It means 'God has sworn,' and has the divine designation El in it. Probably it became common because of the prestige of Saint Elizabeth of Hungary and Queen Elizabeth I of England.

Eisenhower's two forenames belong to these two patterns: one Hebrew and one Greek. David, which means 'beloved,' is the name of the great king of the Jews, and of one important saint. Dwight is probably a diminutive form of the name of the Greek saint Dionysius or Dennis, abbreviated to Dennet and Diot and Dwight. But the name Dwight shows another process at work: the surname of a popular man is taken over and made into a forename. Dwight came into America as a surname. It became famous because of the work and personality of Timothy Dwight, chaplain in a regiment during the War of Independence, and president of Yale from 1795 to 1817. From his family name it was taken over and made into a given name. In the same way, President Roosevelt's Christian name was the surname of the admired Benjamin Franklin; Washington Irving was christened after the first President and Jefferson Davis after the third; there are many men now alive whose first name is the surname of President Lincoln.

Many difficult given names once belonged to the Germanic

and Celtic heroes and heroines of the Dark Ages, although some of them came into England only with the Norman Conqueror—notably William, Robert, Henry, and Gilbert. They recall a language and a style of emotional thinking which are now quite forgotten. The men's names ending in -bert mean 'bright': Robert means 'bright fame,' Hubert 'bright heart,' Herbert 'bright army,' and Gilbert 'bright pledge.' Henry—which has so many forms: Harry, Hal, Hawkins, Harris—means 'home rule,' which I suppose signifies 'ruler of his own house.' William [= Wil-helm] is the simplest of all fighting soldier-names, for it means 'will,' the courage a soldier must have, plus 'helmet,' an essential part of his armor. Charles, which looks and sounds so lofty, is about as low as a name can go before it becomes a number or a grunt, for it means nothing more than 'man,' the German *Kerl*. It became popular because of the power and prestige of the first Holy Roman Emperor, Carolus Magnus or Charlemagne, the Great Man. With James and George we return to Hebrew and Greek. James is rather complicated. It is a variation of Jacob, which means 'he who catches another by the heel = trickster or overreacher'—because Jacob came out of the womb holding his brother's heel, and later cheated him out of both his heritage and his blessing (Genesis xxv. 24–34, xxvii. 36). Dr. Noah Jacobs puts it neatly: the name means 'heel' in both the literal and the slang sense.* However, it became popular because it was borne by two apostles of the church and several important saints. George is simpler. It is the Greek for 'farmer' (a trade name like Plowman or Bauer); but it spread widely, because Saint George was a martyred Roman soldier, admired by the Crusaders and other fighting groups, and because he became the patron saint of England.

A lot of given names are merely place-names adapted, like Tennessee Williams. (Mr. Williams was not given that name by his parents; when she heard he had assumed it, Dorothy Parker said 'I might as well call myself Palestine Parker.') Winston is the name of a small Gloucestershire hamlet, and

---

* *Naming-Day in Eden* (see pp. 108–14 of this book), page 30.

was the *surname* of the mother of the first Duke of Marl-borough, who raised the fortunes of the Churchills from village to palace. Shirley is a place name, 'shire field,' and so is Stanley, 'stony field.' Like Lincoln, they began as place-names and then became surnames and then were adapted into given names.

Many new given names have appeared recently. Sometimes they are fancy spellings of established appellations: so Diana has become Diahann or Dionne. Sometimes they are sad mistakes. The sweet Spanish name Dolores means Sorrows (from Our Lady of the Sorrows); but it is now often misspelt by people who do not know Spanish or care about its derivation, as Delores, to parallel Delilah and Deborah and so forth. Sometimes they combine elements of several names. A friend of mine in Washington during the second world war had just got accustomed to beautiful Southern secretaries with two names, Mary Lou and Jo Anne, when he was overwhelmed by a wave from the deeper South, all with three names, Mary Sue Beth and Cele Anne Lou. Marybeth is now quite usual, made up of whole Mary and half Elizabeth. Marlene, so long associated with an actress playing pretty, languorous, disillusioned prostitutes, is very appropriately a telescoped version of the name of the first prostitute who became a saint, *Mar*-ia Magda-*lene*.

Still some of the most fascinating names of all remain riddles. No one knows what the name of the beautiful Helen means: it must be earlier than the earliest Greek we know. Katharine (with Kate, Kitty, Cathleen, Karen, Katinka, and so on) is another mystery. So are Ruth, and Anthony, and Teresa, and even (in spite of Exodus ii. 10) Moses. Some of the best-known names remain something of a riddle even if we know their surface meanings, because they were originally puns or jokes. Adam meant 'red' or 'red earth'; Isaac meant 'laughter'; Rose was not originally the flower, but the horse admired by the Teutonic peoples; Thomas means 'twin'; and one of the most graceful feminine names, Barbara, equals 'uncivilized foreigner.'

Learning a Language

I HAVE been captured by that delightful constrictor, that subtle serpent, language. Not for the first time, but for the tenth or eleventh time, I am learning a new foreign tongue.

It is always a strange experience to tackle a new language. A man who knew more about linguistics and more about women than I shall ever know once told me that it was more exciting to master a new tongue than to make love to a new woman, usually more difficult and ultimately more satisfying. I am a monogamist, but I try to be a polyglot, and I know what he was trying to convey by this rather wicked comparison. If you are a mountain climber and attack a new mountain, certainly there will be excitement and danger, but ultimately you are going to face problems similar to those you have met before. If you are a chess player and meet a new opponent, your heart may beat harder, but if you lose it will only be because you have mishandled your bishops, as so often before, and if you win it will be because you bring off a two-knight combination which you have often practiced. But if you know two languages and start learning a third, suddenly you will be faced with problems which you did not know could even exist in the fields of thought and speech. Fantastic subtleties, ridiculous laxities, unimaginable complexities, unthought-of strengths and bluntnesses in sound, in significance, and in aesthetic arrangement, confront you. Struggling to turn your thought out of your speech into a new kind of speech, you discover that your thought itself changes. Your mind too changes; and, in changing, it grows.

Friends sometimes ask me why I like learning new languages. I always feel like asking them why they do not like learning new languages, but I never do. For one thing, it would be too much like asking a tone-deaf man why he does not care for Debussy. For another, I know that many of them are actually afraid, and it would be embarrassing to expose their fear. They are timid about sounding like fools or small children while they are learning, and they are reluctant to remold their thinking and their habits of speech. I sympathize with this. Every human being has some inhibitions about learning certain new activities: skiing or dancing, diving or acting, public speaking or private thinking, all repel some of us. Then again, some people of a conservative bent believe subconsciously that there is only one language, their own; and that all others are silly monkey-talk not worth learning. They will not make the effort, any more than they would learn to bark and mew because they had a dog and a cat. This reluctance often appears when two language-groups live together on unsympathetic terms. Not many Peruvians of Spanish descent learn Quechua, the language of the conquered. Not many Englishmen learn Welsh: it was a special diplomatic effort for the present Prince of Wales to master the tongue of his princedom. Not many Jews in old Poland could speak Polish, and very few Poles knew Yiddish. I remember a British officer in Germany who, after some persuasion, though sticking in his big hooves and laying back his long hairy ears, started to learn German. When he was told that *Please* and *Thank you* were *Bitte schön* and *Danke schön,* he asked exactly what the phrases meant. 'What! what!' he grumbled when he heard. *'Pretty please* and *Pretty thanks?* Silly bloody language, I'm damned if I learn another word of it!'

However, why does anyone like learning new languages? Thinking over the people I have known as good linguists, I seem to see four different motives.

Not long ago I said good-bye to a quiet friendly young man whom I had known for some years off and on. He was leaving for the East, on some mission for the Department of State. I asked him how long he had been trained; he told me. I asked what the hardest part of his training had been, and he said it was learning Persian. 'But you aren't going to Iran?' said I. At once I knew I had been indiscreet. The smiling mask of the diplomat remolded his face. He replied, 'No, but it might come in useful.' Then I recalled that I had heard he might be posted to Afghanistan—where the upper classes speak Persian, where Persian is a noble, a cultured, an artistic and diplomatic tongue. If an American arrived in Afghanistan without being able to speak Persian, he might get on very well at the Peace Corps level, but he would scarcely be able to mix with the people who make policy, since they might put him down as an ignorant boor. No doubt my friend also learned the main language of the ordinary people of Afghanistan; but he had to learn Persian. Why? Not to read Omar Khayyam and Firdausi and the Persian poets. If he had been sent to Iceland instead of Afghanistan, he would never have touched Persian; but he had to know it, to talk to the important people whom he would meet.

Only the next day I met a former pupil of mine, good at Greek and Latin. I asked him what he was doing. He said he was learning the Pentateuch by heart in Hebrew, together with the most important commentaries on those five books. 'Have you any plans for going to Israel?' I asked. He replied that he would doubtless go out to Israel some time, but that what he was aiming at now was to have the whole mass of these literary and historical and legal scriptures in his mind, so that he would not have to refer to books and turn pages, but could from memory instantly recall the original words of the texts which were important. He was one of many generations of Hebrew scholars who have done the same thing. They learned the Hebrew language not in order to use it in daily conversation, but so as to read the important books written in it. It is the same with ancient Greek and with Latin. It would be eccentric to try to converse in these tongues, although of course it can be done: Gilbert Murray of Oxford could talk fluently in ancient Greek, and Henry Rowell of Johns Hopkins made fine speeches in Latin apparently without preparation and certainly without notes. But the primary purpose of learning these languages is to read the beautiful irreplaceable prose and poetry which are written in them, and which could not be adequately read in any translation into any other tongue.

My friend learning Persian wanted to speak it. My pupil working on Hebrew wanted to read it. Are there other reasons for learning a foreign language? At once I think of a jolly old philosopher named John Alexander Smith. (I spent an unforgettable year reading Aristotle's *Metaphysics* in a seminar with him and H. H. Joachim.) He was not a dry logic-chopper or a gloomy metaphysical brooder, but a sharp, bold, critical thinker, with some delightful personal eccentricities, such as having a huge library of whodunits, and grading each of them alpha, beta, gamma, or delta after reading it. After he grew to man's estate, he learned a new language every year of his life. He always taught himself, and he always used the same method. Choosing his language, he got hold of a translation of the Bible in it, and started to read, beginning either with the Book of Genesis, or with one of the Gospels, since he knew these books pretty well by heart. By the time he had finished one book of Scripture, he had a grasp of the general pattern of the language. After finishing one of the Testaments, he could read fluently. When he had finished the entire Bible, he could read and write the new language and could make a shot at talking it when necessary. However, his motive in doing this was not to talk this particular tongue (for he might never meet anyone who spoke it) nor to read its classics (for it might have none worth reading). It was to study the structure of the language and to compare it with the many others which he had learned.

No language ever corresponds completely to all the various activities of mankind. No two languages ever express human concerns in exactly the same way. The aim of the linguist is to show how different languages tackle similar problems, and to draw conclusions both about the habits of man as a social animal and about the behavior and potentialities of the human mind. Being a philosopher, J. A. Smith was deeply interested in that complex and fascinating problem, the relation between thought and speech. It is not possible to study this problem productively if you know only one language. It is not possible to go very far into it if you know only two closely related modern languages. You will learn something about it if you know three or four kindred European tongues. You will get much deeper into it if you know several Indo-European languages and several languages outside that big family—for instance, Arabic, Hungarian, Japanese, or Turkish. One set of ideas very hard for most people to grasp, unless they are naturally good at languages or well trained, is that speech, even our own native speech, does not neatly and exactly correspond to thought; that a word in one language does not cover exactly the same area of meaning as the corresponding word in another language (even when most of the meanings of the pair coincide); that some important words in certain languages cannot be adequately translated by single words in other languages (for instance, the English word *home,* the Greek word *logos,* the Latin word *res*).* These ideas cause pain to many a young student of Latin, because he is usually industrious and painstaking and therefore likes order and

---

* There are some excellent pages (50–56) in James Michener's *Iberia* (New York, 1968) where he analyzes certain essential Spanish ideas expressed in certain words untranslatable, except by approximation, into other tongues: *duende, gracia, ambiente, pundonor,* and so on.

system. He would prefer the whole Latin tongue to be neatly docketed into three genders, four conjugations, and five declensions WITH NO IRREGULAR VERBS OR ANOMALOUS NOUNS. When he is told that the Latin language was a coarse, crude instrument, which was only converted with great effort over many generations into a rich and subtle speech, and that it never wholly lost its original imprecision (which for some poets and connoisseurs is part of its charm), he is apt to grow discouraged and to wish he had chosen chemistry, where things can be weighed and measured and put down in neat tables.

It is both a challenge and a discouragement to be a professional analyst of language; for one is constantly learning, there is no danger of ever running out of material, the problems which must be tackled run into the hundreds of thousands, and some of the central puzzles are not anywhere near solution (even the question of grammatical classification of speech). It is, however, humbling to think that no human being, even in the course of a long lifetime of arduous application, could master even half of the languages known and spoken by his fellow men; and it is surely saddening to realize that only an exceptionally gifted linguist could learn even the thirteen chief languages of the world. (These are the languages which are spoken each by over fifty million people. In order of numerical importance they are Chinese, English, Hindustani, Russian, Spanish, German, Japanese, French, Malay, Bengali, Portuguese, Italian, and Arabic.)

I am not a professional linguist, but I have learned and can read eight languages besides English. I have failed with two—Russian and Hebrew: Russian because it is too complex for me to learn it from a handbook without a teacher, and Hebrew because I have a block about the alphabet and the vowel points; but I'll master them both yet! And I still remember the excitement with which, at the age of eleven, I started learning French and Latin and ancient Greek. (Of course, that is the age when foreign languages should be instilled into the young: eleven at latest; ten or nine would be even better. At that period the young mind is flexible and the young character is pretty docile. It is perfectly ridiculous to postpone the study of languages to the high school age, when the mind begins to lose its concentration and the emotions are constantly interfering with its activities.)

Now, at that time I was not interested in linguistic structure. I knew scarcely anything about the excellent books which I was later to read in French and Latin and Greek; and it would probably have been useless to describe them to me. I did not expect ever to talk French to Frenchmen, or of course to use Latin and Greek in conversation. I was simply taking pleasure in using my intellect. And that is the fourth reason for learning a foreign language. At the same period half the boys in my class were busy constructing elaborate maps of both real and imaginary places, working out codes for the sheer joy of handling complex patterns, building models of airplanes and submarines and Norse galleys and 'wooden wall' battleships, and so forth. Just for fun, at that time, I learned off the names and locations of several scores of binary stars, variables, and nebulae: fragments of that perfectly useless knowledge acquired fifty years ago still stick in my mind and have made me, in a small way, an astronomy buff. During the crucial period when the mind is growing rapidly, it needs all the food and exercise it can get. My own son at the same age learned to identify something like a hundred different types of military aircraft, merely from studying their pictures in his spare time. One of the most stimulating and ultimately most useful kinds of exercise the mind can be given is a good complicated nourishing foreign language.

Most people are talkers rather than readers. They find it slightly strange that one should learn a language for the purpose of reading books in it rather than speaking it. How often have I experienced this! One's dinner partner is going to the Berlitz School to learn some Italian conversation before visiting Florence. 'I expect you know Italian?' she says. Yes, I do. 'You visit Italy often?' Well, I used to; but I really learnt

Italian much earlier, so that I could read Dante's *Comedy* in the original. Puzzled silence. . . . The Jews, who have been called the People of the Book, never feel like this, though: one of several reasons why they are so outstandingly good at languages. They know that language is meant both to be spoken, day by day, and to be written, for the centuries.

In fact it is quite mistaken to divide languages into 'living' and 'dead' languages. You might say that a living language was one which is being spoken by a community in which the members understand one another; and that Latin is therefore a dead language, since there is no Latin nation. Yet Latin is still being spoken in parts of the community of the Roman Catholic Church. Hebrew for many centuries was used chiefly in writing and reading and in reciting sacred texts; but quite recently it has become a spoken tongue also. It was never a 'dead language.' It is absurd to suggest that when men die, their thought dies with them even if they have written it down. Therefore any tongue which communicates thought *either* through speech spoken *or* through speech written is a living language. There are no dead languages except those which no one can read and understand. And yet even those languages are potentially alive, because men are fascinated by their mystery and work to bring them back to life. What could have been more dead than the Ancient Egyptian which was written in hieroglyphics incomprehensible even to the descendants of the men who spoke it? Yet Champollion penetrated the secrets of the script, and brought the language back to life. Seventy years ago Arthur Evans, digging in the island of Crete, found many clay tablets inscribed with perfectly unintelligible marks. After they were published people began to try to solve their riddle. Many tried and failed, or succeeded only partially; but in 1952 a brilliant young scholar, Michael Ventris, broke the problem, and the clay tablets inscribed with 'Linear B' began to speak. To the astonishment even of their decipherer, they spoke in archaic Greek.

Human speech is almost a miracle. It would be just as right to call our species Man the Speaker as Man the Artisan (*Homo faber*) or Man the Intelligent (*Homo sapiens*) which he is not always. And now that I remember, it is one of Homer's favorite formulae to describe mankind: *meropes anthropoi,* he says, 'voice-dividing men, articulate-speaking men.' Yet the invention of script to preserve speech is a kindred miracle almost as great. It is because of writing that there are no dead languages, except those spoken by illiterate tribes now vanished. The rest are either living (if spoken and/or read) or in suspended animation, waiting to be called back into life.

J. Chadwick, *The Decipherment of Linear B* (Cambridge University Press, Cambridge, England, 1967²).

J. Friedrich, *Extinct Languages* (translated by F. Gaynor, Philosophical Library, New York, 1957).

S. Potter, *Language in the Modern World* (Penguin Books, Baltimore, Md., 1960).

Name into Word

THERE ARE many kinds of fame, some to be desired, some to be avoided. One of the strangest is that which preserves the name of a man, and only the name, while the man himself is entirely forgotten. There is another, almost equally bizarre, by which the man's name survives as a word used by millions of people, while the man is remembered quite apart from the word. Thus, in most western countries the seventh month of the year is called July and the eighth month August (or close variants of these names); but do we ever remember that July was called after Julius Caesar and August after his heir Augustus?

Occasionally the name is well known, while only a fragment of the man's history is remembered. That is one way in which myths are born. For example, was there ever a real Judge Lynch who administered his own Lynch law? Some authorities give him a local habitation and a full name. They say he was Charles Lynch, a Virginia planter, who was a justice of the peace: in the troubled times of the War of Independence he and other Whigs used to arrest 'Tories and desperadoes,' try them without any of the law's delays, and order immediate punishment. (The punishment, by the way, was usually flog-ging.) This sounds authentic enough; yet there are those who believe that the name Lynch should be traced to other times and other countries, as the practice most certainly can.

When we can discover the man behind a famous name, his life history is sometimes surprising. One of the most notorious names belonged to an apparently insignificant and conven-tional Englishman who died about seventy years ago. Call him X. He was the son of a clergyman in Norfolk, served as an officer in the British army, retired, and got a job as agent for a wealthy landowner. The landowner was having serious trou-ble with his tenants, who demanded an across-the-board re-duction in rents, first ten per cent, and then later twenty-five per cent. He refused to make the concessions. The tenants refused to pay their rent. Now it was the duty of Mr. X to make them pay up, or get out. He procured notices of evic-tion, and sent court officials, accompanied by police, to serve the notices. But an angry crowd gathered and drove both process-servers and police away. The tenant farmers had a powerful union: its leader advised them, if they were refused a reduction in rents, 'to take certain measures against the landlords and their representatives.' It was X who first felt the full brunt of these 'measures.' He had a farm of his own, but he could get no one to work on it. His walls were broken down. His cattle were stampeded, to fret them and make them thin. He could not even buy food in the neighborhood, and had to order everything he needed from many miles away. When he left his house, he was yelled at and spat upon. The climax came in November 1880, when his crops were in danger of rotting in the fields. Fifty volunteers from outside came in to harvest them, protected by a force of nine hundred soldiers with two field guns. (History does not record where X sold his produce, or what he got for it.) X was Captain Charles Cunningham Boycott, the agent for Lord Erne in County Mayo from 1873 to 1886. Ever since his painful adventures, anyone who has been shunned and treated as an outcast has been said to suffer a boycott.

The curious thing about the case of Captain Boycott is that in the end it was less grim than it appeared. In 1880 and 1881, when the Irish Land League agitation was at its hottest, he must often have wondered whether he would ever live to see his fiftieth birthday. He often looked death in the face. He got letters with murder threats in them; he was mobbed when he attended a country auction; and—in a ceremony which appears either silly or sinister, depending where you stand—he was hanged in effigy, and his effigy was burnt to ashes. However, in 1881 the Land League was dissolved. Things returned to normal. Captain Boycott carried on as before. He lived down his unpopularity; and later, when he became a land agent in the southeast of England, he even used to go to Ireland for his vacations. He need not have been very intelligent, Captain Boycott, and most people would say he was the instrument of an evil policy, but there is no doubt of one thing: he had courage.

(His surname, by the way, goes back before the Norman Conquest. It is a place-name. 'Boycott was originally a small cottage in Berkshire where someone called "Boia" or "boy" lived before 1066,' says C. M. Matthews in *English Surnames*, p. 309.)

Many men who were once far more eminent and proud than Captain Boycott are now wholly forgotten except by specialists. Their names alone live on. Even the names would sometimes, in their present form, be almost unrecognizable to the dignitaries who once bore them. Consider the Lord of Villemain, whose name was Jean Nicot. In his day he was both noble and distinguished, for his king sent him to be the ambassador of France at the court of Portugal. But in the Encyclopaedia Britannica there is no entry under his name; his diplomatic achievements (whatever they were) are forgotten; only his name lives, because he brought back to Paris a strange new herb imported from the recently discovered American continent. In his honor the plant was named Nicotiana and the essence of the plant nicotine. Or consider Michel Bégon, who administered the French West Indies for the great Louis XIV. An admirable official, generous and wise; a patron of science; a discriminating collector of rarities: yet he is now recalled only because a botanist to whom he had shown kindness named the begonia after him. His contemporary Pierre Magnol was a quiet professor who worked in Montpellier, and earned the gratitude of *some* gardeners by arranging the plants into families. No doubt naturalists know him well; for others there is only an echo of his surname in that charming group of shrubs and trees called magnolia.

If anyone deserves kindly remembrance, surely we should recall the saints with affection and admiration. Yet poor St. Etheldreda has not inherited such a memory. She was a Saxon lady. Apparently she was beautiful, for she loved dressing up and wearing fine jewelry. But she became more and more withdrawn from the world and devoted to religion. When she was dying, she said that the tumor on her neck was God's punishment for her love of necklaces. After her death she was honored by an annual fair held in the town of Ely, at which people sold cheap necklaces of wood and bone, together with lace neckpieces and trimmings. As time went on, her name Etheldreda was smoothed out into Audrey, and the flimsy goods sold at the fair of St. Audrey were known as tawdry stuff: so now any cheap frippery is called tawdry.

The Russians are very fond of calling other people hooligans and chauvinists. The first hooligan was a tough Irish immigrant to England who lived with his family in south London; he was strong, and his neighbors thought he was unduly addicted to bashing people, and now the name of Patrick Houlihan or Hooligan has become a byword. As for Nicolas Chauvin, he was a veteran of Napoleon's Grand Army, wounded seventeen times. He never ceased to proclaim his loyalty to the Emperor, so much that he made himself absurd, and at last became a character in a French musical show whose author ridiculed extravagant displays of patriotism in the song 'Je suis français, je suis Chauvin!' So now chauvinism is any kind of patriotism of which someone else disapproves.

The Russians do not call their fight against Germany the Great Chauvinist Conflict, but the Great Patriotic War.

Poor Sergeant Chauvin! Poor St. Etheldreda! Yet even the fate which befell them is less fantastic than the destiny of two English noblemen whose names are immortalized by their little domestic inventions: one known and recalled by name ten thousand times a day in Britain, and, although perhaps not quite so widespread in the United States, still far from being fancy or specialized; and the other's title found in nearly every menu from San Francisco to Vienna, multiplied by dozens of inventive variations, and popular in a small way with everyone from the age of seven to the age of seventy. These noblemen were the Earl of Cardigan and the Earl of Sandwich. It is difficult to appreciate and admire proud, pompous, selfish, magnificent European aristocrats, unless (like the Esterházys of Hungary) they harbor a good composer, or (like the Estes of Ferrara) encourage the drama and the visual arts. These two noble earls, although fabulously rich and powerful, were admired by practically no human being except themselves and their toadies. One of them was a handsome, arrogant ass. The other was a shambling, treacherous scoundrel. What is particularly comic is the fact that the sandwich, which we think of as being a nice simple unpretentious kind of food, was invented by (or for) the Earl of Sandwich, who habitually led a life as luxurious as he could possibly manage to achieve on his own large income and the money he screwed out of the British taxpayer. Similarly, the cardigan, the cosy woolen jacket which buttons up the front, and which, in Britain, is often worn by those who like comfort and do not care whether they look smart or not, was invented by (or for) the superb James Thomas Brudenell, seventh Earl of Cardigan, an army officer whose favorite costume was a uniform of cherry-colored trousers, a royal blue jacket edged with gold, a furred pelisse, a short coat thrown over the shoulders and glittering with gold lace, and a high fur hat with brilliant plumes on it. The Earl is never known to have wept; but if he had seen the sad, mousy-brown, sagging, and often slightly smelly garment by which his name is now perpetuated, he would surely have given the performance which accompanied his habitual fits of anger, writhing his body, distorting his handsome features, and making the veins on his temples and forehead bulge with fury.

As for the Earl of Sandwich, there is no biography of him. Someone with a gift for satire and a thorough knowledge of the eighteenth century ought to compose a life of John Montagu, who became the fourth Earl of Sandwich at the age of eleven, and spent over forty years in politics. During his career he helped to lose the American colonies, being a very influential member of Lord North's cabinet, and very nearly wrecked the Royal Navy by allowing a fantastic network of bribery and corruption to be spread all through it. One of the chief British battleships, the *Royal George,* sank in still water at Spithead harbor, because a large piece of her bottom fell out. The only reason Sandwich ever left politics was, not that he was found to be incompetent and dishonest, but that his kept mistress was murdered by an unsuccessful lover, and his peculiar domestic arrangements drew unpleasant publicity upon him. (As Mrs. Patrick Campbell said, the English don't care what you do, so long as you don't do it in the streets and frighten the horses.) The simple and healthful sandwich was invented by the noble Earl about the year 1762, when he spent twenty-four solid hours at the gambling table, without taking any food except slices of roast beef between slices of toast.

That monumental ass, the seventh Earl of Cardigan, has been admirably described with a pen dipped in clear acid by Mrs. Cecil Woodham-Smith, in one of the most intelligent books of historical research I have ever read: *The Reason Why* (McGraw-Hill, 1953). It was Cardigan who led the famous Charge of the Light Brigade. He led it because he was extremely brave and extremely stupid, and because he was in the middle of a violent feud with several other asinine noblemen who held military commands in the same unfortunate army. Knowing and caring nothing about military strategy, he failed to produce any useful result by the charge—apparently because he could not think what to do when it reached its objective, the Russian artillery. He simply rode back again: without his men, whom he left to find their own way home, through shot and shell. Having reached his own lines, he went on to his private yacht, had a bath and dinner with a bottle of champagne, and went to bed. The only reason he invented the cardigan—or had it invented for him—was that, although he lived on his yacht during the Crimean campaign, he found the climate rather chilly.

Suppose for a moment that the Earl of Cardigan had been an ardent gambler, and suppose the Earl of Sandwich had been a dashing cavalryman who fought, occasionally, in the Crimean war. In that case, on a cold winter day, you might have found yourself wearing a sandwich and eating a cardigan.

The Language of Adam

THE HEBREW Scriptures tell us that the first of mankind could talk before there was any other human being for him to converse with. God spoke to Adam and Adam understood, although we do not hear that he answered (Genesis ii. 16–17). Later, he spoke, when God made all the animals and all the birds out of earth. God 'brought them to Adam to see what he would call them; and whatever Adam called every living creature, that was the name of it' (Genesis ii. 19). And so the first man, when he was created, was able to understand language and furthermore he was able to use it for originating new words. This little story is the starting point for a bright and knowledgeable book about that inexhaustible subject, language: it is *Naming-Day in Eden;* its author, Noah Jonathan Jacobs, is a polyglot who was head of the translation office at the Nuremberg trials.

'Articulate-speaking men': Homer's adjective signifies the same as the Hebrew story—that one of the essential properties of mankind, shared by us all and differentiating us radically from the animals, is language. There are no dumb races of mankind. Even although the races of men differ enormously in their range of intellectual experience and their power to think creatively and abstractly, their languages are all (it would seem) equally complex, and for their different purposes equally subtle. Anthropologists constantly note that a primitive tribe which cannot possibly find an equivalent in its language for abstractions such as 'position' or 'motive' has a wide range of words denoting relationships by blood and marriage. We know only slush or snow; but the Eskimos have nearly a dozen words for snow, differentiating between soft snow and hard-packed snow, frozen snow, crusted snow, melting snow, and so forth.

But now that we have been excluded from the Garden of Eden and suffer the curse of Babel, there is no such thing as a central human language. There is not even one speech which uses all the different types of sound that the human larynx and tongue and lips can produce. The Chinese use musical tones as significant parts of speech, while most other people (apart from *emotional* variations of pitch) speak in a monotone. There are elaborate clicks in certain African languages, glottal stops in Danish, complicated L sounds in Gaelic, nasals in French and Portuguese: all these come quite naturally to people who are brought up speaking the languages, but are terribly hard for learners reared in a different linguistic pattern. To us, English seems easy enough, and its sounds straightforward; but foreigners think it is appallingly complex, not only in grammar and syntax but in pronunciation, for it heaps up consonants into masses that most foreign tongues can scarcely cope with and few foreigners can admire: for instance, the combination of two voiced fricatives in *clothes*. It was a distinguished English poet with a fairly good musical ear, Edward Fitzgerald, who inserted into a line beautiful in conception a tangle of consonants so hideous that it is almost unpronounceable even by trained English speakers—STSST:

> And when thyself with shining foot shalt pass
> Among the gue*sts st*ar-scattered on the grass. . . .

And see, a few lines above, how naturally I wrote and you

read another horrid conglomeration: 'its *sounds st*raightfor-ward.'

According to the Bible God created man fully equipped with the power of speech, and apparently with a language of his own, Adamese or Adamaic. What language that was must remain an insoluble mystery, although scholars and screwballs have attempted to solve it. It has (according to Mr. Jacobs) been asserted that Adam spoke German, or Basque, or Celtic (which type of Celtic, p or q, is not stated), or Danish, or Swedish, or Hungarian, or Dutch. Dante had believed it was Hebrew; but when he met father Adam in Paradise and asked him, Adam replied

> The language which I spoke was all extinguished
> before that work never to be completed
> was undertaken by the folk of Nimrod

—meaning the Tower of Babel—and he added, correctly as we now think, that language is not a durable and immutable thing, but changes from time to time and from place to place (*Paradiso* 26. 124–32).

However, those who believe that the races of mankind did not spring from a single original father and mother must ask how it was that man, as he evolved into something like the species to which we belong, developed this amazingly intricate system of communication. Most animals and birds have rudi-mentary languages of their own. It is easy to notice the differ-ence between the ordinary conversational twitter of a bird and its excited cry of alarm; between the playful yapping of a dog, so like human laughter, and the sharp pugnacious far-carrying bark with which it meets a threat or a challenge. But all these animal and avian languages are only varieties of sim-ple *cries*. A man without a tongue could no doubt communi-cate his emotions vocally in a very simple way, by different kinds of shouts, groans, or murmurs. But meaning, true mean-ing, the stuff of the intellect, is carried by *syllables*. And what the linguists want to know is, what was the original connection between syllables and meanings?

Mr. Jacobs is very amusing about this problem. He is a professional linguist, and he knows all the important theoretical suggestions. If he listed them and analyzed them in relentlessly logical order, his book might be heavy going. He does not. Instead he introduces them almost casually, and describes some of them by comical nicknames, the bow-wow theory, the yo-heave-ho theory, and so forth.

He mentions and discards the notion attributed to Plato, that a word somehow expresses in its sound the inner nature of the thing which it names or describes. The argument against this is obvious: there are so many different sounds in different languages to denote the same essential thing that none of them can possibly be more than a label, external to the thing named. A woman is a *femme* in French, a *mujer* in Spanish, a *Weib* or *Frau* in German, a *gyné* in Greek, and so forth. People who accept the idea usually believe that one language, their own, is unique and superior to all others: Plato was a Greek, and the Greeks always tended to believe that Greek was the only truly human tongue; and there are traces of the same notion in certain mystical ideas held by Jews about the Hebrew language. Toward the end of his life Wittgenstein was trying to work out some correspondence between the shape of a sentence in words and the thought which the sentence expressed. As far as I know, he never specified in which language he wished his sentences to be formed. I wonder if he ever realized that the identical same thought could be expressed by sentences of five different shapes if couched in Latin, English, Chinese, Eskimo, and Kwakiutl.

Language was no doubt produced by several converging impulses. One of them was surely imitation: a man made noises imitating the emotions which he wished others to share or understand, and noises imitating the thing which he wished to name. A dog's loud minatory bark combines the two messages *go away* to the intruder and *come here* to the other dogs in the pack. We call the bird which howls and hoots an *owl*; our Teutonic ancestors called it an *ule,* and the Romans, who had ears less full of mud and hair so that they heard its call more clearly, an *ulula.* The very widespread group of words for 'mother' which begin with the syllable *ma* surely come from the first inarticulate noises made by the baby, and form a sonal image of the process of sucking, and pausing for breath in satisfaction. But what of *papa, dada,* and *baba?* Are they images of a primitive call to someone needed but further away than *mama?* Yet many important emotions and ideas have no sound or shape which can be imaged in sound; and the jump from an imitative noise, which is external, to a sound which conveys a complex or abstract meaning, crosses a large and difficult gulf.

One variation of this idea appeals to me, although I know it is not to be taken seriously. This is the notion that some words, when they are written or printed, look like the thing they denote. My favorite is *pool,* where the two o's evoke the deep water with its reflection of the sky, and the downward stroke of the p and the riser of the l resemble the tree reflected in the still lakelet. *Moon* is also very good. *Meat* looks to me like a slab of tenderloin oozing with juice; and now that I think of it, *ooze* looks like something oozing and the word *juice* both looks and sounds like juice. The printed word *potato* is very like a big lumpy Long Island potato with two bumps on it. *Bulb* is just right, whether it means an electric bulb narrowing upwards to its neck, or a bulgy tulip bulb. *Tulip* is pretty good too, both in sound and in appearance. The r's in *mirror* seem to me to mirror the shiny surface of the mirror. *Ankle* and *elbow* both resemble bent joints. *Tongue* looks like the flexible boneless organ which curls and has a thin projecting tip. Dante thought a man's face looked like the old Italian word for man: *omo,* the strong bony nose being the M and the two round O's the eyes on each side of it. One scholar claimed that Hungarian was the ideal language because the Hungarian word for scissors, *ollò,* looked exactly like a pair of scissors. Stop. Stop! That way madness lies!

Another theory of the origin of speech is that each individual language is a convention, something like a code of moral and social laws, which was devised by some ingenious and far-sighted individual or group and imposed upon all the members of their race or nation. This idea was a favorite of certain Greek thinkers. They observed that what was right in one country was wrong in another: the Parsees put their dead out uncovered for vultures to eat, the Greeks burn them to ashes, the Egyptians embalm them, and each would think it foolish and wicked to adopt the practice of the others. Therefore all social customs are merely conventions. Therefore language too is a convention, and the different languages are merely different patterns of speech adopted by different groups. Some supporters of this theory in antiquity insisted too strongly on the notion that a convention such as language implied a single inventor for each tongue, as a code of laws implies a lawgiver. Modern philologists point to the obvious facts: that new words often appear, as it were, out of nowhere, and, if they respond to a need which is keenly felt, will be adopted at once by unspoken and undirected agreement; while, on the other hand, deliberately invented new words are resisted by the public even if they are backed by some strong authority, and are often forgotten within a year or two, or at best remembered with slightly disgusted amusement, like *scofflaw*. Suppose, however, that the theory is true in essence: that the languages of different groups and nations are conventions like their styles of writing and their fashions in dress and their habits in eating and their tastes in music; that no single man or group invented any one *spoken* language (writing is different) but that each community worked out its own system with only a few borrowings from others. The question still remains: how did mankind get the original notion of meaningful syllables?

Some have suggested that words are gestures. For instance, a long word which takes much time to speak and even longer to write might be originally used to signify something large and imposing. Or the movements of the tongue and mouth may imitate the distance between the speaker and the thing he is talking about, so that bed, which we all visit once every twenty-four hours, is named by a close sound, while sky is far off and high up. But if language did begin like that, it retains very few traces of its beginnings nowadays. In Hawaiian (Mr. Jacobs tells us) a large fish is named ô and there is a very tiny one called *humuhumunukunukuapuaa*.

'Honour of mankind, Saint Language!' cried Paul Valéry. But language is neither saint nor angel. It is as imperfect as man. This is one of the chief difficulties confronting poets and ambitious prose writers in any tongue. The ideas which are important and which ought to be written about in noble poetry and majestic prose often have verbal labels which are meager, flat, unexciting, and even downright ugly. Our own language is particularly unlucky. What the French speak of with horror as *la mort,* and the Germans with grim finality as *der Tod,* shrinks in our mouths to *death.* What the Italians affectionately call *mia moglie* (can't you see those soft curves?) and the Germans *meine Frau* (admire that ample bosom!) is for us nothing more sonally inspiring than *my wife.* Two of the master ideas of the world sound puny and insignificant in English: *love* and *God.* Sometimes you wonder how anyone manages to write decent poetry in English. Perhaps the difficulty is a stimulus. Perhaps a perfectly beautiful and appropriate language, such as Adam's must have been, would contain no poetry whatever, because every single sentence would be both meaningful and musical.

Noah Jonathan Jacobs, *Naming-Day in Eden* (Macmillan, New York, revised edition, 1969).

Mario Pei, *The Story of Language* (Lippincott, Philadelphia, revised edition, 1965).

Avocations

Play and Life

———————————

NEARLY every morning as I walk toward my work I pass a pet shop. It is a delightful little place, full of crazy parrots, and graceful fish swimming about in their private universes, and kittens practicing their individual charm, and small dogs. The puppies are always in the window, and they always have a crowd watching them: for they are always enjoying themselves. Sometimes they are asleep; even then they are pleasant to look at. But usually they are playing with one another. Their play is not like that of human children. They do not merely run about and chase one another and try to catch rolling balls or falling leaves. No, they wrestle with one another, they fight, they try to kill one another, biting and clawing. Or so it seems. And yet, if they were really biting and clawing, showing genuine hate for one another and inflicting actual injuries and drawing blood, no one except a sadist would watch them with pleasure. Few would want to buy them. Although they are very young indeed, they know the difference between play and conflict. They know that when they pretend to bite their brother, he is not an enemy fighting for his life and threatening to take theirs, but rather a jolly companion; they also know that even if he is beaten and borne down and compelled to beg for mercy, he is not really conquered by a ruthless attacker, but outdone in a competition which was not fight but play. The people watching the little dogs know this. What seems to be determined fighting is not. The bared teeth do not wound. The deathly grapple turns into something like an affectionate hug between two youngsters who love each other too well to remain apart.

Play is not quite life; but it is part of it. Where does play stop, and life begin?

One of the charms of serious living is that it keeps passing over into play. How often have you seen a beautiful young wife, truly devoted to her husband and children, still enjoying a little innocent play with another man? She will tease him and allow herself to be teased; she will allow him to embrace her in a gesture which, cheek to cheek, is not a real caress but a playful imitation of a caress; she will move about the dance floor in his arms, and then, when the time for play ends, when the music ceases and the crowds disperse, she will smile and stop the game.

An Air Force officer once told me, when I asked him about the methods used in teaching, that his two most difficult jobs were, first, to make the young apprentice pilots work, and, second, to stop them from playing. When they started training, they did not realize how deadly serious a job expert pilotage must be, how they had to calculate every movement and check every possibility as cautiously as a surgeon in a major operation. But then, after they had settled down and learned all those skills, they used to take up valuable aircraft and play games with them. He said they would take a plane worth many thousands of dollars, and skim it below a railway bridge as though they were throwing a ring at a hook in a carnival. They would scarcely apologize when brought in on a charge. 'I'm sorry, chief,' they would say; 'I felt good. I just got through the final test: I was having fun.' They were having fun: playing with fire and explosives, in a modern machine which moved almost as fast as death.

There are not many books that handle this theme. One of the best is a brilliant work called *Homo Ludens*. In biological terms, man is usually called *Homo sapiens:* man (genus) the intelligent (species)—a singularly unconvincing description. Recently he has been sometimes named *Homo faber,* a more appropriate definition, meaning 'man the craftsman,' 'man the tool-maker and -user.' This book suggests that man might be called *Homo ludens,* the human being that plays.* The author is Johan Huizinga, a Dutch historian also known for a remarkable book on the late Middle Ages, called *The Waning of the Middle Ages.*

The whole subject of play is full of paradoxes. It is stimulating to notice them but difficult to explain them. Huizinga makes little attempt to define the essence of play—although he does trace much of it to the fighting instinct which seems to be essential and perennial in mankind, the inborn love of competition which moves both individuals and groups. Often he gives a negative definition to show what is and what is not real play. Professional sport, whether carried out for large wages by carefully selected teams, or (as in the Olympic Games) engaged in by 'amateurs' representing their national groups, is utterly false to the ideal of play. The true player enjoys the game for its own sake, and its own sake alone. If the game is intended to subserve some other purpose, it is ruined. The play spirit has gone. In the next Olympic Games we shall no doubt admire the skill of some of the athletes, but we shall also know that they are not really playing games, not indulging in sport. They are making war. They will not take the half-mile run and the long jump as a combination of fun and exercise, something from which they can return with relief and satisfaction to their normal pursuits outside the sphere of play, as mechanics or librarians or truckdrivers. On the contrary, they will feel that running faster or jumping further than anyone else in the world is the ultimate aim of

---

* The Latin is not very good. *Homo ludens* means 'man while he is (for a little time) playing'; the definition needed is *Homo lusor,* 'man as a sportsman, a lover of play (permanently).'

their existence, and proves something, not only about them personally, but also about millions of their countrymen who are not even present. Usually young men run and jump because they like to try their agility against other young men, just as girls like dancing and singing together with other girls. The notion of training for years to run and jump in order that this activity may serve some *other* aim—particularly an aim so remote from play as political and social aggrandizement—that notion is basically corrupt.

Who enjoys professional team games, such as baseball? Not the players. People try to make their activity look more like play, for instance by giving them the names of localities and then adding a cute and slightly childish group-name such as Orioles or Red Sox. One team is supposed somehow to represent New York, and another to represent Milwaukee; and we have even seen that exquisite paradox, the Philadelphia Athletics. But the members of the teams do not necessarily come from New York or Milwaukee or Philadelphia. They originate from Alabama or California or Cuba or what not; and if enough money changes hands, any one of them will stop pretending to be a Connecticut Nutmeg and start pretending to be a Louisiana Picayune. The people who really enjoy a professional game are the spectators. It is to appeal to the spectators that the so-called players wear local names on their uniforms. A Cincinnati man, watching a group of highly paid experts who may come from anywhere in the United States but are paid to call themselves specifically the Cincinnati Curlers, somehow feels that *he* is playing. They are *his* team, and they satisfy his competitive instinct. As for the professionals, they do not enjoy it as a game. For them, it is a way of making money. That is why team players sometimes ruin the game by deliberately breaking its rules (throwing spitballs) or by turning it from a game into a genuine fight where they can injure and disable their opponents. Occasionally I glance at pro football and ice hockey on television: not much fine play, but a lot of generalized conflict; and I wonder how long it will be before we have trained gladiators paired off and killing each other in close combat.

The fine arts owe a great deal to the spirit of sport. When you see a drama on TV or in the theater, you call it a 'play,' even if it deals with a deadly serious subject such as drug addiction, insanity, or murder; and even although it moves you deeply, its effect is different from the effect of reality. On the screen, you can watch the dope addict writhing and screaming, or you can see the two armed men shooting each other down; and you feel a strong excitement. But your emotion is not that which you would experience in watching a real addict undergoing his pangs, or in seeing real shots, real wounds, real blood, real death. Part of your pleasure is that you know this.

But in creation also, most art must draw some of its strength from the instinct of play. In playing, you must have rules (think of golf, think of chess!). The poet who determines to write the story of his unhappy love in one hundred poems following the strict sonnet form is more likely to compose good and durable poetry than another poet of equal talent who merely writes down a hundred quasi-spontaneous gushes of emotion without rules and without form. The first poet is playing. The second is merely letting off steam—or allowing gas to escape.

On the other hand, one of the strengths of modern painting and sculpture is that its masters have insisted on playing with shapes and colors and materials. By the late nineteenth century much landscape and figure painting had become mere mechanical reproduction. You went out into the fields, selected a view with a clump of trees, some water for sky-reflections, and a few cows (many nineteenth-century artists had a deep spiritual affinity for cows) and then you transferred as faithfully as possible the forms and hues of this view to canvas. Or else you took a pretty model, dressed her as a gipsy, stood her against a white wall or a red curtain, and then produced a lifelike copy of her appearance. This was boring hack work. The rise of photography made it unnecessary. Therefore the true artists started to do something else, which would be less like paid imitation of life and more like playing. Pablo Picasso played all through his life: indeed, one of the hardest criticisms that could be leveled against him is that he played and gambled away his talents. Paul Klee thought seriously about art and the mission of the artist; but his pictures look like jokes and parodies. Matta has even done a group of pictures in the manner of comic strips. The mobiles of Alexander Calder (who at an earlier stage made many small toys and played with them) are essentially play with powerful materials reduced to thin wires and frail plates, moving at random in the air; and Jackson Pollock was playing with paint when he dribbled it onto the canvas. Sometimes when I watch the riffle of the breeze through the grass or the sunlight reflected by the sea-wet sand, I think I see something of his playful purposes.

At its highest, play penetrates the most intense manifestations of life. Thought itself—thought which is not purely mechanical but creative—may often be called playful. There is a wonderful book by Hermann Hesse, *Das Glasperlenspiel,* which tells how an elite order of men, living at some time in the future, contrives to master all the domains of thought, and to transform all ideas into symbols which—like an expert chess master playing a game without a visible board, or a composer hearing with his inner ear the music of a symphony not yet written down—they manipulate and exchange and elaborate and vary and analyze and correlate and transform, all in the spirit of almost angelic play. Indeed, I imagine that one of the visions which may sustain a great scientist—whether he be studying the secrets of the invisible atoms or the secrets of the ultravisible heavens—must be the endlessly various and ceaselessly developing patterns, sometimes inexplicable and nevertheless always fascinating, which make both the smallest particle of matter and the huge structure of the astrophysical universe into a divine dance, infinitely small or infinitely vast, as though the entire cosmos, great and small, were for ever enjoying itself in an endless game.

H. Hesse, *The Glass Bead Game,* translated by R. and C. Winston (Holt, Rinehart & Winston, New York, 1969).

J. M. Huizinga, *Homo Ludens,* translated by R. F. C. Hull (Roy, New York, 1950).

The Art of Persuasion

A CURIOUS enterprise, persuasion.

What makes us think that we can change another man's mind simply by talking to him? Surely it argues a great deal of confidence in our own powers, in his malleability, and in the force of speech or reason or both. It is tricky enough to try to persuade an individual—a wife or husband, a friend or business partner, a rebellious daughter, an angry policeman. But how difficult it is to influence a group of people—a hall full of wildcat strikers, a meeting of creditors, a mutinous crew, or a jury!

Hard it is, surely. Yet it is done, and done constantly. When it is well done, the patient scarcely feels it. Usually he thinks that he has made his own decision, or that he has, through his own perspicacity, managed to discover the truth. Once when Henry Brougham, the brilliant nineteenth-century lawyer, had won a difficult case, one of his juniors fell into conversation with a juryman leaving the courtroom. 'Heavens,' said the juryman, 'what a wonderful lawyer that Mr. Savage is, to be sure! He does make a noble speech!' Brougham's assistant heard this with astonishment, for Savage had been on the losing side.

'Well now,' he said, 'I should have thought Brougham was the better lawyer. Didn't he win the verdict?' 'Oh yes,' said the juryman, 'but then you see it was easy enough for him: he had all the right on his side.' That was a perfect example of persuasion, smoothly applied and painlessly concluded. As long as he lived, that juror would be convinced that he and his peers had merely looked at the facts on both sides and assessed their weight. He would never realize that Henry Brougham had persuaded him to think one set of facts heavier than the other.

Few of us can have such power as that. Yet we all spend much of our lives trying to persuade other people to do things. Parents attempt to influence children; young men woo girls, and vice versa; husbands and wives are continually endeavoring to persuade each other, although a lot of their effort is wasted and some of it backfires. And what is advertising but persuading the public to buy? what is politics but persuading the voters to back this and support that and endure these for the promise of those?

But how is persuasion, really skillful and effective persuasion, managed? If it is a fundamental activity, it must have a few basic principles.

There seem to be two different types of persuasion. One is the ordinary type, which we all try to do. The other is more mysterious and less logical, hard to resist and hard to understand.

In ordinary persuasion, anyone who wishes to win over an individual or a group must have something to offer. He cannot bargain unless he has something to bargain with. Therefore, before starting, he should be quite clear in his own mind what inducement he intends to put before his intended victim. It need not be large. It need not be lasting. But it must be attractive. The simplest and biggest mistakes are usually made at this stage. Sometimes the operator starts talking without having an exact idea of the size and scope of his own offer. He may realize too late that he has not offered enough, and then try to increase his bid, and meet a resistance which has grown to be inflexible. Or sometimes he talks himself into offering far too much, and loses on the deal. (This is reverse persuasion.) Often he attempts to negotiate without offering anything tangible or enticing, and thinks he has been unjustly treated when the persuadee refuses. An even commoner mistake is to choose the wrong inducement. A hook baited with clam will catch a sea bass, but if you drop it into a trout stream you will get no trout. First, then, you must make up your mind about the nature of your inducement. And, second, you should think about it in connection with your patient, until you are quite sure it will really attract him. If it leaves him cold, you will lose. If it repels him, the result may be disastrous.

When husbands and wives try to persuade each other, the chief consideration they have to offer is continuance of their happiness in marriage. 'You ought to do this, darling,' they say, or they imply, 'because it will make us both happy.' That is the standard marriage argument, and is often effective. But there are difficult points in marriage when such inducements have no real effect. A wife or a husband sometimes begins to reflect that the marriage is no good anyhow, so that it is useless to go on tinkering with it. At this point, bad persuasion will cause an explosion. A wife will say to her young husband, 'If you go out drinking again next Saturday, I'll take the baby and go back to mother.' Inwardly, the husband shouts, 'Good, that's exactly what I want!' What started him drinking was the new discomfort of a house with a baby in it and the new responsibilities. Now he is presented with an escape route.

The abruptness and violence of such failures always surprise both parties. There is often another reason for the failures. It is hurry. No important job of persuasion can be done quickly. Few important jobs of persuasion can be done in one stage. To be effective, persuasion must be slow, gradual, easy, patient. That is how the best propagandists work—those who get lasting results. Think of the Christian ministers who have converted ferocious savages, world-weary Chinese mandarins, glum peasants, and vain flippant young noblemen. One of St.

Teresa's operational rules was 'Much can be done by patience.'
The most remarkable conversions of the Jesuit missionaries
were planned years in advance and took many years to execute.
One of the most successful modern persuaders is the labor
mediator Theodore Kheel, who seldom hurries and seldom
gives up and often operates like a man cutting tissue with a
microtome. 'If the parties are, say, ten percentage points apart
on a pay raise, Kheel will not try to work out a compromise
in one stroke but will attempt to narrow the gap point by
point. Often, he will begin with the bargainer whose proposal
is closest to what he thinks the eventual figure should be. "The
other party's offer is so far out of line that it can't be anything
but a bargaining figure," Kheel will then argue to this bargainer. "Give me a point or two to work with and I'm sure
we'll get him moving." ' * Kheel is an unusual man. It is one
of the commonest mistakes made by American publicists,
teachers, and statesmen to believe that, if they simply point
out the right course, everyone will at once follow it. Here is
Democracy, we say. Look at it. It's grand, isn't it? Well, go
ahead, adopt it. And yet. . . .

The second rule of persuasion, then, is that it must be
gradual. And the third rule develops out of that. The third
rule is that persuasion must work on the emotions as well as
on the mind. Human beings were suffering fear and anger,
enjoying hope and pleasure, long before they were able to
work out long logical chains of thought. Their emotions still
lie deeper than their reason, sometimes work against their
reason, and should always, for satisfactory results, be har-
monized with their reason. Persuasion will be most effective
when it begins with the emotions. Therefore—before intro-
ducing any arguments—we ought to start by calming and
soothing, pleasing and even flattering the patient. Surgery
does not begin until the victim is anaesthetized. Persuasion
should never start until the patient has been made receptive.

One of the most widespread but least discussed psychical

* Fred C. Shapiro, 'Mediator,' *The New Yorker*, August 1, 1970, p. 42.

phenomena is self-persuasion: not the delusions of paranoia, but the process by which one element in the psyche imposes itself on others, sometimes in such a way as to produce an important change of character and behavior. Often and often have I listened to such interior dialogues within myself, wondering how one single personality could harbor such diverse and conflicting factors. Some of the conversions discussed by William James in *Varieties of Religious Experience* are the final product of long arguments carried on in silence within the busy and never-resting soul. So also are some decisions, apparently quite trivial, which nevertheless alter a life or two.

There is a Vermont story about a farmer called Snedd who had quarreled with his neighbor Hanley. Once friendly, they would not speak to each other when they met in the store, or help out at harvest-time, or allow their wives to visit. Mrs. Snedd found this painful. She started persuading her husband to make up the quarrel: she reminded him of old times, when the two men had done each other favors; she said it was un-Christian to cherish a grudge, and bad for the health besides, your ulcers have got worse just thinking about it; don't make a big thing of this business, don't expect him to apologize, just be natural as if nothing in the world had happened: look, it's getting well into fall, why not drive over this evening before supper and ask him for a loan of his disk harrow, the one he used to lend you every year? Thinking over this, Snedd nodded, and got out the truck, and started off. But as he drove he started counter-persuading himself. Feel like a fool, asking for the loan of a disk harrow, just as if I couldn't afford to buy one or was too close to spend the money. How do I know he'll be willing to lend the thing anyhow? Why should he? We haven't spoke a civil word for nine months and more. Suppose he tells me he needs the disk harrow himself. Suppose he doesn't, suppose he just looks at me the way you look at a bum asking for a handout and says, 'Snedd, you can go straight to hell!' I'll look all kinds of a fool, taking that from him and then driving back to face Susie with an empty truck and things worse instead of better. I might not take it from him at that. I might just give him a damn good poke in his big fat potato nose. Why should I take his insults as long as I've got my strength? Why, good God— And then he noticed he had reached Hanley's farm. He jumped out of the truck, threw open the door, found the family sitting at supper, and (as they looked up in astonishment) shouted, 'Hanley, I don't want your disk harrow! I wouldn't take it if you gold-plated it and made me a present of it! Keep it! I hope it runs over you some day soon! You and your damned disk harrow can go straight to hell!' Then he drove home again, feeling better.

There is another type of persuasion, much more difficult, which seems to have no rules at all. Yet when it works it is far more effective. We often hear of a man who has been able to persuade hardheaded businessmen or wary old hardhearted dowagers that he is in direct communication with God, that he knows the hiding place of Kubla Khan's treasure, that he can foretell the movements of the stock market through astrology, that he is the child of a multimillionaire but was kidnapped in infancy, that he is the reincarnation of Paracelsus. Vast sums of money, limitless trust and adoration are lavished on these persuaders by their vicitms. And yet they have no real inducements to offer. Frequently they do not even argue. Their emotional appeal is powerful; but it is accompanied by statements so absurd that, standing outside and looking in, we can hardly believe that any sane human being could accept them. Casanova persuaded the Marquise d'Urfé that he could cause her to be reborn as a male, reincarnated in the body of a child to be begotten by Casanova upon an immortal Undine sent to earth by Selenis, spirit of the Moon. The Marquise would then be able to enjoy all the pleasures reserved for the male sex. Therefore she was to make a will leaving all her property to her new baby-self, and appointing Casanova its guardian and trustee until it reached puberty. This elaborate swindle took many months to work out, and failed only because some of Casanova's accomplices betrayed him. (Or so he says.) The 'Count of St. Germain' persuaded numbers of experienced statesmen that he was two thousand years old and possessed the elixir of life. The Tichborne Claimant persuaded Lady Tichborne that she was his mother.

Of the same order, though in a different group, are the great diplomats. We know their names—Richelieu, Bismarck, Disraeli—but we do not fully know their methods. The biographies tell us the external facts of their careers, but seldom explain how they contrived their marvellous successes. How did Bismarck persuade the kings of the other German states to accept the king of Prussia as German Emperor, and to stand behind his throne while he was crowned? Not just by pointing the guns of the Prussian army at them. It was a long process, so tortuous, so varied, and made of so many subtle touches that it has never to my knowledge been adequately described. This was persuasion of a special type, depending little on the ordinary methods: something far more like the art of the man who holds three deuces and persuades his opponent, with a 5-6-7-8-9 straight, to throw in his hand.

It would be easier to understand the art of persuasion if these geniuses did not exist. But they do, and most of us are at their mercy. And they have no technique that we can analyze, no rules—on the contrary, they are always incalculable, bold, and random, almost as though they were inspired. Hitler spoke of himself as a sleepwalker.

They have a few basic traits in common. The chief of these are will-power and concentration. If you really want to persuade people that you are the Messiah or the future ruler of Europe, you must first be one thousand per cent determined to do so. You need not believe it yourself; but you must concentrate on making others believe it. Every act, every word, every gesture must serve that purpose. Most people have weak wills and wandering minds. When they meet someone with concentrated conviction, they tend to believe he is what he appears to be. If they meet someone with a strong will, they feel they must sooner or later give way to him; and sooner or later many of them do. Tall, strong, and burly, Bismarck had a physical advantage over most men with whom he had to negotiate. Also, he was known for his outbreaks of violent anger. Therefore he sometimes contrived to intimidate the other party in a man-to-man discussion. He would summon the Ruritanian Ambassador to an interview at ten a.m. With two attachés, the Ambassador would arrive at a quarter to ten and sit in the antechamber waiting rather anxiously. At ten minutes to ten a footman would pass into Bismarck's room with a bottle of champagne and a tray of glasses for his first drink of the day. A moment later a secretary would enter the room and close the door behind him. Silence. Then suddenly from inside an outburst of roars like an infuriated bear and a tremendous crash of smashing glass. The secretary would emerge white and trembling, and run off clutching a bundle of papers. A short pause. Then, in his long uniform coat, Count Bismarck himself would appear. 'My dear Ambassador, it is always such a pleasure to see you,' he would say with a charming smile. 'A slight contretemps has caused me to be a few minutes late; but please come in: we have much of mutual interest, and I hope benefit, to discuss.' As the Ambassador preceded Bismarck into the study, he was already at least partly dominated and overborne.

Most of this group of persuaders have another trait in common. They are not logical. They do not make clear comprehensible plans and enlist their victims in carrying them out. They offer a safari into the Fabulous Unknown. Not for them a guaranteed return of eight per cent before taxes: they own a map of the route to King Solomon's Mines. They never reveal all their secret plans, but hint at them, tantalizingly. They make us believe myths. Perhaps the cold truth about our daily life is so grim that few of us can face it: we welcome a myth if it is only strong enough. The great top-level persuaders have usually been Quixotes who could make hundreds of poor Sancho Panzas ride along behind them, simply because they seemed to *know* where they were going, even if it was toward the unseen kingdom of Micomicon.

Even on this level, one essential technique of persuasion remains. People will believe anything, however absurd; but they can swallow absurdity only in small doses. When Alice told the White Queen, 'One can't believe impossible things,' the Queen replied, 'I dare say you haven't had much practice. When I was your age I always did it for half an hour a day. Why, sometimes I've believed as many as six impossible things before breakfast.' Therefore a high-level persuader will begin with hints, and rich stimulating morsels, and momentary glimpses into the Luminous Void. Slowly, almost reluctantly, he will lead his Sanchos further on into the Impossible. Soon they will be pushing ahead, jumping the chasms between Inexplicables, swinging boldly across the ravine of the Incomprehensible, glissading upwards on the slopes of the Unutterable. Sometimes, dizzy with the cold thin air, they will pull their master gaily ahead into the Unrealizable, and even if he tries to restrain them, they will link arms and swing him out over the edge of the Abyss.

Of the two types of persuasion, one is simple and reasonable, the other weird and incalculable. Many can do the first; few the second. The second type is far more dangerous than the first; it is the weapon of the spellbinders, the fanatics, the men who turn discontented crowds into rabid violent mobs which they use as their instruments for murder and destruction. It can also be used for good purposes—although that seems to be much less common. The founder of artistic Greek oratory, Gorgias, boasted that, after entreaties from wives and children and advice from doctors had failed, he could through the power of persuasive speech convince a man to undergo (without anaesthetics of course) the surgical operation which might save his life. You and I, just once or twice in our lives, may be able to exercise it—at some memorable crisis, when we feel that everything, *everything* depends on what the girl will answer; or when we see the crowd warming up and a chance phrase seems to draw it together and make it our instrument; or when the tough old man asks us what we have to offer, and then sits back and listens. At such times, with luck, we feel the floodtide flowing through us, we guide it and master it and ride it to triumph and fortune.

Personalities

The Personality of Joyce

JAMES Augustine Joyce died in 1941, at the age of fifty-eight. By the time of his death he had achieved the beginnings of immortality. Nothing is certain in this contingent world, but it seems possible that, hundreds of years in the future, men will still be reading the books of James Joyce. Only last year at Columbia I spent some time analyzing a poem called *Alexandra* by the ancient Greek poet Lycophron. It is nearly fifteen hundred lines long. It is supposed to be a prophecy uttered by the raving prophetess Cassandra of Troy, who always foretold the truth and was never believed: therefore it is all perfectly true, but at first sight perfectly unintelligible. Every sentence contains a solid fact, within a snarl of enigmas interwoven and conflicting like vegetation in the Brazilian jungle. Yet it is a memorable poem, tense with the force of real emotion but controlled by a strong and ingenious creative intellect. In ancient Greek it is the closest thing I know to *Finnegans Wake*. If it has survived, and has been reproduced, and has been held worthy of study for over two thousand years, why not the work of Joyce? He wrote in several other fields on other themes, but his immortality will be based on his three novels about Dublin: one fairly lucid and fairly austere, *A Portrait of the Artist as a Young Man*; one obscure and satiric, *Ulysses*; and one fantastic, comic, all but unintelligible, *Finnegans Wake*. Difficult as they are, these books command respect because of their artistic and intellectual thoroughness; and there is a certain type of reader whom they will always attract because they are puzzles, like the readers of Lycophron.

Some important writers live on only through their books; but Joyce manufactured for himself a double immortality. He made his books, by intense and sustained effort, as nearly permanent as he could; and also he erected to his own Self a monument more lasting than bronze. When he was a little boy, far too small to have his meals with the family, he was allowed to come down to the dining room for dessert: he would walk downstairs one step at a time, calling out at every step, 'Here's me! Here's me!' In the same way, on every page of his Dublin novels, we are aware of an imperious, persuasive, unrelenting, inescapable, confident voice repeating in tones that constantly vary an assertion that is always the same: 'Here's me!' That is why it is legitimate, and necessary, to talk about Joyce's personality when considering his Dublin books. If we tried to examine his books and leave him out, we should be wasting our time and his effort. Works about Joyce published in recent years deal more with his character than his work: for instance, *Our Friend James Joyce* by Padraic and Mary Colum; an unfinished study by his younger brother Stanislaus, called *My Brother's Keeper*—unfinished and unjustifiable; and a keen piece of research into his education, Kevin Sullivan's *Joyce among the Jesuits*.

In spite of Joyce's own books and in spite of all the books about him, nobody has ever managed to explain his character with anything like satisfactory completeness. He was incredibly complex. He was a fox, a snake, an octopus. Could *Finnegans Wake* have been written by anyone except a man of bewildering versatility and protean elusiveness? Almost every assertion you care to make about Joyce can be answered by a qualification or a contradiction or both. Every new book about him contains new information which counters established beliefs about his nature. It is as though we were trying to reconstruct the face and figure of a dead man from a series of photographs, and found that each new picture, instead of adding depth to a contour or emphasizing a feature, compelled us to rub out part of our drawing and begin afresh, with new angles and different colorings, which themselves might prove to be equivocal or false.

Ulysses opens with elaborate blasphemy against the Roman Catholic religious ritual. Buck Mulligan [= Oliver St. John Gogarty], preparing to shave in the presence of his friend Stephen Dedalus [= Joyce], pretends his bowl of lather is the wine of the holy Mass, waits for the transubstantiation of wine into blood to take place, says, 'Slow music, please. Shut your eyes, gents. One moment. A little trouble about those white corpuscles,' whistles to the sky, and ends with 'Thanks, old chap. That will do nicely. Switch off the current, will you?' Elsewhere in Joyce's fiction Christianity (in particular its Roman Catholic version) is ridiculed with much energy and venom; and we knew, or we thought we knew, that after a stringent upbringing in Jesuit schools Joyce lost his religious faith entirely. It is astonishing therefore to learn from his own brother that he made a special point of attending early Mass on Maundy Thursday and Good Friday, and that when his daughter Lucia's health was endangered he lit candles of supplication to her patron saint. Must we believe this? I think we must.

After his mother died, he started drinking hard. His father was a disastrous old soak, his younger brother Charlie also did some convivial boozing, and Joyce was physically too frail to be able to stand much strong liquor, so that he easily became incoherent or unconscious. His brother Stanislaus implies that Joyce was in great danger of becoming an alcoholic, and that in 1907 he was stopped only by the influence of Stanislaus, an influence which was later withdrawn. Joyce never held his liquor very well; drunkenness is one of the key themes in both *Ulysses* and *Finnegans Wake*; but it is quite clear to everyone who studies those intricate books that they were composed by a man who, although his imagination often wandered wildly, was in full command of an astonishingly supple mind and a magnificently stored memory. Alexander Alekhine, the chess master, sometimes played in tournaments when he was full of brandy; but as one of his opponents said, 'even when drunk he could see a great deal further over the board than most chessplayers sober.' * Joyce's drinking was apparently not like the drinking of Scott Fitzgerald or Utrillo or so many other modern writers and artists: it did not deprive the world of fine books and works of art which remained unachieved in limbo because their creator was drugged and paralyzed. It was, apparently, more like the drinking of Rabelais, an excitement which stimulated and liberated his imagination and multiplied his creative powers.

Like Joyce's books, he himself can be understood partly, but not wholly; and although neither he nor they can be said to have real charm, we feel ourselves attracted to both, as the explorer to the unknown hinterland, the cryptanalyst to the cipher, the philologist to the unread language, the diver to the deep sea, the psychoanalyst to the dream.

The more deeply you penetrate into Joyce's life and character, the more dense with contradictions and conflicts the man becomes. Look at what he thought of his own country, Ireland, and the city which was his birthplace, 'dear old dirty Dublin.' Begin with the fact that when he was at the crucial age of thirty-two he left Ireland for ever. Although he made one brief return (to start a motion picture theater, of all things), although later he traveled widely in western Europe, and although he was at least twice invited to return in circumstances of honor, he never thought of Ireland as his permanent home again. All forms of nationalism he despised: Irish nationalism, one of the most vehement, he made into a farce in the Cyclops chapter of *Ulysses*. This chapter parodies the grandiose epic

* H. Golombek, 'Recollections of Alekhine,' quoted from *Chess Review* (1950), in Fred Reinfeld's *Treasury of Chess Lore* (New York, 1951).

poems of Ireland, in which the heroes have superhuman dimensions and adjectives are lavishly used:

> The figure seated on a large boulder at the foot of a round tower was that of a broadshouldered deepchested stronglimbed frankeyed redhaired freelyfreckled shaggybearded widemouthed largenosed longheaded deepvoiced barekneed brawnyhanded hairylegged ruddyfaced sinewyarmed hero. . . . The widewinged nostrils, from which bristles of the same tawny hue projected, were of such capaciousness that within their cavernous obscurity the fieldlark might easily have lodged her nest. The eyes in which a tear and a smile strove ever for the mastery were of the dimensions of a goodsized cauliflower.

It mocks the Sinn Feiners' eloquent devotion to the traditions of their country:

> The citizen was only waiting for the wink of the word and he starts gassing out of him about the invincibles and the old guard and the men of sixty-seven and who fears to speak of ninety-eight and Joe with him about all the fellows that were hanged, drawn and transported for the cause by drumhead courtmartial and a new Ireland and new this, that and the other. Talking about new Ireland he ought to go and get a new dog so he ought. Mangy ravenous brute. . . .

. . . and their aspirations for the future:

> Our harbours that are empty will be full again, Queenstown, Kinsale, Galway, Blacksod Bay, Ventry in the kingdom of Kerry, Killybegs, the third largest harbour in the wide world with a fleet of masts of the Galway Lynches and the Cavan O'Reillys and the O'Kennedys of Dublin when the earl of Desmond could make a treaty with the emperor Charles the Fifth himself. And will again, says he, when the first Irish battleship is seen breasting the waves with our own flag to the fore, none of your Henry Tudor's harps, no, the oldest flag afloat, the flag of the province of Desmond and Thomond, three crowns on a blue field, the three sons of Milesius.

Nor is Irish piety neglected. 'God bless all here,' says one of the drinkers; and off goes Joyce into a pompously elaborate account of a religious procession filled with priests and monks and friars and saints:

> S. Terence and S. Edward and S. Owen Caniculus and S. Anonymous and S. Eponymous and S. Pseudonymous and S. Homonymous and S. Paronymous and S. Synonymous and S. Laurence O'Toole and S. James of Dingle and Compostella. . . .

It is a funny chapter, but the satire is bitter; and if one were a patriotic and God-fearing Irishman it would not be funny at all but hateful. It is introduced by a short and even more trenchant travesty, which comes at the end of the previous chapter. Leopold Bloom, having partly digested his heavy lunch, is overtaken by the urgent necessity to pass wind. At home, it would be easy enough; but he is walking in the streets of Dublin, he is full of intestinal gas ('must be the cider or perhaps the burgund'), and he worries ('Fff. Now if I did that at a banquet'). At last he finds a quiet shop-window, and stops to look into it so that he can relieve his internal pressures while static and not (much more dangerous) ambulant. Yes, but what is in the shop-window? A portrait of the Irish patriot Robert Emmet (1778–1803), with his famous last words inscribed beneath. Bloom stands there as though reverently studying the picture and reading the quotation; but in fact he concentrates on letting out his flatus without making an abrupt explosive noise. So he reads, slowly, and blows, slowly, and welcomes the approach of a trolley car which with its clanging bell will cover the loudest expulsion of air, and (Joyce shows us by skillful typography) contrives to synchronize his long-postponed relief with the dying utterance of the condemned hero.

> Softly. *When my country takes her place among.*
> Prrprr.
> Must be the bur.
> Fff. Oo. Rrpr.
> *Nations of the earth.* No-one behind. She's passed. *Then and not till then.* Tram. Kran, kran, kran. Good oppor. Coming.

Krandlkrankran. I'm sure it's the burgund. Yes. One, two. *Let my epitaph be.* Karaaaaaaa. *Written. I have.*
Pprrpffrrppfff
Done.

Another satirist, thinking of the comic situation of a man compelled to pass wind in public and remembering that Bloom was
a Jew, might well have made him recite one of the special
prayers which the Orthodox are expected to say while per-
forming certain physical functions, or else a quotation from
Holy Writ:

> I am poured out like water, and all my bones are out of joint:
> my heart is like wax; it is melted in the midst of my bowels
> (Ps. xxii. 14).

Or possibly:

> We have been with child, we have been in pain, we have as it
> were brought forth wind (Isa. xxvi. 18).

But no, Joyce's chief aim was to mock Irish chauvinism, and so
he made his anti-hero read the words of the doomed patriot
giving out his last breath. Joyce once described Ireland as 'the
old sow that eats her own farrow,' and in a poem he called it

> this lovely land that always sent
> Her writers and artists to banishment,
> And in a spirit of Irish fun
> Betrayed her leaders one by one.

Consider his three chief characters. Stephen Dedalus, though
born in Dublin, bears the names of a Jew who became a Christian saint, and a Greek inventor; Leopold Bloom [= Virag] is
a Jew of Hungarian background; Humphrey Chimpden Ear-
wicker of *Finnegans Wake,* though a Dubliner too, is not of
Celtic descent, but comes from the Viking invaders who occupied Dublin for centuries. Among the many languages and
secret-bearing names which are interwoven in *Ulysses* and in
Finnegans Wake, Gaelic is present, but far from prominent. At
the very time when almost every Irish-born writer was trying

to penetrate more and more deeply into Irish history and myth, Joyce turned away from Ireland toward a wider horizon.

Nevertheless, it is absolutely impossible to dissociate Joyce's work from Ireland. It is tied fast to Ireland like *Don Quixote* to Spain, or like the *Comedy* of that other great exile, Dante, to Florence. Dante described himself (in the letter to Can Grande of Verona) as 'Florentine by birth but not by nature'; in the same way, Joyce, although anti-nationalist and un-Christian, annually celebrated St. Patrick's Day. Throughout his working life he concentrated on trying to understand and express his native city, and through it (although more distantly and far less completely) Ireland.

But as soon as we say this, we must make another qualification. Joyce's Dublin is not quite an Irishman's Dublin, or a real Dubliner's Dublin. It is seen more from the outside, with wariness, than from the inside, with sympathy. The two men who walk through it watchfully and anxiously in *Ulysses* are displaced persons—one an incomer from a distant land and a different tradition, and the other about to escape (like the primitive Daedalus from his island prison) into a kindlier exile. And in *Finnegans Wake* the little, lonely, beer-sodden city on the very fringe of Europe is weirdly transfigured into a central metropolis typifying the whole of human history. Joyce was trying to have everything both ways, or every way at once: not through cowardice or chicanery, but because he felt that great art is both particular and universal, both parochial and cosmopolitan. He was born in Ireland. He wrote (on the whole) in English. He knew French, Italian, and German, with some Latin and smatterings of other tongues—although it is odd that he wrote about Odysseus without knowing Greek. An early effort to learn Gaelic he abandoned, because he held that his art and the life of his people depended on being connected with the bloodstream of western civilization. The result was a set of Rabelaisian oxymora: cosmopolitan Dublin; international Irishism; James Augustine Joyce, second-class honors in University College, Dublin, a leader of European language and literature.

As a member of society born in an intensely class-conscious city, what was Joyce? What were his manners, his aspirations? Who did he think he was? A poverty-stricken aristocrat like Villiers de l'Isle Adam? An ambitious member of the lower middle class? An aesthete who had cast off all ties of class and rank? Again there is no simple answer. Stephen Dedalus (who is a projection of much of Joyce's character) is a terrible snob in conversation and conduct. Although grindingly poor, he carries a walking stick to show that he is a gentleman; and young Joyce himself used to wear tennis shoes and a yachting cap. Stephen Dedalus usually talks with elaborately exaggerated courtesy; he meets and holds his own with some fine intellects; but with common people he can scarcely bear to converse unless he is drunk or hung over. So apparently the essence of Joyce's work is aristocracy. When he was a young student he published an arrogant attack on the Irish National Theatre, called 'The Day of the Rabblement,' * berating the directors and their supporters for cultivating popular Irish appeal instead of importing difficult foreign novelties. When he grew mature, he wrote books which were intended to be so arduous that the rabblement could not even pretend to understand them. The apparatus of enormous knowledge, interlinked puns in dozens of different languages, complex historical and philosophical allusions, multiple meanings demanding infinite patience and a rare degree of learning to elucidate—all this surely stamps Joyce as one of the choicer spirits of his age, one whose 'soul was like a star, and dwelt apart.'

This was his ambition. But it was fulfilled only in part. Joyce was common. He was vulgar. He was dirty, and he knew it. There is a close parallel: Eugene O'Neill, who sometimes lived like a bum, and a sordid stupid bum at that, and sometimes lived like a remote austere prophet. In its chief char-

---

* The word is suggested by Casca's contemptuous description of a mass meeting in *Julius Caesar* I.ii: 'The rabblement shouted and clapped their chopped hands, and threw up their sweaty night-caps, and uttered such a deal of stinking breath . . . that it had almost choked Caesar; for he swounded and fell down at it; and for mine own part, I durst not laugh, for fear of opening my lips and receiving the bad air.'

acter, O'Neill's play *A Touch of the Poet* personifies the same uncomfortable combination: a gallant gentleman who loves poetry but inhabits the same body as a rough peasant who loves booze and coarse company. This is one of the main difficulties that Joyce's readers have in enjoying his work: not that it is shocking, not that it is obscene (it was intended to be both shocking and obscene, and it succeeded very well for its time), but that it is, beneath a rich veneer of complex intellectual and aesthetic decoration, cheaply coarse, gloatingly low. Joyce's big effects are vulgar effects. At the climax of *Ulysses* Stephen has a vision of his dead mother, who speaks to him about the most sacred of all subjects, religion; but this is in a whorehouse, and he is drunk, and his reply to her is the crudest of English obscenities. The plot of that mighty vision called *Finnegans Wake* is inspired by an Irish comic song about a drunken bricklayer who fell down and died, but at his own wake was revived by the touch of whisky on his lips. (The refrain of the song contains the exquisite line, 'Welt the flure, your trotters shake'—as though the dancers were pigs in a sty.) The truth is that apart from Oliver St. John Gogarty, another dirty talker like himself, and a few mild intellectuals such as the librarians of the National Library, and a handful of nationalist Irish writers with whom he had scant sympathy, Joyce did not have the opportunity of meeting refined and cultivated people. From the sordid little back-street world of *Dubliners* and *Ulysses* and the tight family prison of *A Portrait of the Artist,* one could hardly guess that Joyce grew up in a capital city where there was a great deal of good living and high thinking—or at least high talking—and the vitally active Abbey Theatre producing important new plays and controversies; and that one of the greatest talkers and gayest scholars in Irish history, Francis Mahaffy, was writing and talking and gormandizing with his peers in Dublin's fair city throughout Joyce's youth and young manhood.

Yet can we believe that Joyce himself, that patient remorseless analyst, did not know this? Secretive as he was, would he

not have concealed it if he had wished to do so? Certainly.
Therefore it would be a mistake to think of this dissonance as
hypocrisy, pretense, schizophrenia. Stephen Dedalus with his
noble thoughts and his tramplike habits, his yachting cap on
his head and his pawn-tickets in his pocket, looks like Charlie
Chaplin, who wore a 'toothbrush' mustache (imitating members of the officer class), a walking stick which would not quite
support him, a short black jacket and trousers which would not
fit him exactly, and borrowed or picked-up boots in which he
could hardly walk. Joyce must have known how funny he really
was. His mistress, with whom he lived for many years before,
for financial and social reasons, he married her, was a peasant
girl with the inimitable name of Nora Barnacle;* and sure,
she wasn't very great on the books, she left that to Jim. There is
in Richard Ellmann's biography of Joyce a family photograph
of James Joyce and Nora Barnacle and their son Giorgio and
their daughter Lucia, all dressed up to the nines and facing
the camera with rigid stares of fake elegance, Giorgio wearing
a tight-waisted jacket, pointed shoes, and gray spats, and the
women just a bit overdressed and wrong—it is like a still from
one of Vittorio de Sica's satirical motion pictures. It is impossible to look at it without laughing. As you gaze, you
expect the poses to dissolve, and a conversation in ludicrously
affected accents to begin, all four talking at once and then
moving into a hysterical family quarrel. Joyce was a comic
fellow, and he is a comic artist. His projection of himself in
the *Portrait of the Artist,* although impressive to young idealists and perhaps even to himself when he wrote it, is in some
ways ridiculous. *Ulysses* in most of its chapters is outrageously
comical, its squalor making it more absurd from page to page:
through it Joyce meant to make the city of Dublin itself into
a pompous inflated joke with a bad smell hovering round it.
Finnegans Wake should be compared with the work of
Rabelais, similarly learned, similarly complex, and similarly

---

* Only Dickens could have improved on that, and he did. In *Little
Dorrit,* Part I, chapter 10, we meet Mr. Tite Barnacle of the Circum-
locution Office. His wife, Dickensians will recall, was a Stiltstalking.

obscene. Both books are jokes played on the reader. They say, 'Read this, you muttonhead, and then (if you can) laugh at yourself for reading it!' The vulgarity which Joyce places on top of an intellectual Eiffel Tower, the coarse habits and dirty language of a semi-brilliant young poseur, the reduction of the world's history to the remnant of a vulgar comic song and the troubled sleep of the keeper of an Irish pub—these are comic ideas. Perhaps they will not ultimately prove to be funny. But they were meant to be funny. And only the mistaken reverence with which we approach books that look scholarly keeps us from recognizing their nature. Not Dante, but Rabelais; not Milton, but Ariosto; not Aeschylus, but Aristophanes: these were some of the prototypes of Joyce. Throughout his sufferings and his suppressed remorse and his agonizing self-knowledge and his pervading almost world-wide disgust, he managed to laugh, and to provide material for us, if we have sufficiently strong stomachs and dirty minds, to laugh with him.

Richard Ellmann, *James Joyce* (Oxford University Press, New York, 1959).

Hot Gospeler

ON A FINE spring afternoon a number of years ago, a handsome
blonde woman who lived in southern California went down to
the beach. In the Ocean View hotel she changed into a green
swimsuit. She sat under an umbrella for a time, then went into
the ocean, and after half an hour or so disappeared. Normally
this would have been put down as another case of accidental
drowning, and the woman would soon have been forgotten.
But she was not merely a statistical unit. She was a public
figure and a spiritual force. She was Aimée Semple McPherson,
the pastor of the Angelus Temple in Los Angeles.

Like Mary Pickford and Elizabeth Arden, she was Canadian
by birth. Brought up in poverty, starting married life as a
missionary in China, she had by sheer energy and by an amazing gift of appealing to large audiences become the richest,
most famous, and most successful revivalist preacher in the
United States. Many people thought she was simply turning
religion into a vulgar fun-fair: for instance, she preached a
sermon on the idea that sin is slavery, wearing a pre-Civil
War hoop skirt, and surrounded by a field of artificial cotton
with slaves bending beneath the whip of a Satanic overseer,

while a choir sang spirituals with words written by Aimée herself. But in the 1920's almost anything was accepted if it was loud, and novel, and produced a Thrill. Furthermore, many people were grateful to Aimée because she taught them not to look at Christianity as a creed dedicated exclusively to physical austerity and self-sacrifice. She liked pretty clothes, had her auburn hair beautifully 'styled,' and loved horseback riding and swimming. When she disappeared into the Pacific Ocean multitudes of people were desolated with grief. Divers searched for her body: they could not find even her bathing cap. In the ensuing days thousands of men and women gathered on the beach, expecting her to return walking on the water. One devotee actually claimed to have had a vision of her walking on the waves; another leapt into the ocean, crying 'I am going after her!', and was drowned. Others again thought that her body might have been taken directly up to heaven—like Methuselah's father Enoch, who 'walked with God; and he was not; for God took him' (Gen. v. 24). But her mother Mrs. Kennedy expressed the conviction that Aimée was dead, suggesting at one point that she had been murdered by the dance hall owners of Venice, California, for opposing Sunday dancing. She hired airplanes to strew flowers over the Pacific Ocean. Great funeral services were held, with masses of weeping mourners, and a special choir was formed to be a lasting memorial to her grace and her talent.

But Aimée was not dead. Before the mourning was over, a lawyer in Long Beach, California, told the police that he had been approached by two men who said they had kidnapped her and wanted a ransom of $25,000. After some investigation the police decided this was merely a racket. Then a letter signed *The Avengers* was sent to her mother, demanding half a million dollars in ransom, and adding two pieces of private family information which only Aimée and her mother would be likely to know. Finally, over a month after her disappearance in Venice, California, Aimée walked into a small town in Mexico, just across the border from Douglas, Arizona, and asked for help. She was apparently in good health, with no sunburn, no signs of starvation or thirst or heat prostration, lips not parched, color normal, pulse 72 and temperature 98: she did have two small blisters on her toes. Nevertheless, she asserted that she had been kidnapped from the Venice beach by white slavers who kept her bound hand and foot for many days, until at last she had found an open can with a jagged lid; by sawing her straps and ropes against its sharp edge, she had freed herself, then escaped and run for twelve hours or so through the desert, often falling from sheer exhaustion. It was a startling tale. It was made all the more startling by the fact that her clothes, when the sheriff of Cochise County examined them, were found not to be torn and to bear no stains from perspiration or dust. Kidnapping is a serious offense. A grand jury was summoned to examine the evidence, and, if convinced, to return an indictment against the kidnappers. The jurors interrogated Aimée with great care, questioned her mother, and heard many other witnesses. Then they rejected her story, finding (in the cold phrase of the law) that there was insufficient evidence to warrant an indictment.

This was bad; but then things got worse. The police chief of Monterey, California, uncovered evidence indicating that, during the period when Aimée was missing and presumed dead, she had been living in a seaside cottage in Carmel with a handsome young man called Kenneth Ormiston who had been the radio operator of the Angelus Temple. In spite of her efforts to keep out of sight, several neighbors had seen her and could identify her. In due course Aimée was prosecuted for conspiring to obstruct justice by telling lies to a grand jury.

However, vital witnesses changed their stories, or remained silent when called on for evidence. So many conflicting tales were told that the truth became harder and harder to discover. The judge received death threats, the owner of the Carmel cottage actually died of harassment and exhaustion, and Aimée kept an incessant torrent of propaganda flowing, so that she appeared to be a Christian saint persecuted by the forces of vice and crime and militant atheism. At last, reluctantly, the state of California dropped the case. Aimée said that the Lord had prepared a table for her in the presence of her enemies, and a crowd of her admirers sang 'Jesus Brought the Sunshine In.' Shortly afterward she published her autobiography, *In the Service of the King*. In her first chapter she told how she was kidnapped and held for ransom. From the sinister hut of the malefactors she escaped into the desert. Then she prayed to Almighty God for help.

> O God, Thou who didst lead the Children of Israel across the wilderness and guide them in all their journeys—Thou who didst provide for them insomuch that they were fed from the skies and watered from the rock, and didst even keep their shoes from wearing out*—Thou who didst care for the three Hebrew children, and kept them safe, though cast into the fiery furnace, so that not a hair of their head was singed, nor was the smell of burning upon their garments†—Thou who hast ever looked down in pity upon Thy children in their trials—Thou hast never failed me before and Thou wilt not fail me now—hear my prayer and guide my weary footsteps to safety, for I am lost and sore distressed.

And so the Creator and Maintainer of the Universe miraculously intervened to ensure that, after her long exodus through the Mexican wilderness, Aimée's shoes should not even be scuffed.

The whole story is one of the funniest episodes from the harebrained Twenties. It has been told with much amusing detail, first during Aimée's lifetime by Nancy Barr Mavity in *Sister Aimée*, and more recently by a writer known as Lately Thomas in *The Vanishing Evangelist*. This is highly recommended to students of confidence tricks and mass hallucinations. Even with its religious angle I think it could be made into a rattling good musical, with Tammy Grimes playing

* In Deut. xxix. 5 Moses tells the children of Israel, 'I have led you forty years in the wilderness: your clothes are not waxen old upon you, and thy shoe is not waxen old upon thy foot.'
† Daniel iii. 27.

Aimée, and Busby Berkeley brought out of semiretirement to stage the big scenes of religious ecstasy.

Immediately after the case was dropped, she set off on what she called a world-wide Vindication Tour—which was really designed to let things cool off a bit in California. During that tour I had the pleasure of making her acquaintance. She made a deep impression on me. I did not for a single instant think of her as a pure and noble soul; she did not appear to have the simple sincerity which one sees now in Billy Graham, and many of her methods and her pronouncements struck me as ridiculous and often revoltingly vulgar. But she was the strongest public personality I had ever seen, she made the average professional politician of that period look and sound like a half-starved cat, and in two short afternoons I learned, from watching her work, a great deal about the powers and perils of oratory which I did not fully appreciate until, nearly five years later, as a naïve tourist on my honeymoon in Bavaria, I went to hear a speech delivered by a rabble-rousing Austrian politician named Adolf Hitler.

When Aimée hit Scotland on her way round the world, I was twenty-one years old. The scandal about the fake kidnapping and the surreptitious escapade at Carmel had of course reached the Scottish papers, so that most people were prepared to regard her as a cheap stunt artist. Even when she started to fill large halls with enthusiastic congregations to whom she preached the Four-Square Gospel, ordinary churchgoers and sensible citizens simply ignored her. However, I was interested in the oddities of human behavior, and I went to one of her meetings. In due course I was thrown out, but before that I learned a lot.

I had expected that, after a hymn and a prayer, Aimée would come on wearing a black surplice buttoned up to the neck, and start preaching simple Fundamentalist doctrine. But she knew better. She understood that, in order to control an audience, you must prepare it. She kept us waiting for half an hour or more, which was part of the preparation. The hall was skillfully lit. The seats and the audience were in half darkness, but the platform, covered with masses of expensive flowers and gay satin draperies and showy religious emblems, was brilliantly illuminated. There was (I think) a trained choir in white; there was a loud organ of the movie-house type on the platform; and there was an energetic young man who acted as a conductor and cheerleader. The hymns were all new to me, and tickled my sense of humor, for although their words were religious their tunes were usually profane, brisk and jolly. The cheerleader warmed everyone up by singing himself, waving his arms, and encouraging various parts of the audience to compete with one another: 'let's see who can sing loudest —now the right-hand side of the hall—now the left—ah, that's dandy!—now both together. And now the unmarried ladies against the married ladies—unmarried ladies first!' (much giggling). The spectacle of five thousand brawny Scottish women bawling out 'My Jesus Is Right Up in Heaven' to the tune of 'My Bonnie Lies Over the Ocean' was too much for me, and I was about to leave, when Sister Aimée appeared. If I remember correctly, she was wearing a gleaming white satin costume which made her look like a cross between a hospital matron and a minor European royalty at a flower-show. Her hair, and her teeth, and her vast corsage of hothouse roses, were all dazzling. So was her eloquence. She put on a terrific show. She did not preach at all, as I understood the term. What she did was to retell simple stories from the Bible in such a way as to make them bright and vivid, dramatizing every speech and acting out all the parts and building up every climax with rhetorical questions. 'And *how* did Joshua bring down the walls of Jericho? Did he do it with battering-rams? NO! Did he do it with guns? NO! Did he do it with bombs? NO! He did it BY THE WORD OF GOD!' Her questions were hurled at the audience with such vigor that dozens of staid Scotch bodies were answering them in excited shouts, and her exclamations were so forceful and well-timed that they provoked multitudinous responses, 'Yes, Sister!' and 'Glory, Sister!' The only thing was that her quotations from Holy Scripture were not always accurate. I began to watch for mistakes: after all, I had a sound Presbyterian upbringing and an excellent memory. Then I began to correct them, audibly. Two burly men in blue serge suits moved up beside me, and asked me what was on my mind. I replied, very civilly, that if Mrs. McPherson wanted to quote the Word of God, she ought to quote it correctly. They withdrew and discussed this for a while. Then they returned to the attack. 'What don't you like about the Sister's preaching, brother?' said one of them. I knew I couldn't last five minutes now: so I pointed to the platform, where Aimée was on her knees, shouting at the top of her voice, with four floodlights trained on her, and replied, 'Jesus once said "When thou prayest, thou shalt not be as the hypocrites are: for they love to pray standing in the synagogues . . . , that they may be seen of men." ' In twenty seconds, without a struggle, I was outside in the street.

A few days later I saw Aimée's astonishing energy and versatility exercised in a far more difficult situation. She came up to Glasgow University, and tried to evangelize the students. I don't honestly remember whether she was invited, or invited herself. In any case, she met an audience which was in part openly hostile and in part cheerfully contemptuous. Most of us thought it was a piece of impudence for a hot gospeler from California to try to bring true religion to the land of John Knox; that a woman preacher who looked like a movie star was bound to be a fake; that Aimée's tirades against cigarette-smoking and whisky-drinking were poor substitutes for genuine, deeply felt Christianity; and that the scandal about her kidnapping made her not only a fake but a liar. There were some also who remembered the words of St. Paul in First Corinthians, chapter fifteen:

> Let your women keep silence in the churches: for it is not permitted unto them to speak; but they are commanded to be under obedience, as also saith the law. And if they will learn any thing, let them ask their husbands at home: for it is a shame for women to speak in the church.

So we received her with a tremendous ovation, which would have daunted almost any other speaker. The hall was festooned with derisive posters, and our gayest co-eds sat in the front seats ostentatiously smoking cigarettes and drinking tea out of whisky glasses. Sister Aimée opened cold, to a crowd of about a thousand youngsters whom she had not prepared, and therefore could not control. It was an extraordinarily difficult problem that she faced. For some time, we sang profane ditties to the tunes of well-known hymns, thus reversing her own technique. (Nothing scurrilous, of course, but things like 'Oh, Why Are We Waiting?' to the tune of 'Oh, Come, All ye Faithful!') Whenever, between verses, she managed to say a few sentences, her accent, with its piercing nasal twang, sounded so funny that her words were drowned in laughter and applause. After about twenty minutes the entire meeting was about to dissolve into chaos, so that even the rather light-headed authorities of the student council were worried. But Aimée would not be beaten. She would not walk off in silence, defeated. (Although we did not know it then, she had faced equally difficult assemblies in her own country, and, if not vindicated, had come out even.) But what was she to do? How could she even begin to dominate such an audience? Whenever she addressed it directly she was laughed down. If she merely stood still and waited for attention and silence, she would never get a hearing, for young people get more and more excited with the inflammatory infection of laughter and irresponsibility. I watched her try three times, six times, eight times, to gain their attention, and fail. She did not falter. She did not lose her temper. She faced them. She maintained her composure, so that even the rowdiest began to quieten down at intervals. And then there came a short pause, lasting less than a minute. Into that pause, with a wonderful sense of timing, Aimée injected the only words which would silence an irresponsible but good-hearted audience. She said, 'Almighty God! We pray you. . . .'

Within twenty seconds the hall was silent. Within ninety seconds heads were bowed and eyes were thoughtful while, in her harsh but apparently sincere voice, Sister Aimée asked the Almighty to bless us all and to lead us in the paths of righteousness. A prayer to God, a communion with the Father of all, could not be interrupted. When she ended, her last words were spoken quietly but triumphantly within a serious or embarrassed hush. And then, briskly, before she could lose the domination she had won with such effort and difficulty, she tripped off the platform and hopped into a taxi and sped away to continue her world-wide Vindication Tour.

Although we had felt her power, we did not consider her vindicated; and indeed we had had no chance to examine the evidence. But we had seen a first-rate orator at work. We had felt something of the mysterious quality which the sociologists call *charisma*, the magnetic force which makes some great actors, and revivalists, and politicians. It is a power which has nothing whatever to do with truth or falsehood, good or evil. It exists, or it does not. Anyone who possesses it, even if he or she is a fraud or a half-educated paranoiac, will be believed, and will prosper for a time. It is for us, the ordinary people, to be wary of such men and such women, for they are not like us, and usually we are nothing to them: nothing, except instruments to be used.

R. C. Hazeltine, *Aimée Semple McPherson's Kidnapping* (Carlton Press, New York, 1965): this is a short book by a believer, who some time after Aimée's disappearance miraculously heard her voice 'speaking with tongues.'

Nancy Barr Mavity, *Sister Aimée* (Doubleday, Doran, Garden City, N.Y., 1931).

Lately Thomas, *The Vanishing Evangelist* (Viking, New York, 1959).

Careless Marjory

———————————

YOU MEET such charming people in books.

One of my favorites is a little girl who lived a hundred and sixty years ago. She might have become a poet, or conceivably an actress; but she died before she was nine. Even so, she left something of herself.

Her name was Marjory Fleming. She was born in 1803 at Kirkcaldy, a quaint old town in eastern Scotland. Her father was an accountant whose brother was the parish minister; her mother was the daughter of an Edinburgh surgeon: solid middle class. Marjory was a cheerful, healthy, energetic little creature. In her diary she wrote, 'I am very strong & robust & not of the delicate sex nor of the fair but of the deficent in look. People who are deficient in looks,' she adds (correcting her spelling), 'can make up for it by virtue.' Marjory's mother taught her to read when she was about four years old; she was allowed the free choice of any book in her father's large library; and often in the evenings her father used to read to her—not stuff thinned out and watered down for children, but adult poems and histories. Even if she did not understand them all, Marjory enjoyed them. Hearing them read aloud gave her the experience of rich rhythm and melody; if she could not absorb all their intellectual content, she could sense the grandeur of their emotions, and dream with their imaginative fervors: she used to learn passages of poetry by heart, simply for the fun of it, and she soon started writing poems of her own.

When she was about five, her cousin Isabella Keith (a girl of about eighteen) came to visit the family. She was charmed by Marjory and offered to take her back to Edinburgh for a long stay. The two were soon devoted to each other, as though they had been sisters, or a young mother and an affectionate little daughter. They slept in the same room, and, when they went off for a holiday in the country, in the same bed: but at opposite ends, as Marjory recorded in her diary. 'At Breahead I lay at the foot of the bed becase Isabella says that I disturbed her repose at night by contunial figiting and kicking but I was very well & contunaly at work reading the Arabin nights entertainments which I could not have done had I slept at the top.' The experience inspired one of her earliest poems:

> I love in Isas bed to lie
> O such a joy & luxury
> The botton of the bed I sleep
> And with great care I myself keep
> Oft I embrace her feet of lillys
> But she has goton all the pillies
> Her neck I never can embrace
> But I do hug her feet in place [= instead].

Marjory read a lot and wrote very neatly and clearly indeed; but she did not spell very well. Isabella hit on a plan for correcting this defect. She persuaded Marjory to write a diary, a page every day; and then she herself checked the spelling, underlining mistakes, writing in 'fie' for particularly bad boners, and once making the child rebuke herself by writing over a whole page of the diary

CARELESS
MARJORY.

Though begun as a chore, the diary became a pleasure. The little girl was a chatterbox, and she put down her thoughts just as they occurred to her, together with snatches of literary criticism, occasional jokes and poems by herself, news flashes about the Napoleonic wars, and many highly moral remarks showing her struggling to discipline herself. She lived in Scotland, and the Scots have never been averse from indulging in strong and even somber moralizing.

She filled three little manuscript books with her journal. It is still in existence, and has been published several times. With all its mistakes in spelling (fie, Marjory!) and its curiously adult didacticism, it makes amusing reading, like listening to the talk of an intelligent and attractive child. Boys and girls of that age often talk to themselves, and then they are even funnier than when they are talking directly to an adult: some of the diary is therefore a monologue. And her letters are inimitable. After she settled down in Edinburgh, her cousin urged her to write home to her family, telling them how she was. It is always difficult to get high-spirited children to write home to their families, but finally Isabella managed it. Here is the result, in the form of a letter to Marjory's elder sister:

> I now sit down on my botom to answer all your kind and beloved letters which you was so good as to write to me. This is the first time I ever wrote a letter in my life.—There are a great many Girls in the Square and they cry just like a pig when we are under the painfull necessity of putting it to Death.—Miss Potune a Lady of my acquaintance praises me dreadfully.—I repeated something out of Deen Sweft* and she said I was fit for the Stage and you may think I was primmed up with majestick Pride but upon my word I felt myselfe turn a little birsay
> > birsay is a word which is a word that William composed which is as you may suppose a little enraged.—This horid fat Simpliton says that my Aunt is beautifull which is intirely impossible for that is not her nature.

---

* Dean Swift. In her journal she says 'Doctor Swifts works are very funny & amusing & I get some by hart': probably bits from Lilliput and Brobdingnag.

Marjory is like many of the Scots—customarily writing standard English, but not above using an old dialect word. 'Birsy' was not made up by William, whoever William was: it is a good Scots word meaning 'bristly (with anger).' Elsewhere she writes of the springtime, 'The hedges are spruting like chicks from the eggs when they are newly hatched or as the vulgar says clacked.' The 'vulgar' are the ordinary folk who spoke broad Scots. But Marjory herself evidently pronounced many words in the Scots fashion: 'spruting' instead of 'sprouting.'

She loved animals and birds. They inspired some of her best poems. Once after three turkey chickens were killed by rats, she produced a short but poignant elegy on them.

> Three Turkeys fair their last have breathed
> And now this worled for ever leaved
> Their Father & their Mother too
> Will sigh & weep as well as you
> Mourning for their osprings fair
> Whom they did nurse with tender care
> Indeed the rats their bones have cranched
> To eternity are they launched
> There [fie] graceful form & pretty eyes
> Their fellow pows* did not despise
> A direful death indeed they had
> that would put any parent mad
> But she was more then usual calm
> Sse did not give a singel dam
> She is as gentel as a lamb†
> Here ends this melancholy lay
> Farewell poor Turkeys I must say.

She has an even finer poem eulogizing the beauty of a pet monkey. She calls it a sonnet, and indeed it will stand comparison with some love-sonnets I have read.

* She means powt = poult (as in poultry) = chicken.
† I think I know where Marjory got this comical rhyme. Elsewhere she says she admired Scott's poem 'Hellvellyn' and quotes its last stanza: 'to lay down thy head like the meek mountain lamb . . . [who] draws his last sob by the side of his dam.'

O lovely O most charming pug*
Thy gracefull air & heavenly mug
The beauties of his mind do shine
And every bit is shaped so fine
Your very tail is most devine
Your teeth is whiter then the snow
Yor are a great buck & a bow [= beau]
Your eyes are of so fine a shape
More like a christains then an ape
His cheeks is like the roses blume
Your hair is like the ravens plume
His noses cast is of the roman
He is a very pretty weomen
I could not get a ryhme for roman
And was oblidged to call it weoman

This was evidently written when she was beginning to master the complexities of spelling, but before she started on punctuation. Later she wrote, 'Isa is teaching me to make Simmecolings nots of interrigations peorids & commoes &c.'; and indeed she became very strong on both peorids and Simmecolings.

The most touching and amusing thing in her journal is her moral struggles. She was an impetuous little creature, with frequent outbreaks of hot temper. Perhaps she would have been improved by an occasional smack on the place where she sat down to write her letters; but instead of that her cousin Isa gave her short sermons, which Marjory reflected on, and then transferred into sad religious and ethical meditations in her diary. Once, for instance, after she had been restless in church, whispering and fidgeting, she wrote: 'Yesterday I behave extremely ill in Gods most holy church for I would never attand myself nor let Isabella attand which was a great crime for she often often tells me that when to or three are geathered together God is in the midst of them and it was the very same Divel that tempted Job that tempted me I am sure but he resisted satan though he had boils and many many other misfortunes which I have escaped. ——————— ' At this point

*'Pug' meant 'monkey' long before it was applied to a breed of dog.

Marjory stops for a moment (there is a long dash on the page and a space) and reflects on the misfortunes which make her life nearly as wretched as Job's. One of them is arithmetic. 'I am now going to tell you about the horible and wretched plaege that my multiplication gives me you cant conceive it —the most Devilish thing is 8 times 8 & 7 times 7 it is what nature itselfe cant endure.'

Not long after this she had a row with a small cousin, and recorded it with remorse. 'To Day I pronunced a word which should never come out of a ladys lips it was that I called John a Impudent Bitch and Isabella afterwards told me that I should never say it even in joke but she kindly forgave me.' Marjory blamed this particular outburst not on the Divel, but on having had to drink two cups of a foul-tasting purgative called senna tea.

Later she corrected herself after commenting strongly on the sciolism of Miss Potune, the 'Lady of her acquaintance.' She wrote, 'Miss Potune is very fat she pretends to be very learned she says she saw a stone that dropt from the skies, but she is a good christian.' A charitable comment; and it made Marjory reflect on her own religious affiliations. 'An annibabtist is a thing I am not a member of:—I am a Pisplikan just now & a Prisbeteren at Kercaldy my native town.' But she was always very conscious of the stern absolutes of Scottish religion. 'God Almighty,' she remarks in her diary, 'knows every thing that we do or say & he can kill you in a moment'; and later, in a sudden apostrophe, 'Joy depends on thou O virtue!'

However, all the week is not Sunday, even in Scotland; and all Marjory's days were not spent in sad self-examination, vowing (as she once said) to 'turn over a new life and be obedient.' There were visitors; there were parties; the behavior of the gentlemen was keenly observed and recorded. 'Yesterday there was campony Mr & Mrs Bonner & Mr Philip Caddle who paid no little attention to me he took my hand and led me down stairs & shook my hand cordialy. . . . Yesterday a marrade man named Mr John Balfour Esge offered to kiss me, &

offered to marry me though the man was espused, & his wife was present, & said he must ask her permision but he did not I think he was ashamed or confounded before 3 gentelman Mr Jobson & two Mr. Kings.' Romance was much in the air; Marjory read romantic novels; and in spite of Isabella's admonitions she kept thinking about love. It keeps coming into her diary, and whenever it appears she crushes it down with an obvious effort. Once a young man who was in the Navy called at the house in Edinburgh on his way out to foreign service. This is how she recorded it: 'A sailor called here to say farewell, it must be dreadfull to leave his native country where he might get a wife or perhaps me, for I love him very much & with all my heart, but O I forgot Isabella forbid me to speak about love.—' (Pause.) 'A great many bals & routs are geven this winter & the last winter too,—Many people think beuty is better then virtue.' (Pause.) 'Isabella is always readng & writing in her room, & does not come down for long & I wish every body would follow her example & be as good as pious & virtious as she is & they would get husbands soon enough, love is a very papithatick thing as well as troubelsom & tiresome but O Isabella forbid me to speak about it.'

Long after Marjory was dead, the Scottish doctor and author John Brown published an essay on her, saying that the greathearted poet and romancer Walter Scott had known the little girl and loved her. Being a friend of the family, he used to call for her and carry her over to his house (said Brown) wrapped in his plaid, like a shepherd carrying a lamb through the snow. She would sit in his big chair and teach him nursery rhymes; he would pretend to get them wrong and be scolded; he would make up for it by reading her the fine old ballads which none knew better than he himself; finally she would recite great poetry for him. Scott (said John Brown) declared that he could not keep from weeping when Marjory spoke the speech of the despairing Queen Constance in Shakespeare's *King John*:

> For I am sick, and capable of fears,
> Oppressed with wrongs, and therefore full of fears,

A widow, husbandless, subject to fears,
A woman, naturally born to fears.

This sounds charming. Unfortunately it is very nearly incredible. Marjory, who talks of so many people she knew, never mentions Scott in her journal except as the author of 'Hellvellyn,' the poem she liked. She is not even mentioned in the biography of Scott written by his son-in-law Lockhart; and Scott had two 'osprings fair' of his own whom he dearly loved and kept close to him. And somehow it is very difficult to imagine the comical cheeky little girl who wrote doggerel verses about turkeys and monkeys being able and willing to speak the grievous utterance of a Shakespearean tragic queen in such a way as to satisfy a poet such as Walter Scott. The nineteenth century was in some ways the Age of Fable.

But there were many who loved Marjory Fleming. She died of meningitis supervening on measles when she was one month short of being nine years old; but she was not forgotten. Her mother kept her letters and diaries and poems, and a lock of her bright brown hair. Nearly fifty years after her death, extracts from her writings and reconstructions of her life began to be published, and her quaint bold sweet character gradually became known. And now her relics are in the National Library of Scotland. That would really have surprised Marjory. She might well say (as she once wrote in her journal), 'It is Malancholy to think, that I have so many talents, & many there are that have not had the attention paid to them that I have, & yet they contrive to be better than me.'

Frank Sidgwick, *The Complete Marjory Fleming* (Oxford University Press, New York, 1935).

The Life of a Yogi

A YOGI is a man who practices the Hindu mental and physical discipline called yoga. According to one difinition, yoga is a method of attaining union with God: the Sanskrit word *yoga* is cognate with *yoke* and *join* and means 'union.' Union with God, not in the hereafter, when we shall presumably be liberated from our miserable mundane limitations of body and spirit, space and time, but now, in our present life and in this world. I know nothing whatever directly about this peculiar mystical creed; but I was introduced to it some years ago by reading *The Autobiography of a Yogi*. This book is published by a society which is based in California and was founded by an immigrant Indian yogi under the title of The Self-Realization Fellowship. Its author signed it not with his original given name but with his religious title, Paramhansa Yogananda, which is said to mean The Supreme Swan who Attains Bliss through Union with God.

The book is often advertised in literary periodicals, for the Self-Realization Fellowship appears to be well endowed and to be passionately convinced of the importance of its founder. Put it down to my weakness or my overwork or my worldliness that I should never have paid it any attention at all, if the publishers had not sent me several copies at intervals. I glanced at the first two or three and then gave them away. Yet something about them stayed in my mind; and when the next copy arrived I read it and thought about it. Its contents were unlike anything I had read for a long time (a substantial recommendation for any critic); and its jacket was curious, because it bore a photograph of someone who looked like one of the best schoolteachers in my old school: Miss Agnes Colquhoun. I still remember her, with her oval face, her large deep eyes, her long black wavy hair, and her full soft lips. It was not a picture of Miss Colquhoun. It was not a picture of a woman at all, but a portrait of the yogi, the Supreme Swan. Even that fact was interesting: so was the book.

Most yogis appear to have one single and continuous career. They mature, they attain enlightenment, and then they settle down in a small hermitage in a Hindu area of the Indian subcontinent, teaching any pupils who come to them and seem worthy of their attention. This particular yogi, however, began his career in India and then moved far away to instruct foreigners: he died in exile, self-chosen. Even with the help of his book, his biography is not easy to trace in detail. Yogis, like all inward-looking men and women, consider their emotional and moral development far more important than their physical and social experiences: so Paramhansa tells us a great deal about religious doctrines imparted to him by others, and miracles which happened to him and his friends, and interviews which he had with extraordinary practitioners of mysticism; but he is quite casual about giving his own vital statistics, and omits, or at least minimizes, many data which would be highly important for a normal extrovert's life. Thus, he spends twelve pages recounting an interview with a Hindu woman who gave up eating at the age of twelve, after being reproached for gluttony by her mother-in-law, and neither ate food nor drank water for fifty-six years; but he tells us hardly anything about the four years he himself spent in poverty at the beginning of his mission. This makes the book confusing and difficult to read. It is like a mixture of William James's *Varieties of Religious Experience* with St. Augustine's *Confessions,* all steeped in the bland Indian butter and flavored with the sweet Indian honey.

But some essential facts of the yogi's life can be extracted from his book. He was born in 1893 in northern India. His father was an executive on one of the railroads built by the British. The family name was Ghosh; the future yogi was Mukunda Lal Ghosh. Like other Indians during that period, he had a double education. His parents tried to make him a Britisher and he made himself a Hindu. Without bitterness, and indeed with touches of charming humor, he explains that he attended the Scottish Church College and then a branch of Calcutta University, but that he was able to graduate only through several personal miracles. (No wonder: one of the examination questions he had to answer was to trace on the map the entire route of Byron's romantic traveler Childe Harold.) In the meantime he was spending the greater part of every day with an Indian teacher, Sri Yukteswar Giri, preferring his oral instruction to English-language books and lectures, sometimes passing the entire night in his house, and once sleeping in his bed.

After miraculously graduating, young Ghosh wondered what to do with his life. His father wanted him to become an official in the British administration; gently but firmly he rejected that. Some Indian revolutionaries invited him to join their cause, and to use German guns to separate India from the British Empire; he rejected that also, believing that violence was tactically useless and morally wrong. During the first world war, he suffered vicariously for the men who were fighting. He even records a dream in which he experienced the agony and death of a naval officer on a battleship sunk by heavy gunfire —British or German, Russian, Japanese, or French, who knows? In the midst of this time of killing and destruction he decided to do something positive, and opened a school for boys. It must have been a strange institution. Apparently he attempted to adapt the principles of yoga (usually considered a painfully difficult discipline for grown men) to children: tiny boys, he says, would sit for hours in meditative positions, endeavoring to come closer to the essence of God. The school was largely supported by an Indian Maharajah. However, it did not give Ghosh sufficient scope for his talents; or perhaps he saw it was a mistake. He determined to enlarge his career.

On the first ship which sailed after the war, he left India, and, with money supplied by his father, moved to the United States. He began in Boston by attending a Congress of Religions—apparently as a delegate representing himself. He stayed in America for the rest of his earthly life. After lecturing up and down the country, he established the Self-Realization Fellowship in Los Angeles. (This was in 1925, when he was at the climacteric age of thirty-two. The International Church of the Four-Square Gospel was founded in the following year in the same city by Aimée Semple McPherson.) He says very little of how the place was organized, how it was financed, and what was taught in it—doubtless because he thinks that finance is unimportant and that the teachings are (in the exact sense) esoteric, intelligible only to the initiates. He does spend much space on describing a world tour which he made in 1935. He passed a day with the Scottish folk singer Harry Lauder, and also visited the stigmatist Therese Neumann. The yogi was accompanied by a male secretary and 'an elderly lady from Cincinnati, Miss Ettie Bletch.' Having returned to California, Paramhansa lived and taught happily for many years, until in 1952, after making a speech at a banquet honoring the Indian ambassador to the United States, he left his earthly body. According to a statement made by an undertaker in Los Angeles, his corpse remained without signs of corruption for many days.

Externally this is not unlike the biography of many other teachers who have come to the United States during this century to lecture, to write books, and (with luck) to find a permanent position and form a group of followers.

But internally, the life of Paramhansa is peculiar because of its motivation. He was not out for money or comfort, or wide recognition. He seems to have thought all these things totally unimportant. What he was endeavoring to do was to assert two singular theories.

The first of these theories was personal. It involved his own qualifications. Suppose someone had questioned him at the end of a public lecture, and asked, 'Why should we listen to you? Who are you, anyhow? Are you anything more than a half-educated Bengali, who balked at government work, failed at teaching, and then came to America to prey on the gullible?' What would Paramhansa have answered? Because he despised hostility and hated conflict with the unenlightened, I think he would have said nothing, or else produced a bland, evasive, generalized reply. But to the enlightened he would have explained that he was the latest (although not the last) of a succession of exalted spiritual teachers who lived far above the ordinary plane of existence and were in regular communion with Almighty God. Before Paramhansa there was his teacher Sri Yukteswar Giri, who died in 1936; before him, Yukteswar's teacher, Lahiri Mahasaya, who 'gave up his body' in 1895; and before him, a mysterious personage known as Babaji. (The name seems to mean Papa = Pope, or Father.) Babaji is stated to be virtually immortal, having already existed for many centuries, and to have been the modern founder or revealer of yoga. The book asserts that Babaji has performed many miracles, and has appeared in visionary form to several of his pupils. Therefore, the first theory of Paramhansa was that he was the chief earthly leader of a supernatural church having a superhuman founder and being in communion with God.

The second theory he does not state directly, but allows it to be perceived through implications. Although he declared that all religions were more or less equivalent, although he spoke sympathetically of Christianity and Mohammedanism, although he stated that the mission imposed on him by Babaji was 'to point out the basic unity of the Christian and the Vedic scriptures,' yet in fact most of his teaching (at least as it appears in print) was aimed at demonstrating that Indian religion, Indian theology, Indian mysticism, and Indian civilization generally were central, and basic, and superior to all others: that they should not be questioned, while others ought to be interpreted through them. There are serious obstacles to this theory, but the yogi seems to have ignored them. Christians and Jews and Moslems believe there is one God, and one alone. Hindus believe there are many. There are pictures of several Hindu divinities, widely different in aspect and personality, in the yogi's autobiography; and it is impossible without abuse of language and logic to assert that the destructive goddess Kali and her husband Shiva prostrate under her feet are simply 'aspects of the same eternal being.' But Paramhansa never tried, it would seem, to explain the difference between the creeds or to suggest which of the two conflicting beliefs was right. He also professed to discover Hindu doctrines in the Bible. For instance, he asserted that St. John the Baptist and Jesus were Elijah and Elisha reincarnated. (No doubt this notion was based on the fact that Elisha succeeded Elijah [2 Kings ii. 12–15] and on the utterance of Jesus that Elijah had come again as St. John [Matt. xvii. 10–13]; but it entirely overlooks the repeated statement of the Gospels that Jesus was not inferior to, but greater than, Elijah.) The yogi's church was Hindu. His teaching, although it made conciliatory gestures to other religions, was basically Hindu. His most important convert, an American insurance man named James Lynn, actually turned into a Hindu mystic, took the name of Rajasi Janakananda, and was photographed sitting half-naked on a Californian beach with his eyes closed and the beatific smile of yoga-union on his face.

In his autobiography Paramhansa says surprisingly little that is revealing about the highly specialized side of yoga teaching: the complicated physical exercises which have purposes that seem obscure and even perverted to many western minds. There is a penetrating and unsympathetic study of them by Arthur Koestler in *The Lotus and the Robot* (Macmillan, New York, 1961): see in particular Part I, chapter 2, 'Yoga Unexpurgated,' and chapter 3, 'Yoga Research.' A single sentence from page 100 will illustrate both Mr. Koestler's trenchant style and his hostile attitude to this ancient doctrine:

> The Indian mystic is taught to force his tongue into the cranial cavity, to drink his bindu [seminal fluid] and to blink with his anus, [in order] to achieve union with Brahma.

Perhaps such teachings were reserved for the elite, and were too esoteric to be discussed with the general public.

The yogi Paramhansa was a significant phenomenon in the conflict between east and west. Unwillingly educated at a Christian and western school, he resisted what he felt to be western dominance. He became a Hindu missionary, working to convert western Christians to a higher form of Hinduism. Similarly, Gandhi in his autobiography records how, when he was a young man in Britain, he attempted to remake himself completely: to transform himself from a Hindu into a European. He tried to learn to waltz, and posed for a picture wearing a top hat and tailcoat. But then he decided that his nature and his mission were incompatible with such practices; and he became the man we remember, wearing plain homespun peasant clothing and sitting at a primitive spinning wheel. As Toynbee might put it, his response to the challenges of the west was not to try to beat the westerners at their own game, but to play that game which, by birth and early training, was his own. The career of Paramhansa seems to have been inspired by the same challenge and to have followed a comparable strategic plan. Gandhi and Paramhansa were not the first to answer the western challenge in this way. In fact, I wonder if the 'miraculous' revelation of yoga by Babaji, which took place in 1861, was not a spiritual sequel to the Indian Mutiny, the violent rebellion which lasted from 1857 to 1859 and which, although using physical methods and western weapons, failed. Gandhi and Paramhansa were not the first; and most assuredly they will not be the last.

A Surrealist Memory

────────────────

THE MOST famous surrealist now at work is the Spanish (or Catalan?) Salvador Dali, who is a fantastically skillful painter, an offensively decadent writer, and an inexhaustible self-advertiser, concealing shrewdness beneath a mask of lunatic eccentricity. The difference between Dali and a madman (as he himself says) is that Dali is not mad. For various doctrinal and personal reasons he has never been the official chief of the surrealist movement; indeed, he was excommunicated from it more or less formally. But he seems to me to be the sole surviving member of the group who has carried out most of the original surrealist ideals both of life and of art.

One of his earliest attempts at self-advertisement very nearly finished him altogether. From one point of view it was a ridiculous failure; from another, a glorious triumph of surrealism. Here is an eye-witness account of it.

In June 1936 a display of surrealist art was announced in London. Many well-known and many unknown surrealists were to take part; it was to be held in a distinguished West End gallery under distinguished patronage; there was a sizable admission fee; the whole thing had *cachet,* it had *ton,* it had *éclat* and *élan* and *verve*. Herbert Read blew shrill trumpets before and after the event. 'A month of torrid heat, of sudden efflorescence, of clarifying storms. In this same month the International Surrealist Exhibition broke over London, electrifying the dry intellectual atmosphere, stirring our sluggish minds to wonder, enchantment and derision.' Dali concentrated a disproportionate share of the publicity on himself by not only exhibiting his pictures but making an appearance on the lecture platform. As I was paying my admission, I saw an announcement at the door saying that Mr. Salvador Dali was to deliver a lecture on either *Harpo Marx* or *Charlie Chaplin* or *Memories of My Childhood*. The choice of the particular theme depended on Dali's mood, although a close inspection might show that there was not such an enormous difference between the three subjects he had proposed. All the better, I thought aleatorily, as I worked my way through the crowd and looked at the exhibits.

The crowd was almost as well worth seeing as the exhibits. There were a number of beautiful girls trying to look ugly, and ugly girls trying to look beautiful, and ugly girls trying to look still more ugly. There was a stunning brunette who had two kidneys swinging from her ears, as earrings. (It was not apparent whether they were the ordinary *rognons de veau* or a pair of human kidneys, perhaps a memento of someone near and dear.) There was a blonde with a smooth calm face and smooth pale hair, as tranquil as a statue—except that her hair was decorated with the entire works of a clock. (No doubt her face was the dial, and she had an alarm somewhere at the nape of her neck.) There were little frail feminine men, and big bristly masculine women. There was a man with a beard like a goat and a waistcoat like the skin of a leopard; there was a woman who appeared to be wearing nothing but a huge black cloak in the manner of Count Dracula, plus a pair of pointed black boots. It was very brisk and original, the exact reverse of a showing at the Royal Academy, where the spectators are usually engaged in relocating one another socially while the pictures gaze at them with lofty disdain.

As usual at a surrealist exhibition, some of the objects on display were trivial, some were disgusting, some were comical, some were brilliant and perverse, and some were hauntingly poetic. There were some visible paradoxes: I think that the famous cup and saucer and teaspoon made of fur were there,* and I am pretty sure it was there I first saw the flatiron with the huge nails protruding out of its flat surface.† There were some parodies similar to Marcel Duchamp's *Mona Lisa* with the added moustache, some found objects from seashores, dumps, and attics, some *collages* apparently done by children on wet Sunday afternoons, and some lumps by the Master of the Lumps, Hans Arp. There were some quietly crazy Magritte paintings, some exotic Tanguys which I longed to possess, and I think some enticing Paul Klees (*The Mask of Fear*, perhaps) —but in those days I had no money with which to buy pictures. I contented myself with admiration. I moved all the movable objects, and all the exhibits which were meant to swing and tinkle, I tinkled and swung.

It was getting rather hot. There must have been at least two hundred of us milling around. The exhibition was held in the top-floor studio of the gallery, which had a glass roof. It was one of the few really warm days of an English summer. People began to perspire; bearded men furtively scratched their secondary sexual characteristics, and some elaborately structured feminine hair arrangements became gradually unstuck. I was just thinking of smashing a window in order to get some fresh air—for of course a true surrealist will not hesitate to alter his environment in the most original and drastic way that occurs to him—when there was a stir at one end of the room, and a uniformed man appeared on a platform and put out chairs and a table and a glass of water. Evidently Salvador Dali's lecture was about to begin. After some slightly irritable maneuvering we all found seats. Several people sat down on artistic exhibits, which immediately tickled them or pinched them or collapsed with a low reptilian hiss. After cautiously

---

* Meret Oppenheim's only famous work.
† *Cadeau,* by Man Ray.

testing it, I took a chair off to one side and put it where I could watch both the speaker and the audience.

We did not yet know what Dali was going to lecture about. No announcement was made, and he was not visible. A cackle of noted critics and artists sat down in the front row, all looking stridently original and all combining attractiveness with repulsiveness in a peculiarly appropriate way, like a plate of chocolate ice-cream with a fried egg in its center. Gala (Mrs. Dali) materialized, looking weirdly beautiful and beautifully weird. Then the chairman (it may have been the ubiquitous Edward Marsh, with his fluty voice and his glittering monocle) hopped up and made a fluttery introductory speech, saying that surrealism was a step toward world peace, because it reminded all human beings that they suffered from similar illusions during the daytime and had the same kind of bad dreams at night . . . something of that kind . . . the details have become blurred in my mind, because by now it was growing very hot indeed under the sunlit glass roof. Then the chairman announced Monsieur Salvador Dali.

Off stage, a clanking sound was heard. Everyone sat up straight. The clanging grew louder and louder; it was mingled with a bestial panting noise and a heavy obscure rustle; we heard the steps leading up to the platform squeak and quiver. And then, very slowly, Salvador Dali moved onto the platform. He was invisible inside a huge deep-sea-diver's suit. In his belt were planted two daggers (perhaps a reminiscence of Captain Nemo in *Twenty Thousand Leagues under the Sea*), and he was leading, or being led by, two enormous wolfhounds. I have seen lecturers who were nervous, and lecturers who were preoccupied, and lecturers who were partly drunk, but I have never before or since seen one who had to be helped onto the rostrum because he was wearing a rubber-and-metal suit, with lead shoes so heavy he could scarcely shift his feet. At once I applauded like mad, because almost anything is better than the conventional lecture—and, after all, this was a meeting of surrealists, where almost anything goes or ought to go. After some hesitation the rest of the audience joined in. Dali could not hear us, and he could not bow; he could hardly walk; but weightily and ponderously, like the Golem or the Frankenstein monster, he clumped toward the speaker's table and turned to face the microphone.

The chairman now opened the little glass window in front of Dali's helmet. The well-known bizarre face appeared. But it had suffered a sea-change. It was dark crimson with exertion and heat. The temperature in the gallery was by this time about 90°; inside the diver's suit it must have been about 150°. The chairman held the microphone toward Dali's mouth, and a few croaks came out of it. The musketeer moustache, soaked with perspiration, drooped vertically downward like seaweed from a floating corpse. The bright bulging slightly goofy eyes were half-closed with heat exhaustion. At the sight of this, I applauded even more enthusiastically—remember, the essence of surrealism is to welcome, and even to induce, the unexpected and the unsystematic; the surrealist lives in a world of improvisation surrounded by unpredictable dreamlike events —and the audience followed me. The temperature rose to 95°. Both the hon. chairman and Mrs. Dali saw that Dali was about to pass into another phase of consciousness, and they buzzed around him, trying to take off his helmet by the force of their delicate hands alone. This was hopeless. Someone then took up a curved billiard-cue which was one of the exhibits, and tried to pry off the helmet by forcing the point between the neckring and the headpiece; but although this was a resourceful idea it risked either breaking Dali's neck or stabbing him in the tonsils, and somebody brushed this energetic helper away, so that he fell off the platform, breaking the billiard-cue. By now everyone was experiencing events with great intensity. The chairman was almost hysterical, the wolfhounds were leaping about barking madly and jumping up on everyone near by, Dali was sinking into total collapse, and the audience was applauding and stamping and manifesting the profoundest surrealist sympathy. (At one of the earliest Dada exhibitions, all those who entered were given an ax with which to destroy any object they did not approve of, and in theory the principle should carry over into surrealism: we were merely putting it into active practice.) Somebody with presence of mind had meanwhile gone down to the basement and got the janitor, who now appeared, carrying a basket of tools and looking rather like Buster Keaton. He loosened the bolts which held the helmet in place, and then turned it slowly round so that it screwed off. This was a delicate operation, since Dali was so frail that it would have been perfectly easy to unscrew his head at the same time. At last, however, helmet and head were separated. The janitor bowed to our applause, which was tumultuous. Dali, panting for breath, drank a glass of water, and began his lecture.

He did not open cold, in any sense of the phrase. No lecturer ever had a more appreciative audience. We were all in a riotous mood of enjoyment: the girl with the kidney earrings took them off and slung them across the room at a total stranger, everyone was laughing and chattering, and the Spirit of the Absurd flapped his cockamamie wings above our heads. Clearing his parched throat, Dali began in a peculiar French, heavily accentuated with Catalan or Spanish, saying, 'Je vais vous mantrer quelques souvenirrs de man anfance [= Oi shall show you some rremembrrances of moy choildhood].' He had decided not to do Charlie Chaplin or Harpo Marx but one of their successors. Then, after explaining that one of the most potent of his youthful memories was the putrefying corpse of a donkey past which his father compelled him to walk, on his way to school each morning, he clapped his hands for the slide to illustrate his depiction of this object. There was a click. A slide appeared. It was a beautiful reproduction of *Las Meninas* by Velazquez. At this I instantly applauded warmly, and the audience joined me. Dali was perturbed, crying out, 'Nong, nong, vous avez torrt,' at which the operator whipped out the slide, and put it on again upside down. By this time the applause was spontaneous, and shook the roof. This festive mood continued throughout the lecture. It was enhanced by the fact that, because of his accent, nobody could understand more than half of what Dali was saying; and the half which was understandable sounded funny. And all the pictures were either wrong side up, or in the wrong order, or both. It was a truly delightful afternoon.

Dali remembered the occasion. And one of the few things that make me distrust his genius is that he does not realize how beautiful it was. He describes it in the twelfth chapter of his autobiography. He says that, while his friends and assistants were struggling to get the helmet off, 'the audience was convinced that all this was part of the show, and was loudly applauding, extremely amused at the pantomime that we were playing so realistically.' No, Master, we were extremely amused by the pantomime, and we were well aware that it was part of the show; but we knew perfectly well you did *not* intend it. A good surrealist seizes on the unexpected, savors it, and helps to create it. Once in my life at least I can-claim to have been a surrealist artist, perhaps all the greater because my finest creation was spontaneous, fanciful, libertarian, and as evanescent as a comic dream.

S. Dali, *The Secret Life of Salvador Dali* (Dial Press, New York, 1942).
H. Read, ed. and introd., *Surrealism* (Faber & Faber, London, 1936).

The Stationary Man

———————————

NOT ALL the best books are produced by powerful and imposing personalities. There is at least one immortal classic in English whose author was a quiet, unobtrusive, almost insignificant little man with practically no professional literary experience, no mighty ambitions, and no special training. This is *The Natural History of Selborne,* published in 1789. Selborne is a parish in the English county of Hampshire, about fifty miles southwest of London. The book is simply a description of the parish as seen by an amateur naturalist with some antiquarian tastes: its inhabitants, its weather, its birds, its trees and plants, its animals and insects, and such oddities as a visit from the gipsies, the behavior of a tame bat, and the best method of building a pair of 'heliotropes' to indicate the apparent pauses in the movement of the sun at the summer and winter solstices.

Its author was called Gilbert White. He was born in 1720, in the parsonage of Selborne, where his grandfather was the vicar; becoming curate of Selborne himself when he was just over thirty, he lived in the parish for fifty years. Although he was poor nearly all his life, he was well educated. He went to

Oxford and became a Fellow of Oriel College (those were the days when the Fellows did not have to do any teaching), serving as Dean for some time, and once even aspiring to the headship of the College. But he would not have been happy living continuously in the city and the academic community of Oxford; he was miserable even when staying in the parish of West Deane in Wiltshire, less than a hundred miles from Selborne. Not that he did not travel. He rambled in youth over much of southern England and some of the Midlands, riding horseback, observing nature, and occasionally preaching a sermon when he visited another clergyman's parish at week's end. He rode so far and so cheerfully that a friend called him 'a hussar parson.' But he could never settle down anywhere but Selborne. As Fellow of Oriel, he was offered a number of comfortable benefices which were in the gift of the College, and refused them all. He could not be happy anywhere except in his country home.

The Natural History of Selborne is the only book he ever published. It was scarcely planned as a book; he was a little dismayed when the proposal was made that he should bring it out, but at the age of sixty-eight he made the effort; it was a success, and his one work has been read constantly ever since.

The Natural History of Selborne was not composed. It just grew. It was based on two excellent ideas, though. One of these was an idea worth adopting by every man or woman who has a little house in the country or at the seashore: the regular practice of keeping a diary of nature. It is delightful to enjoy the fresh air, the green things or the sand and the waves, the birds and the other beings who share our dwelling-place with us. But there is a further delight, less often cultivated because it requires a longer view: this is to watch the swing of the seasons and the richly varied yet usually regular procession of life, year by year. The return of the swallows to their California summer home at San Juan Capistrano is always recorded in the newspapers and noted with pleasure even by those who have never seen Capistrano. It is easy, if one has a place of one's own, to have similar pleasures every day or every weekend for months at a time—welcoming the first buds on the hedges, the first flowering shrub, the first visit from a migrant bird; noting how nesting and singing go together; checking on the growth of young trees; watching the steady climb of the sun into mid-sky; observing that, as the land and water change, so do not only the sights to be seen, but the sounds and the scents of nature. A small garden or a narrow strip of lake front can be a miniature world, exemplifying the march of the months and never growing old.

Gilbert White began to observe and record the processes of nature when he was at school. After he went to Selborne as curate, he started a 'Garden Kalendar,' writing regular notes on pages stitched together, and kept this going for sixteen years. Then he went on to something more elaborate, a 'Naturalist's Journal,' which apparently had blanks for various types of entry and was specially prepared for him every year. After maintaining that for twenty years or so, he knew a good deal about his parish. As he says himself (p. 130), 'For many months I carried a list in my pocket of the birds that were to be remarked, and, as I rode or walked about my business, I noted each day the continuance or omission of each bird's song; so that I am as sure of the certainty of my facts as a man can be of any transaction whatsoever.' It was a good observation-post, too. He noted that more than 120 species of birds had been observed in Selborne parish, 'near half the species that were ever known in *Great-Britain*' (p. 111).

That was one of his good ideas. The other was to correspond with friends who were equally interested in wild nature, asking and answering questions. He spent much time enquiring into the migration of birds. It does seem improbable on the face of it that small creatures who fly only short distances in the summer should 'be able to traverse vast seas and continents in order to enjoy milder seasons' in the winter. There are still a few people who deny it. The American naturalist Edwin Way Teale followed the movement of spring, and with it the north-bound birds, from Florida to Maine. He spent many days watching and accompanying huge flocks of migrants; and then in North Carolina he met a Tar Heel who disbelieved the whole thing.

> He had noticed the swarms of birds that day. But he assured us that migration had nothing to do with it. Why? Because there is no such thing as migration.
> 'The birds are here all the time,' he said.
> 'Why don't we see them in the winter?'
> 'That's simple. They're just farther back in the woods.' *

So Gilbert White's contemporary, Dr. Samuel Johnson, with his usual taurine assurance, explained why swallows were not found in England except during the summer months: it was, he said, because they 'certainly sleep all the winter.' If so, one might think they would have been found in their hibernacular nests; but no, Dr. Johnson explained that too. He said, 'A number of them conglobulate together, by flying round and round, and then all in a heap throw themselves under water, and lye in the bed of a river.' At the same time as Dr. Johnson was maintaining this absurdity, Gilbert White was going into the problem intelligently and open-mindedly, reading books about the appearance of such birds as the woodcock in other countries and exchanging letters with friends elsewhere in England about the exact times when birds disappeared in the autumn and reappeared in the spring. He was greatly encouraged also by reports from his brother who lived in southern Spain, and wrote him that 'for many weeks together, both spring and fall, . . . myriads of the swallow kind traverse the Straits [of Gibraltar] from north to south, and from south to north, according to the season.'

When at last he came to compile his *Natural History,* he simply edited and rearranged his letters to two of his fellow naturalists. Since he wrote in a friendly conversational tone, his book is pleasant and apparently effortless. Also, he did not claim to be a scientific expert, collecting, classifying, and describing dead specimens in a zoological museum. 'All that,' he

*Edwin Way Teale, *North with the Spring* (Dodd, Mead, 1951), pp. 180–81.

remarks (p. 150), 'may be done at home in a man's study, but the investigation of the life and conversation of animals, is a concern of much more trouble and difficulty, and is not to be attained but by the active and inquisitive, and by those that reside much in the country'; and he professes to be 'an *outdoor naturalist,* one that takes his observations from the subject itself, and not from the writings of others' (p. 123). Therefore his book, like the birds and animals, insects and fish and reptiles, which populate it, is alive. It is one of the easiest to read of all the classics.

Its attractively simple language and unpretentious format are the first reason for the long-continued success of White's book. Another reason is that he genuinely loved his subject, with a self-forgetting love which embraced almost all physical nature. Although he was a clergyman, one would not call his book a very pious one. God is rarely mentioned in it, and the doctrines of the Church of England never. Yet you cannot read it without seeing that his affectionate admiration of the ways of animals and plants was really religious. It was full of wonder. It was full of reverence. It contained a sense of the infinite which verged closely upon awe—for we may be in awe of the power of creation as seen in the habits of a tiny bird as well as in the motions of a galaxy.

In particular White was fascinated by the strange mixture of instinct and intelligence which he saw in little creatures. Some things, he observed, they always did in practically the same way, without being taught, and usually from their earliest days of life: these acts are instinctive. Once, for example, he killed a pregnant viper, cut it open, and found fifteen unborn viper babies inside it. 'This little fry issued into the world with the true viper-spirit about them, shewing great alertness as soon as disengaged from the belly of the dam; they twisted and wriggled about, and set themselves up, and gaped very wide when touched with a stick, shewing manifest tokens of menace and defiance, though as yet they had no manner of fangs that we could find, even with the help of our glasses' (pp. 208–9). Similarly, watching the feeding habits of animals, he concluded they were almost wholly instinctive.

> There are three creatures, the *squirrel*, the *field-mouse,* and the bird called the *nut-hatch* (*sitta Europæa*), which live much on hazle-nuts; and yet they open them each in a different way. The first, after rasping off the small end, splits the shell in two with his long fore-teeth, as a man does with his knife; the second nibbles a hole with his teeth, so regular as if drilled with a wimble [= gimlet], and yet so small that one would wonder how the kernel can be extracted through it; while the last picks an irregular ragged hole with it's bill: but as this artist has no paws to hold the nut firm while he pierces it, like an adroit workman, he fixes it, as it were in a vice, in some cleft of a tree, or in some crevice; when, standing over it, he perforates the stubborn shell. (P. 263.)

Although each of these acts looked intelligent enough, they were all three repetitive, compulsive, and so undoubtedly instinctive. But White saw something like the power of reason in such a specialized action as this:

> A willow-wren . . . had built in a bank in my fields. This bird a friend and myself had observed as she sat in her nest; but were particularly careful not to disturb her, though we saw she eyed us with some degree of jealousy. Some days after as we passed that way we were desirous of remarking how this brood went on; but no nest could be found, till I happened to take up a large bundle of long green moss, as it were, carelessly thrown over the nest in order to dodge the eye of any impertinent intruder. (P. 156.)

White also found it delightful to watch how small birds would educate their smaller children. Swallows, for instance, never settle on the ground to catch and eat insects. They take all their food on the wing. They must therefore teach their young both to fly and to catch insects while flying, and they do this by stages. First (says White) the young ones are fed in the nest, which is often in a chimney where they will be safe from owls. When they are ready to leave the nest, they first move to the top of the chimney and are fed there for a day or two. Next, they

> are conducted to the dead leafless bough of some tree, where, sitting in a row, they are attended with great assiduity, and may then be called *perchers*.* In a day or two more they become *flyers,* but are still unable to take [i.e. capture] their own food; therefore they play about near the place where the dams are hawking for flies; and, when a mouthful is collected, at a certain signal given, the dam and the nestling advance, rising towards each other, and meeting at an angle; the young one all the while uttering such a little quick note of gratitude and complacency, that a person must have paid very little regard to the wonders of Nature that has not often remarked this feat. (P. 173.)

White enjoyed the songs and cries of birds until fits of deafness began to deny him that pleasure (p. 191); but his eyesight remained, 'thank God, quick and good.' He used it well. He could distinguish and describe the peculiar gait and flight of many different species.

> *Rooks* sometimes dive and tumble in a frolicksome manner; *crows* and *daws* swagger in their walk [like our grackles]; *woodpeckers* fly *volatu undoso* [in a wavy flight], opening and closing their wings at every stroke, and so are always rising or falling in curves. (P. 232.)

Most of all he admired quick agile flyers. He noticed that swifts copulate while actually flying in the air.

> The swift is almost continually on the wing; and as it never settles on the ground, on trees, or roofs, would seldom find opportunity for amorous rites, was it not enabled to indulge them in the air. If any person would watch these birds of a fine morning in *May,* as they are sailing round at a great height from the ground, he would see, every now and then, one drop on the back of another, and both of them sink down together for many fathoms with a loud piercing shriek. This I take to be the juncture when the business of generation is carrying on. (Pp. 183–84.)

---

* Nowadays swallows prefer telephone wires at this stage: the young ones look like a row of crotchets on a musical staff.

THE STATIONARY MAN / 185

Naturalists are often so engrossed in observing animals and birds that they have little leisure to look at their fellow men and women. And sometimes, when you are reading Gilbert White, you feel as though he lived entirely alone in a world of creatures, he the only human being, a five-foot-three Adam in his private Garden of Eden. However, this impression is corrected by C. S. Emden's *Gilbert White in his Village,* which shows how much he depended on the farmers and villagers of Selborne to help him in his observations. He found that, like all peasants, they had their areas of blindness. Describing a tiny elusive bird with a soft whispering song, called the grasshopper-lark, he says, 'The country people laugh when you tell them that it is the note of a bird' (p. 56). Yet we are apt to forget how little education the country folk of his time really had, and how recently they had risen upward out of medieval filth and poverty. Speaking of scabies and other endemic skin diseases, he says it was not long before his own lifetime that the ordinary English people started to wash and change their linen shirts and underwear: until then they had worn wool.

> The use of linen changes, shirts [for men] or shifts [for women], in the room of sordid and filthy woollen, long worn next the skin, is a matter of neatness comparatively modern; but must prove a great means of preventing cutaneous ails. At this very time [1778] woollen instead of linen prevails among the poorer *Welch,* who are subject to foul eruptions. (P. 218.)

And he adds,

> Potatoes have prevailed in this little district, by means of premiums [= subsidies], within these twenty years only, and are much esteemed here now by the poor, who would scarce have ventured to taste them in the last reign [of George II, 1727–60]. (P. 219.)

We have come a very long way in our knowledge of health and diet since 1778; men and women are taller and stronger and more long-lived than in Gilbert White's time, and the population of his England and other lands has increased almost out of all measure. But other things have not changed so greatly: the movement of the seasons, the departure and return of 'birds of passage,' the growth and sleep of plants, the annual breathing and turning of the earth. Even if we cannot be 'stationary men' like Gilbert White, his advice and example are good for those of us who can find a home somewhere outside the mechanical noise and hurry and smell of cities. He was convinced (p. 14) that we should 'pay a more ready attention to the wonders of the Creation, too frequently overlooked as common occurrences.'

Gilbert White, *The Natural History of Selborne in the County of Southampton* (Oxford University Press, World's Classics series no. 22).

C. S. Emden, *Gilbert White in his Village* (Oxford University Press, New York, 1956).

Ishmael

'CALL ME Ishmael.'

That is the opening sentence of the most famous American romantic novel, *Moby Dick.*

'Call me Ishmael.' Few know the Bible well enough to get the full force of the name. It comes from the Book of Genesis. The first son of Abram was borne to him by an Egyptian maid-servant; the child and his mother were driven out of the camp into the desert, and there saved only by a miracle. The boy was named Ishmael, 'God Hears,' because of his mother's loneliness and divinely ordered preservation; but it was fore-told that he would be 'a wild man; his hand [would] be against every man, and every man's hand against him.' Ishmael grew up in the desert, a hunter and a wanderer.

The modern American Ishmael was a hunter and a wanderer too, sailing on a ship with a Red Indian name, the *Pequod,* out of Nantucket, in pursuit of sperm whales. His is a magnificent story, fantastically remote from normal life and yet intensely real. No one who has read it can ever forget the strange figures who sail on the *Pequod*: the thin dry Quaker mate Starbuck; the harpooner, a tattooed savage from the

South Seas, Queequeg, with his two wild comrades, the Red Indian Tashtego and the gigantic Negro Daggoo; and the diabolical Captain Ahab with his leg of ivory and his heart of red-hot steel. Wild men; weird men. What do they want of life?

Not long ago I came across another book about whale hunting which does something to answer the question: not fiction, but fact, together with strong doses of salty personal opinion. This is an account of an eight-month whaling expedition in the Antarctic Ocean, told by the senior medical officer, R. B. Robertson, and called *Of Whales and Men*. Dr. Robertson is a physician and surgeon with wide experience: he has seen much bodily suffering; one of the most gripping passages in his book is his description of how, in the tiny cabin of a little ship rolling in a heavy gale, he attended and ultimately saved a sailor who had had both legs smashed and pulped by a broken harpoon rope. But he is also a psychiatrist, and on that long voyage he had a priceless opportunity to study the gallant but eccentric men who make those long gloomy sojourns on the lonely frontiers of the world. His explanation of their character is not fully satisfactory, but it does start us thinking. He calls them 'psychopaths'—which means 'soul-sufferers' and to most of us implies weakness and illness; and he even compares these tough whalemen to Dostoievski and Kafka, two mental invalids who reek of decay. And yet he says that most of them are *too healthy* to accept and endure the civilization in which we live, so that they are compelled to escape from it.

Psychopaths? Perhaps Melville was nearer the truth when he said that such men were Ishmaelites—a separate breed with different aims. While Abraham and Isaac and Jacob were building an increasingly complex civilization, Ishmael and his people preferred to be free hunters and wanderers.

Such men love the desert, the forest, the ocean, the wilderness, the lost parts of the earth. To this breed belong the mountain climbers, who feel fully alive only when they are painfully inching their way up the steep side of a gigantic rock massif, with pinnacles of ice far above and the chill breath of the uninhabited upper air on their faces. Such are the explorers, who cannot look at the outline map of an uncrossed tropical island without planning to find a way where no way exists, who choose only what is remote and unvisited, who grapple with extremes of weather and hunger and thirst and disease and exhaustion and peril from savage animals and savager men. Such are the heroes who now go where men hitherto have only dreamed of going—in rocket ships through space, in diving spheres toward the bottom of the sea, and with rope and lantern into caves far below the roots of the mountains along underground rivers flowing from the dark wells of prehistory.

They love danger. Some of us unconsciously like it: challenge it when we drive too fast along a difficult road or swim in a rough sea. These men court it, seek it out, delight in it. In one of the favorite adventure stories of my boyhood, Conan Doyle's *The Lost World,* there is a memorable passage in which a small expedition, making its way by canoe up one of the tributaries of the Amazon, is accompanied and menaced by a deep throbbing in the air, rhythmic and solemn: the beat of war drums. The explorers see no Indians: nothing but the quiet dark curtain of vegetation on each side of the river; but the drums endlessly repeat, 'We will kill you if we can. We will kill you if we can.' In spite of that, the explorers press on. To such men danger gives zest. Many famous commanders of irregular soldiers have felt this zest: Wingate, who fought in Palestine and Burma; T. E. Lawrence; and Col. Robert Rogers, the hero of Kenneth Roberts's *Northwest Passage.* Whale hunting may sound easier nowadays than it was when Ishmael sailed from Nantucket. It is more efficient, in that it kills more whales; there is less danger in shooting a whale with an explosive harpoon from some distance away than in rowing up to it and giving it the cold steel; but the harpoon rope still breaks and can murder anyone it hits, flying blades and whirling machinery do not make restful surroundings, the ship itself is loaded with oil that might turn it into a blazing torch, icebergs the size of islands pitch through the waves by day and by night, and the tempests of the Antarctic Ocean scream like fiends and shake the ship and its crew like maddened giants.

Most Ishmaelites have a tight emotional link with the animal world. Their prehistoric ancestor was the hunter of the Stone Age who loved and worshipped what he killed. Captain Ahab dispatched other whales, because they exercised his crew and brought money to enable him to sail on; but what he dreamed of with passion was the great antagonist, the unique White Whale. Outside the realm of fiction, the autobiographical tales of the Indian tiger-hunter Jim Corbett are valuable documents for this relationship of hunter and hunted. Corbett could speak some of the language of tigers. He would call male tigers up close to him by imitating the cry of a tigress—not to shoot them, but because he felt kinship with them. There is an extraordinary chapter in his *Man-Eaters of Kumaon* which tells how he not only knew one particular tiger for fifteen years, but helped to educate it. It was a yearling cub set adrift by its mother. Having killed a deer, it ate some of the meat and then went away to sleep off its meal. Jim Corbett came upon the kill, and waited. The cub was only a year old, inexperienced and rash. Without looking to the right or to the left, it walked out into the open toward its kill. Corbett waited until it stopped to sniff at the blood, and then—without killing it— educated it. 'As he raised his head to smell the tree-stump, my bullet crashed into the hard wood an inch from his nose. Only once in the years that followed did the cub forget that lesson.'

Men were hunters for many thousands of years before they settled down to till the fields and build the villages. The sons of Ishmael are not rebels or outcasts. More positively, they are upholders and transmitters of an old tradition—a tradition that gave mankind many of its finest qualities—energy, alertness, resolution. Most of them shun the regular, multitudinous, routine-dominated civilization in which we live: they do not like having a home in a street, with a wife and a family and friends all as ordinary as apple pie. Yet though wild, most of them are sociable enough with their own kind. They hate the faceless crowd, but they enjoy small companies of primitive men like themselves: rough bravoes with whom they sometimes fight, but who will bear a hand with them in time of common danger. Out west, many of the cowboys are like that. Their home is the bunkhouse, which is like the fo'c'sle of a whaling ship.

But there are some, a stranger breed yet, who have no friends: hermits and solitaries they are, who speak to few and live in a self-made desert. In *Of Whales and Men* there is one such man, an expert flenser, who is highly paid for his skill in cutting up the captured whales. He scarcely ever appears except to do his job, and remains an enigma until the end of the book. Out west, one sometimes runs across a lonely cabin put up by a man of this type. He felt even the little cow towns and the bunkhouses too crowded for him; found a canyon far from any trail; built his own home; and settled down to live with nothing but the trees, the mountains, and the changing sky. Among the Big Horn mountains of Wyoming, my wife and I sometimes used to ride up and spend the day at 'Ginger's Cabin,' built by such a hermit, and then deserted although not yet decayed. It was supremely alone; and yet, set beside a little stream, surrounded by whispering aspens, sunlit on one side and mountain-shadowed on the other, it was a peaceable and a happy place.

Yet some solitaries are for ever gloomy, full of grief, hate, perhaps fear. The Vikings of old were sociable bravoes. But among them there appeared grim and dangerous solitaries, the berserks, who fought less like strong men than like mad wolves. Sometimes, during a long voyage, a berserk would turn against his comrades. Then they would tie him down roaring and foaming, or else put him ashore on an island, where he would slash the trees and rive the rocks until his fury wore itself out. Put a berserk in command of a whaling ship, inject him with perverted Christianity, and you have Captain Ahab of the *Pequod*. These are the true soul-sufferers. To hate all mankind is to be truly sick, for it is to hate oneself.

There is a strange travel book by an Englishman, so eccentric that it has never been widely read. In *Travels in Arabia Deserta* Charles Montagu Doughty told how in 1876–78 he traveled by foot and camel from Damascus southward many hundred rough desert miles, almost to the holy city of Mecca. Being unable to approach it, since he made no secret of being a Christian, he by-passed it and returned to civilization at the port of Jidda. For many months he had been wandering alone and friendless among cruel and capricious men who hated infidels worse than poison. Doughty had nothing to defend himself with, except a pistol which he never fired, a Turkish passport which few could read, a little store of drugs and medical knowledge, and a mild calm courage which could suffer insults and even blows and make them seem unworthy of the giver. Khalîl (his Arabic name) seemed to the wild tribesmen, the Bedouin, to be a spy.

> Ullah bring thee home, Khalîl! and being come again to thy house, if the Lord will, in peace, thou wilt have much to relate of the Aarab's land? and wilt thou not receive some large reward? for else, we think, thou wouldst never adventure to pass by this wilderness, wherein even we, the Beduw, are all our lives in danger of robbers: thou art alone, and if thou wast made away, there is none would avenge thee. There is not, Khalîl, a man of us all which sit here, that meeting thee abroad in the khála [empty desert], had not slain thee. Thy camel bags, they say, are full of money, but, billah, were it only for the beast which is under thee; and lucky were he that should possess them. *The stranger is for the wolf!* you heard not this proverb in your own country?—'By God (one cries), I had killed Khalîl!'—'And I' (said another).—'Wellah, I had waylaid him (says another); I think I see Khalîl come riding, and I with my matchlock am hidden behind some crag or bush; he had never seen it:—*deh!* Khalîl tumbles shot through the body and his camel and the gear had been all mine: and were it not lawful, what think ye, mates? to have killed him, a God's adversary? This had been the end of Khalîl.'

To travel for years alone among narrow-hearted alien folk, to be at any moment in danger of wounding or annihilation for a grudge or a whim, to see no friends but only strangers or enemies, marks a special temperament shared by few and understood by few. The Arabs themselves (says Doughty) can scarcely exist without their tribe: unless when they go on pilgrimage to the Holy City and become part of a larger community. He himself, a wanderer without a tribe and a pilgrim without a sanctuary, often found every man's hand against him, and took a superhuman pride in showing himself, among the Ishmaelites, a solitary Ishmael.

J. Corbett, *Man-Eaters of Kumaon* (Oxford University Press, New York, 1946).

C. M. Doughty, *Travels in Arabia Deserta* (Cambridge University Press, Cambridge, England, 2 vols., 1888).

R. B. Robertson, *Of Whales and Men* (Knopf, New York, 1954).

The Philosopher on the Throne

A MAN I know suffers from anxiety dreams. He has a wide repertoire of them; and he says that the worst of all is, happily, the least frequent. He could not endure it if it came more often. He dreams that he is the leader of a great country and the supreme commander of its armed forces; that he is expected to make a series of interlinked decisions, both political and military, involving millions of lives, huge sums of money, and the entire future of his nation; that he has no real advisers, nothing but vacillating subordinates; and that he himself has not the remotest idea what ought to be done. As he thinks and suffers, the problems grow in importance and increase in number and become at once more urgent and more insoluble; messengers arrive with reports that darken the situation still further, news of battles which he has not foreseen and rebellions which he cannot control; some of the incoming intelligence is so obscure as to be incomprehensible, he begins to see that his own assistants are plotting against him, anything he does will be both useless and dangerous, he is tempted to fly out into a fearful rage and order a general, massive, irrevocable destruction, and just as the tension becomes unendurable, he wakes, with a heart-pounding shudder of agony which very slowly changes into awe-inspired relief.

Yes. But suppose he did not wake up? Suppose his dream continued, and was confirmed by the various evidences of reality, and was proved to be the real life he was living? What kind of existence has the man in such a position—a supreme commander, a powerful governor, an absolute monarch, surrounded by threats and loaded as heavily as Atlas with responsibilities? This is one of the most important questions in several different fields: in history, in political science, in psychology, in biography and autobiography. Documents for its study come from the lives of many presidents of the United States; of the Popes; of many kings and caliphs; and of the emperors of China and of Rome.

One of these documents has been for many years among the favorite books of the western world—never widely popular, but deeply respected, often quoted, constantly reprinted and translated right down to the present day. This is a sort of spiritual diary or self-educator written for his own private use by one of the greatest emperors of ancient Rome. He was Marcus Aurelius Antoninus, who lived from A.D. 121 to 180 and reigned from 161 to 180. His book is usually translated under the title of *Meditations,* but he seems to have called it simply *To Himself.* In it he often addresses himself, saying 'Do this' or 'Remember this': so that we are tempted to call it *Conversations with Himself.* It is an interior dialogue, partly written down.

It is not really a book in the sense of having a beginning and a middle and an end; and quite obviously it was not designed as a aesthetic whole, or written in one continuous effort of concentration. But it is a book because it has one central purpose and two or three important central themes which interlock. The central purpose is one of the noblest which any book can have. In it the emperor was endeavoring to discipline and strengthen his own character, raising it above his weaknesses and making it impervious to shocks and temptations from without. Although he did not write the book to help other people, those who published it (no doubt after his death) felt that it would do so; and they were right. For many centuries the dialogues of the monarch with himself have been consoling and uplifting men and women who need advice and example and spiritual exercise.

They are mostly set out in short sections: one sentence long, or one paragraph, or one or two pages. Each section is generally a unit, self-contained. It looks as though Marcus wrote down each of these pithy little thoughts after he had worked it out in his mind, often with application to some problem he was confronting; and each of them is just about enough for us to read and think over in a single mental operation. It would be a mistake to read the *Meditations* straight through from beginning to end—except perhaps at the first meeting, when we wish to get the spiritual flavor of the man's mind and a general view of the book's character. After that, it should be sipped, not drunk down at a draught; chewed and digested, not swallowed at a gulp. To read one section and think it through provides almost enough healthy intellectual and moral nourishment for one day.

Here is one such paragraph. It starts from the fact which most people never understand, although thinking men and women grasp it firmly: that we are liable to be afflicted and injured by spiritual diseases which are *self*-caused, *self*-inflicted, and have to spend much effort trying to treat them and cure them. A healthy body seems to live on almost automatically, and will do its best to repair minor injuries; but the human spirit often seems to try to tear itself apart, to make itself sick, to wound itself and destroy itself. Marcus sets out to classify these destructive impulses (2.16).

> The human soul brutally injures itself, first when (as far as it can) it becomes an abscess, so to speak, and a tumor on the universe: for being annoyed about anything that happens is a departure from nature, which includes the natures of all subordinate beings. And next, when it turns away from any human being, or even opposes him and tries to hurt him, as people do in anger. Thirdly, when it gives way to pleasure or pain.

Fourthly, when it puts up a pretense, and does or says anything insincere or untrue. Fifthly, when it fails to aim its acts and energies at a target, but functions inconsequentially and at random, although even the smallest deeds should be directed to a purpose. The purpose of reasonable beings is to follow the rule and law of the most venerable city and state.*

Of course Marcus did not work out this philosophical argument and the others which he uses, all alone. Very few men have been capable of elaborating an entirely original system of thought with little co-operation and suggestion from others; and those who have usually prove to be professional philosophers like Leibniz and Kant. Marcus was here discussing with himself one of the principles of the philosophical system which he adopted at the age of twenty-five. It is called Stoicism. Its aim is to exclude emotion from life, to exalt man's highest quality, reason, to diminish suffering, to sanctify duty, and to increase our participation in and enjoyment of the communal life of the universe. Although he was the most powerful man in the western world, although he was necessarily the richest and could have been the most utterly wolfish, hedonistic, lazy, irresponsible, and depraved character of his generation, instead he dedicated his life to cultivating pure intellect, to expunging all emotion from his soul, to ignoring Time and the present moment in order to fix his gaze on Eternity, to crushing out both those liars, fear and hope, and those deceivers, pleasure and pain, and to thinking of happiness only as the cool dry satisfaction of having had a thought or having completed an act which was perfectly in tune with the vast harmonious activity of that infinitely superhuman mind, the universe. He was alone, but not self-centered; independent and wealthy, but dedicated and frugal; surrounded by the apparatus of every pleasure conceivable to western man in his time, and yet contemptuous of such distractions as the adult despises the pleasures of the baby in its playpen. Marcus was not wholly an orthodox Stoic—for there are paragraphs in his book where

* He means by this the community of the universe and of all living things within it.

we see him arguing out some of the more complex points of Stoic doctrine with himself, and not always reaching a firm conclusion; he even quotes the opponent of the Stoics, Epicurus, with approval. But in life and in most of his thought he was an austere and devoted Stoic worthy of the best ideals of his creed.

Now, Stoicism is not for every man. It has never really appealed to the public at large. It has still less appeal today, when most people appear in practice to be Epicureans, if not Cyrenaics devoted to the pleasure of the passing moment and oblivious of the future. Marcus Aurelius has therefore often been called a prig, a pompous self-satisfied puritan safe in his own ivory-lined steel-walled tower. His conversations with himself have been criticized as cold, remote, inhuman, useless. This is a massive misinterpretation. To understand why, we must consider when and how and why he wrote his book. Marcus Aurelius was the sixteenth in a line of absolute monarchs governing the vast and wealthy western world from Rome. He had, among his predecessors, wise men such as Augustus and Hadrian, wise fools such as Claudius, criminals and maniacs such as Caligula and Nero. He *could* have done anything he wanted, anything humanly possible in the world.* But he chose to give up his life to the endlessly laborious business of government, and to the duty of defending civilization against the savages who keep trying to break in and destroy it—as we see today. He could have sent out generals and administrators to fight the wars of the frontiers and arrange the affairs of the threatened provinces. For the first few years of his reign he did so. Then, in A.D. 167, when he was in his middle forties, the empire was beset by relentless dangers. There had been two years of bad harvests and famine in Italy. Plague broke in from the Middle East and devastated the population. The tribes of northeastern Europe and southern Russia started moving west

---

* His disastrous son Commodus, who succeeded him, tried to call the twelve months of the year after the twelve names in his official title, renamed Rome 'Commodus' Colony,' and appeared in public dressed as Hercules, with gold dust in his hair to give him a halo.

and south in great masses. Some attacked Rumania; others pushed across the Alps into Italy, so that even Verona was threatened. Marcus took personal command. Although the sad bearded face of his portraits and the somber thoughtful words of his *Meditations* give us the impression of a retiring intellectual, he was also a superb military commander, a fine disciplinarian, a master of tactics and terrain, and a first-rank strategist for the long term. Visitors to modern Rome are emphatically reminded of this: in the Piazza Colonna stands a huge marble pillar decorated with sculptures in relief showing Marcus's northern victories, and in the square of the Campidoglio is the man himself in bronze, on horseback as a commanding general. He beat back the invaders, and followed them to the frontiers, and strengthened the defenses, and then made expeditions into enemy territory which were so successful that they provided a zone of security that was likely to last for a long time. He was still at work, in sight of final triumph, when he died at the age of fifty-eight. Marcus was not an idealistic recluse but a front-line philosopher.

The more powerful you are, the more difficult it is to be polite and considerate, or even mild and fair, to your inferiors: particularly if you mistrust them or they fail you. Napoleon and Stalin used to fly into terrible rages, when they shouted the vilest obscenities at their wretched victims; and the worst of the Roman emperors would have men flogged to death or burned alive for an insult real or imagined. Marcus Aurelius was well aware of this threat to his own equanimity. When you are ruler of the world it is simple to say, 'Off with his head!' Therefore he warned himself (2.1):

> Tell yourself this, first thing in the morning: I shall meet men who are busybodies, ungrateful, insolent, treacherous, malicious, self-seeking. All these defects come because they do not know the nature of good and evil. But I have looked into the very essence of goodness, seeing that it is beautiful and noble, and of evil, that it is ugly and base; and into the nature of the man who errs, seeing that it is akin to me—not because it shares blood or

sperm with me, but because it participates in reason, which is a share of divinity—and that I cannot be injured by any of these men. For no man can inflict shame on me;* nor can I be angry with a kinsman or hate him. We are born to work together, like feet or hands or eyelids, or the two rows of teeth. It is contrary to nature for us to work against one another: for instance, by being angry and resentful.

Later he repeated his warning to himself in more drastic terms (5.28):

Are you angry with a man who smells goatish, or whose mouth stinks? What does it matter to you? His mouth is like that, his armpits are like that, and the consequence follows naturally.

For such a man, life was a constant effort. For most people it is a constant effort, but they are not so keenly aware of it. Marcus was. He talked to himself like a coach to an athlete (7.61):

The job of living is more like wrestling than dancing: you have to be on guard against unforeseen attacks, and keep your balance.

He scarcely mentions the grosser temptations which beset every powerful man: gluttony, drunkenness, and sexual indulgence. One rather touching note, clearer to Marcus than to us, appears in his first notebook, when he is remembering people who have helped him and things for which he ought to be grateful. One of these things is (1.16.7) 'that I did not touch Benedicta or Theodotus'—perhaps a pretty slave-girl and slave-boy. He adds, 'and that later, when I was infected by the disease of sexual passion, I recovered.' When he was writing the *Meditations* he was middle-aged. At that stage one of his strongest temptations was simply to lie late in the morning. Late, for the upper-class Roman with intellectual or administrative interests, meant after daylight. Many of them got up

* A favorite theme of the Stoics. What about Socrates' pupil Phaedo, who was captured in a war, enslaved, and sold into a male brothel? No doubt the Stoics would say that he could and should escape, through suicide.

at three or four in the morning, to read or to handle official correspondence. Marcus himself when he was a young student reported to his tutor what appears to have been part of his normal routine: he rose at 3 a.m., had breakfast, and then studied until 8. Yet it is sometimes hard to rise early, particularly if (like Marcus) you have a low reservoir of vitality. And so he begins his fifth notebook (5.1):

> In the morning when you are reluctant to wake up, be ready with this thought: 'I am getting up to do a man's work. Why should I complain about proceeding to the actions which I was born to do and for whose sake I was brought into the world? or was I designed simply to lie in blankets and keep warm?' 'Well, it is more enjoyable.' 'Oh, so you were born to enjoy yourself? to be passive, not active? Look at the plants, the sparrows, the ants, the spiders, and the bees, all doing their own job and organizing their own worlds; and you shrink from doing a man's job? Why not follow the lead of your own nature?' 'Yes, but I have to rest.' 'Certainly; but nature has set limits to the amount of rest you can take, just as it has for eating and drinking: you are going beyond the necessary limits.'

This rigid self-discipline was characteristic of those who practiced Stoicism. (The word means only 'the doctrine first preached in the Portico,' for a *stoa* was a pillared hall or portico, and the founder of Stoicism taught in the Painted Portico at Athens; but now 'stoical' has come to mean 'rigidly self-controlled,' which after all is one of the essentials of the creed.) However, Marcus allowed himself so few relaxations that he became not merely indifferent to externals, but contemptuous of them and hostile to the material world (9.36):

> Each of us is made of rotten material: water, dust, bones, stench. And furthermore: marble is only a deposit in the earth, gold and silver merely sediment; and our clothes are hair, and purple dye is blood, and all the rest things of the same kind. Our life breath is like that too, changing and changing.

From this it is not far to the world-hatred shown by so many of the early Christians, who despised the flesh, would not wash, denied themselves food and sleep, lashed and tormented their bodies, and sometimes left human society altogether to live in caves and on the tops of high pillars. Marcus did not persecute the Christians. His predecessor Antoninus Pius (when Marcus was a junior partner) had ordered that they should be left alone; and later he himself was too busy fighting the barbarians. Although he never mentions them explicitly in his *Meditations* (the one occurrence of the name is a later insertion), it has been argued that, when he says a calm and righteous mind can remain independent even though mobs shout and wild beasts tear the clay that grows round the soul (7.28), and in a few other such passages, he is expressing admiration for Christian martyrs. Possible, though far from certain: the just man's patience under public obloquy and torture had been a philosophical theme for many centuries. But the spiritual kinship between the austere Stoic and the Christian ascetics is too clear to be denied. The world had become materialistic and luxurious, as it has today. The only way to be strong in it was to be self-sufficient, and to give up desire for the pleasures of the flesh.

Apart from his father Antoninus, he speaks without admiration of the mighty Roman emperors. The good ones such as Trajan and Hadrian he views rather coolly: they worked hard, their world was busy, and now they and their world are gone like smoke. The bad ones he contemns: Tiberius in Capri was crazy, Nero was a puppet pulled by the strings of lust (just like a wild beast or a passive homosexual, he adds). He himself is more of a Stoic than an emperor. A hundred years and more before his time, the opposition party—the few Romans who still longed for the republic to be restored and still fought against the encroachment of one-man absolute power—had been devoted, passionless, courageous Stoics: Cato, Brutus, Thrasea, Helvidius. They were all exterminated in blood. Now history was strangely reversed. The monarch of the western world spoke of past emperors rather patronizingly or pityingly or contemptuously, but he revered the great republican Stoics as immortal souls whom it was a privilege to imitate

(1.14). For one of the few times in human history when such a blessing was conferred upon mankind, the absurd but inspiring ideal of Plato had been realized, and a philosopher sat upon the throne.

Like many great books, Marcus Aurelius' *To Himself* is not straightforward and consistent, but full of contrasts and conflicts, some obvious, some concealed. Its author was a Roman born and bred, but he wrote in Greek: it was the language of philosophy, and, for subtle reflections, it was more expressive than Latin. He was a monarch, but he admired the enemies of monarchy as noble idealists. He was a man devoted to public duty, but his main work is a private notebook containing his personal doubts and sufferings, and obscure and painful affirmations, angry self-reproach and cold self-consolation. Outside were the usurpers and the barbarians: these Marcus Aurelius could fight and conquer. Within, his own passions and fears: his weaker self, over which he won a greater victory.

Red Dawn

————————————————

IT IS ALWAYS hard to be a poet; and in Soviet Russia it is very hard indeed. The Russian tongue itself is extremely complex; and some experts say that if you want to remain active in poetry you must learn to write two languages concurrently, normal Russian and official Soviet. Under this burden, some aspiring poets have bugged out altogether and settled into lifetime jobs as proof correctors on the *Great Soviet Encyclopaedia*. But others, who have faced the manifold challenges, have the right to call themselves Soviet poets. Among these the most original and daring is N. V. Ponimaiu, leader of the Vitalist School and the coryphaeus (as he is styled) of the post-Stalin generation of Soviet writers.

'Others,' says Nye Ponimaiu with a smile in which there is no trace of malice, 'can talk about poetry for many hours at a time. I find it is better to *live* poetry. And life is work, is it not?' Already some farsighted Russian critics are forecasting that he will (if he lives) attain the same degree of national popularity and international significance as Shostakovich in music or Spassky in chess. Much depends on the success of his self-designed self-educational program, which his friends humor-

ously call his Ten-Year Plan, or sometimes (from its three
stated aims, to travel among men and cities, to learn life, and
to toughen his moral fiber) TravLerTuf. In the poem which
announced his dedication to the plan (and which won for him
the first annual All-Union Brezhnev Award), he voiced an
ideal which has inspired many young Soviet citizens of today.

> Away!
>
>   (leaving the cosy dacha
>   to steam
>   in comfort
>   unreal
>   unhealthy)
>   Go!
>   See!
>   Dare!
>   Up and forward!
>   A hundred thousand versts!
>   A million!

Yet his poetry has not always had those clean lines and that
flashing speed. When he published his first book, *Sour Cream
and Sunflower Seeds* (1954), he was denounced as a degenerate.
The Young Pioneers of Krasnoyarsk, his native town, removed
his name from their honor-roll. A severe editorial in the
Literaturnya Gazeta, in that magazine's most trenchant style,
described him as 'a reactionary wolf in progressive sheep's
clothing'; all unsold copies of his book were removed from the
shelves of the state bookstores and pulped. Nye Ponimaiu himself said nothing, then or thereafter. He is content to await the
verdict of history. Nevertheless, from this distance in time, it
is difficult to see why those early lyrics were counted so offensive. One of them has already crept back into favor. At avant-
garde parties in Leningrad (always the more boldly experi-
mental of the two great Soviet cities) the exquisite diseuse Olga
Marmeladovnitchka often recites his *Damp Fog in Thin
Pyjamas,* with its haunting refrain:

> vagabond O vagabond I
> flotsam adrift between earth and sky

> leaf in the breezes to and fro
> vagabond I vagabond O

Another man, a weaker man, might have abandoned all hopes of a poetic career after such a disaster as the condemnation of his first book. But N. V. Ponimaiu instinctively knew the road to true greatness, which lies across deserts and through forbidding mountains. He set his face to the future. He met its frown with a courageous smile.

A year passed; and then another. With a gesture as startling as the first Sputnik, he launched his manifesto. It was the ode called *A Hundred Thousand Versts*. Courageously, he sent it to the *Literaturnya Gazeta*. Wisely, that periodical did not decline it. In this bold lyric he defined the duty of the new Soviet poet as he had conceived it. This was simple: perhaps so simple that it had eluded most of his contemporaries. Although a poem has, or ought to have, no logical skeleton, yet such an important poem as this has a complex thought behind it; and N. V. Ponimaiu's thought could be defined in an enthymeme.

> To be a poet one must know life.
> To be a Soviet poet one must know the life of the Soviet Union.
> Therefore. . . .

Therefore, Nye Ponimaiu asserted with unimpeachable logic, he must set out to learn the life of the Soviet Union, by traveling through the entire territory inhabited by Soviet men and women, and working at various trades and professions during his educational and poetic journey.

Nyashka began his odyssey like Homer's Odysseus, by going to the far west. He adventured into the Autonomous Soviet Socialist Republic of Lithuania. In a spirited ballad—already set to music by some of the energetic young guitarniks among his admirers—he evoked the rhythms of pounding heart and rolling wheel which exalted him at this time.

> West and away to the tomb of the day
> out of the Mother's arms
> into the distance, dangerous challenge,

> thundering onwards on Soviet wheels!
> Express West!

The fact that he could not speak Lithuanian, although it necessarily narrowed the field of his new acquaintances at this
time, did not diminish the intensity of his poetic experience.
Its immediate issue was the libretto for the opera *Forward to
Paganism,* celebrating the abolition of the Christian superstition, once forced upon the unhappy Lithuanian people by
their feudal overlords.

Next Ponimaiu turned eastward, to see (as he put it) the
other pole of Soviet power. He journeyed to Vladivostok in the
Maritime Territory, where he served for some time in a whale
cannery,

> taming the sea monster
> harvesting the Pacific
> lavishing
>   protein on the masses. . . .

Unfortunately a persistent infection in the poet's right hand,
which refused to yield to the most advanced Soviet medical
treatment, made it imperative for him to move to a milder
climate and to change his occupation. We next find him working as a peach pitter in the Autonomous Soviet Socialist Republic of Georgia. There he soon recovered health and spirits,
but (no doubt because of the prolonged effort of convalescence)
produced no poetry except a choral ode to peach brandy—
which, after initial publication in *The Georgian Aesthetic and
Cultural Program-Journal,* he decided to withdraw and has not
republished. 'In the life of every artist,' he says with a wry
smile, 'there are mistakes. As the Georgian proverb puts it, a
busy builder sometimes forgets the roof.'

Today, however, Nyashka is happy and productive again. He
has spent two terms in heavy industry: one in the gold-mining
area within the Arctic Circle, where, although he gathered
much material, a severe attack of pneumonia temporarily prevented him from converting it into poetry; and the other in

the Donets Basin, where he produced a superb dithyramb on the important Russian invention of aluminum:

> White as our souls
> light as our hearts
> bright as our future—
>   aluminum!

After the instantaneous success of the abstractionist ballet *Storm of Bauxite,* during which this noble lyric was sung by the choir of the Donbas Light-Metal-Workers-and-Cryolite-Processors' Union, N. V. Ponimaiu was given a remarkable distinction. He was appointed a Poet of the Soviet Union, and presented with a three-roomed dacha in the woods near Tsarskoe Selo. Then, after a two-week vacation on the Crimean Peninsula, he was sent on an official mission to the Middle East. Well versed in the Arabic language—although not yet, as he candidly admits, able to compose poetry worthy of its strength and charm—he has been in contact with many important leaders of the peace movement in the Arab world. Ever since the U.S.S.R. single-handedly overthrew the German and Japanese warmakers in 1945, Nye Ponimaiu has been dedicated to promoting world peace; and now, from his flower-bedecked room in Cairo, he is pressing the cause with all his energy. Already one of his new compositions is frequently heard on Middle Eastern radios, his *Song of Youth:*

> We are front-line fighters for peace!
> Yes, front-line fighters for peace!
> We'll hang, we'll shoot, we'll bomb, we'll burn
> All enemies of peace!

Poems like this have made Nyashka Ponimaiu not only a leading Russian writer, but a sonorous and memorable voice of the whole progressive world.

Miller's Tropics

WHEN YOU first read Henry Miller's *Tropic of Cancer,* you are apt to judge that it was written during a series of lengthy drinking-bouts.

> Could man be drunk for ever
> With liquor, love, or fights,
> Lief should I rouse at morning
> And lief lie down of nights.

So wrote A. E. Housman, concluding sadly that it was impossible, because 'men at whiles are sober, and think by fits and starts. . . .' But Henry Miller seems at first to have mastered this impossibility, and to differ from ordinary men as a perpetual drunkard from a total abstainer. Occasionally in the lounge car of a train, while you are peacefully reading *Encounter,* someone who has had too many highballs bumps his fat behind into the chair beside you and begins telling you a long incoherent story about this girl in the office, name's Delores, and what the poor broad said to the floor-manager, wasn't her fault anyhow, never saw such a lousy deal, reminds me of a time once out in Seattle when the salesmen all got stoned at the Christmas party, boy, should have seen them, boy, never forget it. Waiter, let's have another round here, sure you won't? I still got forty minutes, but as I was saying this stinking brother-in-law of mine. . . .

Much of Miller's writing reads like that. It is an endless gush of reminiscence about personal acquaintances whom he knows well, but who are never introduced to the reader and are sometimes hardly credible. Some of them appear in full light, and are drawn in vivid detail, and then vanish for ever. Others fly into the story and out again in a few moments, like a bat in a night-lit garage. Neither *Tropic of Cancer* nor its sequel *Tropic of Capricorn* is a novel in any ordinary sense: that is, a story with a coherent plot developed in time, and a cast of characters interacting with one another. They are sections of a non-stop monologue going on in Miller's head. Basically, this monologue is like the gabble of the drunkard on the train, but with two important additions. One is that its style, its use of language, is marvelous. The other is that its subject matter rises far higher than that of the average monologist and also sinks far lower. Much of it consists of rhapsodic prose poems about Life, and Art, and Individuality, and the Horrors of the Modern World, and so forth: crabby, opinionated, half-educated, not very original but very forceful in the good old tradition of the village rebel and the street-corner atheist. Much of the rest is conversation so filthy that it is never heard outside prisons, barrack rooms, and the lowest slums: together with brilliantly vivid narratives of mean and degrading actions. It is often very funny, at least to men. Taken as a whole, it makes you detest and despise Henry Miller (or the fictional narrator, if there is a difference). You try to pity him, but you cannot. Not at first; less and less as the books proceed; perhaps not ever. He likes being despised, and telling despicable things about himself.

Open *Tropic of Cancer* at its first page.

> I am living at the Villa Borghese. There is not a crumb of dirt anywhere, not a chair misplaced. We are all alone here and we are dead.

Last night Boris discovered that he was lousy. I had to shave
his armpits and even then the itching did not stop.

What sense does this make? How in twenty devils' name can
Henry Miller (or his fictional narrator) be living with someone called Boris at the Villa Borghese? It is a beautiful spot
in Rome, just outside the Pincian Gate. You can walk to it
from the Via Veneto, turning right at the horse-ring, the Ga-
loppatoio. It is full of superb paintings and sculptures and
lamentable tourists; it is the property of the Republic of Italy,
and it is carefully controlled by the Department of Fine Arts.
What are Henry Miller and his lousy friend doing in it?* And
how can the two men be dead if one of them is verminous?
Body vermin always leave a corpse at once. All right, then, it
is a hyperbole: they are both lonely and clean, therefore dead,
like well-washed cadavers in a funeral home. Then if they are
both so rigorously and ritually clean, how does one of them
harbor lice? And then, curiouser and curiouser, why does
Henry Miller have to shave the other man's armpits? Boris is
pediculous, but is he also paralyzed, so that he cannot shave
his own armpits? The operation presents few technical difficulties; and most people who had lice in their armpits would
prefer to shave their own armpits. Or does Henry Miller like
telling us on the first page of his book that he was so degraded
—living on another man's charity—that he was compelled to
shave the armpits of his host? Perhaps his relationship with
Boris was like that of the clients described by Juvenal (3.104–8)
who were ready to throw up their hands in praise if their patron and host managed to emit a satisfactory belch or to uri-
nate straight and clear and good and fine: a peaceful, although
unappetizing, symbiosis. But is that all he did for Boris? Why
does he stop there? Perhaps he is squeamish?

No. Reading on in *Tropic of Cancer,* we realize that Henry
is not squeamish. He may not always be logical, but he is

---

* From Alfred Perles's book *My Friend Henry Miller* we learn that
Miller does not mean the Villa Borghese in Rome, but uses the name to
describe a place in Paris called the Villa Seurat. Mystifying, ho ho, but
not very funny.

immune to the etiolating vice of fastidiousness. On this first page, perhaps he wishes to puzzle his readers or to leave something to their imagination. Later on he makes no such concessions.

Yet, having read these first sentences of *Tropic of Cancer,* you will remember them. Henry Miller can use the language. He writes strong, biting, durable prose. Often it is unjust to begin criticizing a book by taking out the first few sentences. But Henry Miller is a rhetorician. He knows that the exordium is important. His books and his separate chapters begin dramatically, pungently. Style, style, style: brushwork, the drive of the hand into the clay, the thrust of the lines of structure against one another, the movement of the phrase between keys and modes, the balance and rivalry of colors, the rise and fall and rhythm of an actor's voice—style is a chief aim of all good artists in all media. This Henry Miller has achieved: he is a wonderful stylist, and also (as represented by his fictional narrator) a filthy swine.

Spontaneous, his style appears to be. He writes prose which often seems to run quite naturally, like the flow of eager conversation or a rapidly written letter or the current of non-logical ideas in one's own mind. If in the future he is remembered for anything more than his interest in low life, he will be recalled as an agile, often graceful, sometimes powerful manipulator of word and phrase and sentence and paragraph, and sometimes (although less often) of those larger units which are called chapters. He seems to be talking to you as you read him. He can even get away with such old-fashioned tricks as the address (no doubt half-ironical) 'Dear reader.' It is easy to believe that he is an enthusiastic letter writer and has poured out tens of thousands of pages of correspondence to his friends. Much of it has been preserved, and will no doubt in time be acquired by Yale University. Writing even one letter a day is practice for an author, provided it is not formal or commercial, but intimate and friendly. Renoir said that if he did not draw something every day, even if it were only an apple on a plate, he would forget how to draw. So it is with writing. But inditing as many letters as Miller has done is like a violinist's playing three hours of exercises every morning. Some of his most ardent admirers are professional authors: Lawrence Durrell, Karl Shapiro, and others. They too have struggled with the Laocoön serpent of language, trying to master it before it inwound and paralyzed them, and they delight in Miller's superb conquest of it. Even one of his short works, such as *The Air-Conditioned Nightmare,* makes your heart beat faster and your brain move more rapidly—if you like language. Stylistically, compared with most regular novels, *Tropic of Cancer* and *Tropic of Capricorn* are like two big symphonies for eighty-piece orchestras, contrasted with two chamber works by Karl Ditters von Dittersdorf.

True, he rambles. Frequently, and most of all in *Capricorn,* he wanders off into illogical rhodomontades which remind us partly of Thomas Wolfe's barbaric yawp and partly of those old Dadaist and surrealist prose poems which nowadays seem like a waste of ink and paper. But, like a number of half-crazy stump speakers, he is a skillful rhetorician. Open either *Tropic* at random and begin to read. The only reason you will stop is that you are either exhausted or nauseated. I take up *Capricorn* and let it fall open, really at random. Page 256: 'I remember Sunday mornings in the little old house near the cemetery. I remember sitting at the piano in my nightshirt, working away at the pedals with bare feet, and the folks lying in bed toasting themselves in the next room . . .' and off he goes into four grand continuous pages about music and Wittgenstein and Prokofiev and a scherzo Henry improvised to a louse discovered in his underwear—a real bravura piece of writing, impossible to interrupt or ignore or despise. And then it modulates straight into a piece of narrative about his first sexual experience, with his music teacher: which both in language and in content is base and revolting. Yet it is written with the same driving energy, the same rich variety of phrasing, the same lively offbeat sentence structure, the same admirable spontaneity, and the same crazy humor.

This is the paradox of Henry Miller. The two *Tropics* are

among the foulest books ever written in English, because they describe such foul actions in such foul language. *Cancer* is bad enough, but *Capricorn* gets worse as it goes on, and reaches depths of vileness which are really indescribable. Lawrence's obscenity in *Lady Chatterley's Lover* was meant to be natural, unaffected, life-enhancing, inspiring. The obscenity of Aristophanes and Rabelais is heroically comic, often shocking, but never nauseating. Much of Miller's obscenity is abnormal: he tells us about the kind of thing which goes on among base and perverted moral lepers. And he himself (or his fictional narrator) is usually among the basest, doing their things.

Why did he write all this? For instance, why did he trouble to describe himself as going with a miserable prostitute, and then stealing the wage he had given her? He has talent. Why does he want to make himself out to be a swine? To this question, which occurs to his narrator several times, he gives several different answers: the customary flapdoodle about the Artist being a separate species of humanity with unique privileges; the bold assertion that the entire world is all wrong, and the sooner it is blown up the better; the adolescent notion, so delightful for a few years, that sex alone 'holds the world together'; and so on. But as you read you feel that these are only rationalizations of psychotic drives which lie much deeper. The line between genius and derangement is often hard to draw; and the literary evidence suggests that Miller was close to derangement when he wrote these books. The two *Tropics* represent two distinct stages of his malady. The explanation will not be found in *Tropic of Cancer*, which contains only evidence of the middle period of his aberration. The truth is concealed in *Capricorn*. There were several convergent causes for his trouble, but the strongest is hinted at only within the final thirty pages, as though (consciously or unconsciously) he had held it back to the very end. It comes in a hideous waking dream of his adolescent years.

> I seemed to have absolute liberty and the authority of a god, and yet by some capricious turn of events the end would be that I'd be lying on the sacrificial block and one of my charming

uterine relatives would be bending over me with a gleaming knife to cut out my heart.

Now, Miller says he had two 'uterine relatives' (curiously evasive term). One of them was an idiot sister, whom his mother used to beat savagely. The other was his own mother. Whose face did he see bending over him with the knife?

The End of the World Is at Hand

THE PSYCHOLOGIST and almost-philosopher C. G. Jung had a favorite story, half funny, half grim. Long ago (he said) a warrior knight was captured by his enemies, and put in a dark dungeon, chained to the wall. Year after year, he sat there in prison enduring his evil fate. At last he beat his fists upon his knees and cried, 'Oh heavens, when will these damned Middle Ages come to an end?'

Jung told the story to illustrate the paradox that people seldom understand the historical period in which they live. At this moment we may be inhabiting what future generations (if any) will describe as the pre-planetary age, *or* the last era of world anarchy, *or* the transition period between mass disease and mass starvation, *or* the new enlightenment, *or*—who knows? So the men of what we call the Middle Ages, between A.D. 1000 and 1400 or so, did not know that they were living in what we should see as an intermediary period between the Dark Age following the collapse of the Greco-Roman civilization and the reappearance in the West of classical culture together with the birth of modern science. On the other hand, they did not make the mistake which some of our ancestors, and some of us, have made: the mistake of believing that they were perfect: the acme, the ultimate, superior to the people of all previous historical periods; the end-product of the long evolutionary process; the top of the progress-graph. Instead, they were apt to believe that they were living in the last days. The world, they often thought, was coming to an end.

Many of those who expected the end of the world were simple devout Christian folk. They looked forward with fear and hope to the Second Coming of Jesus, which he himself had foretold (Matthew xxiv) and which was linked with the Last Judgment in the Book of Revelation (chapters xix and xx). This mighty event could occur any day. Jesus himself commanded, 'Watch: for ye know not what hour your Lord doth come' (Matt. xxiv. 42). The Judgment was always present in men's imaginations; it was pictured on the walls of churches and carved on the porches of cathedrals; and it was powerfully hymned in *Dies Irae* as 'The day of wrath, that dreadful day,/ When heaven and earth shall pass away.'

There were some who believed that it was their duty to hasten the end of the world, and endeavored to do so by almost every means they could devise. Some lashed their bodies with spiked whips, some murdered priests, Jews, and Moslems, some starved themselves, some indulged in every form of luxury, some shunned the face of mankind and became solitaries, some formed communes where many moral restraints were obliterated. In the passion of their belief and hope, they lived lives in which the normal routine was completely overthrown, often deliberately reversed. The end of the world did not come. All these people are now a pitiful and sometimes revolting episode in the long tragicomedy of man's history. It was not the first, and it was not the last.

For a Christian it was difficult to believe that Christ would return triumphantly to rule in glory as long as the holy city of Jerusalem was occupied by infidel Mohammedans. Devout men and women often made pilgrimages to the Holy Land in order to see the very sites where Jesus had lived and taught and died and risen again. But in A.D. 1095 Pope Urban II, with many supporters, proclaimed the ideal of a war to set the holy places free again: the First Crusade. The thought that the home of Christ might be recaptured from non-Christians, detestable and damned, inspired a great mass of enthusiasts, who left their homes and their families and set off to reach Jerusalem. They were not sure where it was; they had scarcely any idea of how to reach it except by covering many hundred miles of land and sea; but they were certain that, when it was reached and liberated, a new heaven and a new earth would be revealed to mankind. As they went on their toilsome journey, they saw a mystic city floating in the sky above them.

In history books and romantic novels, the Crusaders mostly seem to be members of an elite, the aristocrats of the sword: men with horses, and expensive armor, and heraldic devices to show their nobility; knights and squires, earls and marquises, princes, even, and kings like Richard Lionheart. We do not usually read that these men, with their fairly well-trained forces, were accompanied rather against their will by a less skillful but sometimes more energetic force, the Poor Crusaders: beggar Christians, without weapons or armor, wearing sackcloth or rags, with no supplies and no organization, with nothing except an inflexible and unreasonable will to get to Jerusalem and set it free, either killing or converting all who stood in their way. The Arabs protested to the knightly Crusaders about the behavior of these forces—the Tafurs as they were called—because they were perfectly ruthless, killing every living thing they met, eating roots and grass and even the corpses of those whom they killed. Quite truthfully, the Crusaders replied that they had no means of controlling these fanatics. In fact they were urged, enlivened, inspired by forces perfectly irrational and irresistible, just as the Moslems themselves had been some four hundred years earlier, when in a single generation they surged over many hundreds of miles of conquest. Such insane mobs can be stopped by main force, or slowed down by dogged resistance: they can never be reasoned with.

There were several crusades of poor people, of shepherds, even of children. They ended in complete disaster, the children being sold as slaves to the infidels, and the others either dispersed into wandering bands of desperate DPs, or killed, or lost in limbo. Often in medieval stories we read of 'wild men of the woods' who, within a fairly civilized country with laws and cities, still lived Mesolithic lives deep in the forest, hunting and hiding, waylaying travelers, raping and murdering, sometimes eating their victims. Some of these may have been devout young farm boys who set out to save Jerusalem, and when their crusade dissolved into chaos, lost all faith in God and trust in man, becoming savages.

Yet the belief that the end of the world was at hand often took a different form. Some excited spirits announced that the end of the world had actually occurred, and that a new moral, social, and political order was in force.

In France about A.D. 1140 there appeared a man who said he was the son of God. His name was Eudes de l'Étoile, but he called himself Eon, a mystical Greek name meaning either The Age or Eternity; and he had a church of his own, with bishops called either by the names of the apostles of Jesus or by appellations such as Wisdom, Knowledge, and Judgment. He was not a howling psychotic, but a calm intelligent man who was also powerfully magnetic. To himself he attracted thousands of the farmers of southern and western France, who were starving because of several hard winters and several generations of inefficient and unequal government. With his worshipping followers he formed a state within a state. They devastated and plundered much of western France, helped by the fact that the Bretons did not feel themselves truly fellow-citizens or rightfully subjects of the men in Paris, and also assisted by the notion that Eon himself could perform miracles. After reigning for some years he was captured. In the cathedral of Rheims he was examined by church authorities. He stated that he was the Messiah, sharing the government of the universe with Almighty God. He was sent to prison: there, being

fed on water and little else, he soon died. His principal disciples were captured with him. They refused to deny his
teaching. They were burned alive. As one of them was being
led toward the stake and the pile of wood, he called out to
the ground beneath his feet to swallow up the 'heretics' who
were attacking him. 'Earth,' he cried, 'divide yourself! Earth,
split open!' Soon after that, he was ashes and dust.

The same spiritual energies which drove crusades of rich
and poor out toward Jerusalem kept other devotees at home,
and persuaded them that their own country was ready to become the Holy Land and their own city the New Jerusalem.
Each of these movements generally followed the same chiliastic
pattern. Its leader declared that the end of the world had arrived; that he himself was God, or the Messiah, or an apostle
of God in immediate communication with the Almighty—
although this last (perhaps because it resembled the mission of
Mohammed) was less usual. Those who opposed him were
obviously doomed and damned, and must be utterly rooted
out. But those who followed him were saints, and had the perfect blessedness of saints. Since the Kingdom of God had come,
the sin of Adam and all its attendant penalties and prohibi-
tions were removed; and the sanctified could do whatever they
wished. Sometimes marriage was abolished; sometimes polyg-
amy was instituted, for the leaders at least. Sometimes all property was communized; sometimes the leaders had the best of
everything. John of Leiden, the Anabaptist king of Münster,
renamed the days of the week, minted new coinage with millennial symbols, dressed in magnificent clothes, and had a
harem of lovely wives, none over twenty years of age. Meanwhile he confiscated all the belongings of his followers, explaining that pomp and luxury were permissible for him,
since he was wholly dead to the world and the flesh. After he
attempted to extend his dominion over other cities and was
defeated, he still for many months held his central Jerusalem
against the besieging forces of the Holy Roman Empire. He
maintained his power over his subjects until the vast majority
of them had starved to death or had been killed by his own

police. When his city was captured, he was taken and tortured to death with red-hot irons. Throughout his agony, he uttered no sound and made no movement. The cage in which his corpse was suspended can still be seen in a Münster church.*

There is a valuable study of these enthusiasts of the Middle Ages: *The Pursuit of the Millennium,* written by an eloquent and well-balanced historian called Norman Cohn, first published in 1957 and since then so successful that it has been revised, and enlarged, and reissued. The illustrations include one depicting the Pope as Antichrist, and another showing Jews committing the ritual murder of a Christian child. They are simply revolting. Yet they demonstrate the peculiar blend of fantastic image-building, fierce emotion, and quasi-intellectual control which explains both the frenzy and the power of such end-of-the-world revolutions.

The dismal medieval stories, what do they mean to us? They are so far away, so clouded with bogus theology and small local politics, that they can surely tell us little about our present and our future? So we might think if we looked at them superficially. But Mr. Cohn points out that these millennial movements have many things in common with the political upheavals under which so many of us have suffered. In essence—apart from the belief in God—they are the same as the belief of the modern authoritarian and totalitarian states that the new world is about to arrive, or, after the Revolution under the inspired and superhuman Leader, has already appeared. There are two views of human history, Mr. Cohn observes. One is that it moves slowly and painfully, often going backward or sideways or for a long time pausing fruitlessly, sometimes making mistakes, but usually, although not inevitably, improving. The other is that it is pointing toward a single divine event, which we can hasten if we work a speedy and drastic change. The average man holds the former view

* A century or so later a false Messiah arose among the Jews, Sabbatai Zevi. He, after a longer and more brilliant career than John of Leiden, shrank from the face of death, and lived on, basest of humiliations, as a Moslem convert.

of history; the fanatics hold the second, and they are prepared to do and suffer anything to bring it about. If you think the Golden Age is about to dawn, or the Messiah is about to appear (in close connection with yourself), you will do *anything* to further that event. Therefore, if you happen to be mistaken, you may do horrible things, both unreasonable and cruel. Yet you will believe you cannot possibly be wrong. The opponents are fiends; you are an angel; they are the devil; you are the representative of God, or possibly God himself. Whatever you will, is right.

At this point political thought and planning passes into insanity. Mr. Cohn is a very calm and charitable historian; but his study of these painfully misdirected movements has led him to conclude that such political programs are not a phenomenon confined to the Middle Ages. They recur. They reappeared in this century, as the Nazi and the Communist and other such philosophies of politics. The cruelties and violences that accompany such movements are (says Mr. Cohn) 'consequences not of ordinary human fallibility or ignorance but of a chronically impaired sense of reality; illustrations, in fact, of the irresistibly compelling nature of that peculiar type of vision, at once rigorously self-consistent and fatally distorting, which is so characteristic of paranoia.'

And now, in the last few years, the same spirit has been reborn. Destroy first, and then build a new world! This system is all bad; the new society will be perfect! The old are rich and corrupt; the young are not concerned with money, and are pure! Bold, these antitheses; simple, easy to grasp, tempting to believe—especially if you do not know how complex human motives and desires always are, and cannot realize that all forms of human association are inevitably faulty. Often, however, the men and women who preach these simplistic contrasts do so with the frenetic energy and glassy-eyed conviction which indicate grave mental disorder. Carried on partly by the excitement generated by a crowd in motion and partly by an earnest sense of social injustice, one of my own pupils at Columbia joined the radical revolutionaries at the first outbreak of disorder in 1968. Some weeks later, his face drawn and pale and his voice somber, his whole gait and expression those of a much older man, he told me how he had heard one of the fanatical leaders expound, with great glee, a plan for completely destroying the main library of Columbia University, tier by tier; how he had suggested that some of the books at least might be worth saving; and how he had been silenced with a stream of vile obscenities. As he talked, he gazed in his mind's eye at the figure of the leader, dressed as fantastically as a character in a surrealist ballet, but also foul with body-dirt and dizzy with drugs. Burn the library! Destroy the books! At that moment, my pupil decided that the whole movement had gone crazy. I never saw anyone get a practical education in politics so rapidly and effectively.

Sometimes, as I look back over history and consider the extraordinary effect which men on the verge of lunacy have had on it—men like Hitler and Ivan the Terrible and Stalin —I wonder whether, to explain the events of the past, we should employ social scientists, or historians, or literary men, or psychologists. Mankind tries to be sane, but sometimes it is led by madmen.

Norman Cohn, *The Pursuit of the Millennium* (Oxford University Press, New York, 1970 ²).

The Man in the Gray Velvet Suit

THERE HE stands in the photograph, wearing a gray velvet suit, which is rather wrinkled but undeniably distinguished. With his pointed beard and his myopic eyes and his fantastic costume, he contrives to look both silly and dignified. Many people have been puzzled by him, some outraged, and some contemptuously amused. His friends once asked him to explain how he lived. He replied by writing an article called 'Memoirs of a man with amnesia.'

An artist must live a regular life.

Here is the exact time-table of my daily routine.

7:18 a.m., I get up. 10:23 to 11:47, I am inspired. I have lunch at 12:11 and leave the table at 12:14.

From 1:19 p.m. to 2:53 I ride horseback in my park, for health and exercise. From 3:12 to 4:07 I am inspired again.

Various occupations (fencing, meditation, immobility, visits, contemplation, dexterity, swimming, etc.) from 4:21 to 6:47.

Dinner is served at 7:16 and finished at 7:20, followed by symphonic readings, aloud, from 8:09 to 9:59.

I go to bed regularly at 10:37. Once a week (on Tuesdays) I wake with a start at 3:19 a.m.

I eat only white food: eggs, sugar, powered bones; the fat of dead animals; veal, salt, coconuts, chicken cooked in clear water; fruit-mold, rice, turnips; camphorated sausages, pastry, cheese (white varieties), cotton salad, and certain fish (skinned).

I always have my wine boiled, and drink it cold with juice of the fuchsia plant. I have a good appetite; but I never speak while I am eating, in case I choke.

I breathe carefully, in limited quantities. I dance very seldom. While walking, I hold my sides and look steadily behind me.

My expression is very serious; when I do laugh, it is an accident. I always apologize, very affably.

I sleep with one eye open, very deeply. My bed is round, with a hole for my head to go through. Every hour a servant takes my temperature and gives me another.

For a long time I have subscribed to a fashion magazine. I wear a white cap, white stockings, and a white waistcoat.

My doctor has always told me to smoke. He adds, 'Smoke, my friend; if you do not, somebody else will.'

Surely that gives a clear impression of the man in the gray velvet suit? No?

He was a musician: let us look at his work. His compositions include these: *Bureaucratic Sonatina* for piano solo; *Dressed Like a Horse,* two chorales and fugues for piano duet; *Furniture Music,* for piano, three violins and trombone; *Things Seen to Right and Left (without glasses)* for piano and violin; and *Three Pear-Shaped Pieces* for piano duet. A mere clown, a cheap parodist, a vulgar sensationalist: both he and his work are equally worthless. No: by the judgment of able musicians this is mistaken. He was a friend of Claude Debussy, and influenced some of Debussy's most important work, including *Pelleas and Melisande*; Maurice Ravel admired him greatly, and played some of his music at concerts; Darius Milhaud said he had set the future course of French music; Francis Poulenc and Roger Desormière were proud to be his pupils. Evidently he was a clown with a strong mind, a powerful will, a serious heart.

His name was Erik Alfred Leslie Satie. He was born in Normandy in 1866. His father was a shipbroker in Honfleur, his mother a woman of Scots descent. When Erik Satie was a boy, she died, and was replaced by a very earnest, strong-willed, and boring stepmother who was determined to make Erik into a serious musician. She and his father dragged him to concerts of conventional classical music, endeavored to impose accepted aesthetic standards upon him, and sent him to the Paris Conservatoire, where he made a faint but paradoxical impression. (His piano teacher thought he might be a good composer, while his professor of harmony suggested he had a gift for the piano.)

At the age of twenty-one he published what were to become two of his most famous works: a group of three dances for piano solo called *Sarabands,* and another called *Gymnopaidiai.** Today they sound simple enough, and even a little thin; but in 1887 they contained startling innovations in harmony and style: strangely resolved chords of the ninth, which Debussy was to use fourteen years later; delicate, almost imperceptible melodies; an air of reticence which was quite unlike the confident Olympian style of Wagner and Brahms and Saint-Saëns; an eerie, almost unearthly simplicity and purity. The first of Debussy's *Preludes* published in 1910, *Dancers of Delphi,* is closely reminiscent of the *Gymnopaidiai;* and the *Sarabands* were the forerunners of such works as the *Saraband* in Debussy's *Suite for Piano* and Ravel's famous *Pavan for a Dead Infanta.* These were only the first of many unusual and original works which Satie was to compose. He felt power within him. It must be wonderful to be twenty-one and to have written music you know to be pure fresh creation.

The unhappy result was that he went mad, or very nearly mad, with ambition. For the next ten years or so he lived in Montmartre, playing the piano in cabarets for a living, writing lofty mystical music, and doing everything he could to have himself acclaimed as a supreme genius. When he was twenty-eight he proposed himself as a member of the Institute

---

* The *Gymnopaidiai* were a festival in ancient Sparta at which groups of boys and men danced and sang naked.

in succession to the composer Gounod; and, when rejected, he wrote to Saint-Saëns warning him that the rejection showed Saint-Saëns was ignorant of God and was in danger of hell fire. (Saint-Saëns had already completed *The Carnival of the Animals,* or he might have put Satie into it as a goose or a cockatoo.) His most ambitious work was a ballet in three acts, which contained only one human character, together with multitudes of angels, demons, saints, and martyrs—something to outdo both Goethe's *Faust* as set by Gounod and Flaubert's *Temptation of St. Anthony.* He offered this to the Opera in Paris. When he did not even get an acknowledgment of its receipt, he challenged the director of the Opera to a duel. At the age of twenty-nine or so, he founded a church of his own, called The Metropolitan Artistic Church of Jesus Conductor and Guide. Apparently he conceived himself as its leader, the vicar of God on earth, and he published official utterances in the manner of papal bulls. (Some of them were devoted to solemn denunciations of Colette's first husband, the revolting 'Willy.') About the same time he had a love affair with the well-known model Suzanne Valadon, the mother of Maurice Utrillo.

Then, when he was about thirty, Satie stopped composing, for a time. His madness abandoned him. Or, more correctly, he mastered it and turned it into controlled eccentricity, deliberate deviation. He realized that he would never be accepted as a genius equivalent to Richard Wagner. He saw that the effort involved in composing vast amorphous works trending into infinity was like the self-inflation of having one's own personal church. He became convinced that his talent, while original, depended on economy and control. Perhaps this realization was confirmed by his friendship with Debussy, which has been compared to the relationship of a poor brother and a rich brother. Satie dined regularly at Debussy's house, where, with a characteristically French gesture, Debussy gave him a carafe of *vin ordinaire* and kept the vintage wines for his other guests, and of course for himself.

Satie now moved from Montmartre, then the gayest and most rackety district of Paris, to one of the poorest, dingiest, and most repulsive suburbs, Arcueil, far to the south. He went into Paris every day and back, usually on foot. He lived in a single room over a bar, at 22 Rue Cauchy, among factories and tanneries and dreary little vegetable gardens. There was no running water in his room; like everyone else, he drew his water from the public fountain in the square. He did his own cleaning, and no human being except himself ever set foot inside his room until he died. He was known as the Velvet Gentleman, because he usually wore a gray velvet suit. He had inherited a little money from a relative, and spent it on a dozen gray velvet suits—most of which were never worn, and were eventually consumed by myriads of clothes moths. To wear gray velvet while living in what is almost a slum; to have hundreds of stiff collars and piles and piles of shirts, in a neighborhood where most people never dress up except on Bastille Day; to clean one's own room rather than admit a stranger; to wash one's hands with pumice rather than soap: these are the marks of a man who has been so deeply disappointed by life that he has withdrawn from it to set up a self-oriented protective routine of his own. The absurd parodic autobiographical sketch of his daily routine contains well-known symptoms of withdrawal, not too carefully concealed. Lunch takes only three minutes and dinner only four: Dean Swift toward the end would not even sit down to eat his meals, but consumed them standing up or walking round the table. 'I eat only white food'—rather than taste blood and rich reality. 'I always have my wine boiled and drink it cold' —for the sake of purity. (There is nothing special about the fuchsia plant, except that it is mostly an indoor luxury rather than a hardy outdoor flower.) 'I breathe carefully, in limited quantities'—rather than open my lungs and my heart to the air of life. 'I ride horseback in my park' like a nobleman with a large estate, when in fact he trudged back and forward from Arcueil to Paris on foot.

However, Satie was not completely withdrawing, in flight from the whole world. He was retreating because his first entry had been a failure, and he now wished to make a second and more prudent attack. He dropped all the vague mystical ambitious stuff he had written in order to astonish the world. He composed carefully and published slowly, starting with a work called *Frightening Tunes*: they are not really very frightening, but their title signifies hostility. He began his musical education all over again, spending three years in the Schola Cantorum under Vincent d'Indy and Albert Roussel, and graduating with high honors in counterpoint (the careful man's speciality) at the age of forty-two. Roussel said he was 'a prodigious musician.' Thenceforward his reputation began to grow, outside official circles, always among the advance guard, the daring adventurers. His work did for music something of what the cubists were to do for painting and sculpture. Yet, because of its built-in orderliness and simplicity, it was less disruptive, less explosive, more sympathetic, more positively creative.

The work of Erik Satie was known to few people outside France until quite recently. I bought and played his *Dried Embryos* and *Cold Pieces* (*Frightening Tunes*) in 1926, but could never see more in them than very mild joking and bleak neo-classicism: certainly they compared very poorly with the genuine humor and whimsicality of Debussy's *Homage to S. Pickwick, Esq.* and *General Lavine, Eccentric,* and with the atmospheric charm and complex harmonic textures of Ravel's *Mirrors*—or, for that matter, with the curious involutions of Bix Beiderbecke's *In a Mist,* which I was tackling about the same time. Much of his music reminds me of the shallow prose of Gertrude Stein: for instance, 'Pigeons on the grass, alas!'— on which James Thurber commented that pigeons on the grass were not alas, they were not ho ho or hurrah or even woe's me, they were simply pigeons and that was all. Satie's piano music can now be heard on records, and is becoming much more widely known. I note that a popular singing group, Blood, Sweat, and Tears, has variations on a theme by Satie in its repertoire. His most famous orchestral work, the 'realistic ballet' *Parade* (produced by Diaghilev, scenario by Cocteau, sets and costumes by Picasso, choreography by Massine), now sounds cheap and garish, but it was the forerunner of other such works, for instance Milhaud's *Creation of the World*. The English music critic Rollo Myers has high praise for Satie's setting of three of Plato's tributes to his master, a piece called *Socrates* for four sopranos and small orchestra: he calls it 'solitary music' conceived by a mind 'dwelling in a rarefied isolation,' which is the reverse of both Socrates and Plato, though it might do for Heraclitus or Plotinus. Unhappily I have never heard it performed or seen its score.

The one thing most musicians know about Satie was that he made more jokes in and about music than anyone else. He gave grotesque titles to compositions which without them might have been taken seriously, and he added to many of his scores perfectly absurd notes of expression and technical directions. He will tell the pianist, 'Play like a nightingale with toothache,' or 'Open your head,' or 'With one hand on your conscience.' The last twelve chords of the second *Frightening Tune* are to be played 'in the deepest silence.'

When he chose his fanciful titles, he was satirizing musicians such as Debussy, who gave to short romantic pieces pretentious names: *Sounds and scents turn in the evening air* (*Preludes* 1.4) and *What the west wind saw* (*Preludes* 1.7). (Debussy has since been outdone by Olivier Messiaen, who entitles two of his *Preludes for Piano Song of ecstasy in a gloomy landscape* and *Bells of anguish and tears of farewell*.) His crazy suggestions for performance and other comments in the scores also parodied the hypersensitive interpretative hints which some composers liked to include. For instance, in *Preludes* 1.6, *Footsteps in the Snow,* Debussy writes 'Like a tender and sad regret.' (Again Debussy has been excelled by Messiaen: a direction in one of his bird pieces, *The Tawny Owl,* reads 'Like the cry of a murdered child.')

Such tricks were part of Satie's protective armor. If people took his music seriously, then it would be played and become immortal without the printed directions. If they did not, then he was safeguarded by the implication that he was a joker, who did not even take his own compositions seriously. In this he prefigures Marcel Duchamp, who spent much of his career in parodying the pretensions of visual art: he parodied painting by submitting to an exhibition a reproduction of the *Mona Lisa* with the addition of a moustache, and he parodied sculpture by submitting to another exhibition a porcelain wall-urinal, signed. Duchamp ended with desperate attempts to create an anti-art which could not be appreciated unless the viewer threw away all the standards derived from the great sculpture and painting of two millennia, and contented himself with admiring one man's fairly ingenious tricks. Such people come at the end of an art which has been overblown and elevated into a religion, as by Wagner and Scriabin. Their function is to make it brittle, to undermine it, to try to loosen the links which connect it with traditional standards of aesthetics, even of morality. They are also trying to make it less of a transcendental experience and more part of the life of every day.

As I write, I am listening to Gieseking play Ravel's *Tombeau de Couperin,* which contains more harmonic innovation and rhythmic invention than all the work of Satie: it makes me even more intensely aware of Satie's defects. He played the piano in cabarets for some time, which easily becomes a tedious and obsessive mechanical exercise: its effects can be traced in his rhythmically and harmonically monotonous scoring for the left hand. He scarcely attempted to exploit the new tonalities worked out by Debussy and Ravel, although in his early work he had been their precursor. Some of his work is trivial, all of it small in scope. Yet again and again there appear in it hints and anticipations of the music written by his great contemporaries and successors. He quotes French folk songs jokingly: so does Debussy, tenderly, in *Gardens under Rain.* He writes pure naïve short-step melodies with minimal harmonic background: so does Ravel in *Mother Goose.* He parodies popular songs and dances, and couples the

---

parodies with satiric texts: so does Walton in *Façade*. Satie was an original, and a clever original. He might have developed his talent, if he had not believed in his genius.

Aldo Ciccolini, *Piano Music of Erik Satie*: three LP records: Angel S-36482, S-36459, and S-36485.

William Masselos, *Masselos plays Satie*: RCA record: LSC-3127.

Rollo H. Myers, *Erik Satie* (Dennis Dobson Ltd., London, 1948)—to which I am much indebted in this essay.

New Year's Day with Mr. Pepys

SOME VERY readable books are unreadable as books. They cannot be read straight through in one continuous effort, but must be dipped into or visited for an hour or two. One of the most famous such books is the diary kept by a British government official who served under Charles II: Samuel Pepys. Both for its liveliness and for its occasional prudery, both for its wisdom and for its folly, and above all for its keen wide-ranging observation, it is one of the most diverting books ever composed. He started it at the beginning of the year 1660, writing in cipher so that no one who casually picked it up could read it, and he kept it until the end of May 1669, when he felt he was beginning to go blind from overwork. (Fortunately his sight was saved.) There are entries for almost every day during those nine years, sometimes only a few sentences, sometimes several pages of close political and social analysis. Only it can scarcely be read straight through: it is too jerky and fragmentary, sometimes too repetitious and sometimes too detailed, and occasionally too cryptic and incomplete. It is Notes for an Autobiography which never got written.

What I like to do is to choose one single day—often the particular day on which I happen to pick up the volumes—and then look up that same day in each year of the diary; and mighty strange it is (as Pepys himself would put it) to see what various adventures can surround the same man on the same day at intervals of a twelvemonth. Now he is in love, now in danger of public disgrace; now anxious about his house in the Great Fire, now in fear of his life in the Great Plague; sometimes he is being short-changed at the theater, sometimes he is visiting the king's court and horrified to see the courtiers playing cards on Sunday. Since Pepys was an ambitious and methodical man, he believed that the end of the old year and the beginning of the new were an important and valuable time to balance his budget, looking backward over his successes in order to gain courage for the struggles of the future. Therefore it is most interesting to read the entries he made when he was in his most regularly serious frame of mind, on December 31st and January 1st. These, almost better than anything else in his diary, give us the true measure of the man.

The ancient Greeks used to sing a song at parties, listing the four most important things in the world. 'Best of all things is health,' it began. Next to health (although perhaps only the ancient Greeks would think so) came personal beauty; third was clean money, 'wealth without guilt'; and fourth was to be young with one's friends. Pepys agreed with only two of these: health and money were the things he prized. He had too few close friends and too many rivals to attach much importance to friendship; and he had seen too many handsome rakehells about Charles's court to want to be handsome—although he did dress as well as he could.

His first entry in the diary deals with his physical condition. He says he is, thank God, in good health, without any of his old pain, except when he catches a chill. His old pain. Nearly two years before this, he had been cut for the stone. It sounds bad, and it must have been frightful. There were no anaesthetics of the modern type. Poor Pepys must have been strapped down on a table, and had his body cut open, and his urethra incised, the stone taken out, and the wound stitched up or padded and bandaged—all this while (unless drowsed by drink or opium) he was fully conscious. His friend John Evelyn (who also wrote an attractive diary) saw the stone that was taken out of Pepys and records that it was as big as a tennis-ball. Still Pepys lived to be seventy. Toward the end of his life the old wound opened again, and after he died the doctors found four ounces of stones in his left kidney; but the original operation, terrible as it was, could be called successful. At the end of his diary what worried him most was the condition of his eyes. Lighting in those days was miserably inefficient; paper was poor; everything had to be written with a quill pen; and Pepys often records that he worked till midnight. Strange that he does not mention the commonest modern symptom of strain and overwork, a blinding headache; but that may be what he means by his numerous complaints that he is 'unable to see almost.' There is something truly sad about the final entry in the diary.

> May 31st 1669. And thus ends all that I doubt I shall ever be able to do with my own eyes in the keeping of my Journal, I being not able to do it any longer, having done now so long as to undo my eyes almost every time that I take a pen in my hand; and, therefore, whatever comes of it, I must forbear. . . . And so I betake myself to that course, which is almost as much as to see myself go into my grave: for which, and all the discomforts that will accompany by being blind, the good God prepare me!

However, he did not go blind, although he had to be far more cautious about his eyesight. He survived, and did the work of two or three men until, after the accession of William of Orange, he was forced by political pressure to retire at the age of fifty-six.

Next in importance to health, for Samuel Pepys, was money. (Religion was important too, but it was a vexed problem. Charles II was a secret Roman Catholic and the Queen openly a Catholic, while the mass of the people were Protestants; and they were torn by disputes between Presbyterians, Episcopalians, Quakers, and cranks like the Fifth-Monarchy men.) In those days anyone who was in government service expected to make money out of it: not only his salary for his regular work, but perquisites given to him by those who dealt regularly with his office, if he was at the policy-making level, and shares of any enterprise undertaken with governmental approval and support, and retainers or sweeteners passed to him at Christmas time, and anything else that happened to come in, sent round in a basket of flowers or inside a gift parcel containing a pair of gloves. (Remember the crooked Egyptian official in Lawrence Durrell's *Alexandria Quartet* who collected rare editions of the Koran, with Swiss bearer bonds between the pages?) To us nowadays this must seem shocking and repulsive. For us it is inconceivable that any official, entrusted by his fellow-citizens with the administration of public affairs, should even remotely contemplate the possibility of accepting a perquisite in cash, or a privilege, or a gift. But in good King Charles's golden days, things were more lax. Mr. Pepys did quite well both above and under the table.

The other chief interests of his life were his family and his work. In fact he thought more about his work. By the end of has career he was a really distinguished public servant: he has been called the Nestor of the Navy. He worked like a dog at his office, and took work home, and brooded about it much of the time—sometimes all the more earnestly because some of his superiors were lackadaisical noblemen who would not work hard at anything—and he often neglected his young wife in order to attend to business. His own blood-relatives were fairly numerous, and since he was the most competent and influential he had to look out for the others: that took time and thought and energy. His wife was another kind of problem. She was French, the daughter of an eccentric Huguenot. Pepys married her without a dowry when she was fifteen years old and he was twenty-two, without a fixed income. It must have been a love match.* But the atmosphere

* The editors of his diary are surprised that both he and his wife thought their wedding-day was October 10th, whereas the register of St. Margaret's Church, Westminster, gives it as December 1st. Lord Bray-

of Charles's court was filled with flirtations and seductions and anti-Puritan escapades; and Pepys found it very difficult to remain faithful. Actresses, and pretty wives of shopkeepers, and housemaids living in his own home, were most apt to ensnare him, and often he went out of his way to fall into their snares. He worried about this throughout the period of the diary, and never solved the problem. He did try.

The first entry in his diary is for January 1st, 1660. He is twenty-six years old, a meager little clerk in the civil service (Office of the Exchequer) living in the garret of a house in Westminster with his wife and one maidservant. His wife has just had a miscarriage. His 'private condition,' or his status, is 'very handsome, and esteemed rich, but indeed very poor': he has no money on hand or in the bank, nothing except his furniture and his job in the Exchequer 'which at present is somewhat uncertain.' However, he dressed well. He 'put on his suit with great skirts, having not lately worn any other clothes but them,' and went to chapel, where he heard a sermon on the Circumcision. His wife stayed at home to get dinner ready, as he records. 'Dined at home in the garret, where my wife dressed [= cooked] the remains of a turkey, and in the doing of it she burned her hand.' He spent the whole afternoon going over his accounts, and then took his wife to supper at his father's house. 'And so to our own home' in the garret.

A year later he is doing much better. He has a more or less permanent government post and has moved into government housing, as one of the officials in the administration of the Navy. He has now two more servants, is 'in constant good health' and 'worth £300 clear in money.' What £300 in those days meant I can scarcely conjecture, but I think it was at

---

brooke thinks the register must be wrong, and adds, 'Surely a man who kept a diary could not have made such a blunder.' But Pepys was an eager amorist; and perhaps the day that he and Elizabeth remembered was not the day of the ceremony in church, but another day much more important and delightful.

least as much as $15,000 today. He could afford to invite
guests to celebrate New Year's Day: his father, his brother,
his uncle with his uncle's two sons ('Anthony's only child
dying this morning, yet he was so civil to come') all visited him
for breakfast. 'I had for them a barrel of oysters, a dish of
neat's tongues [= beef tongues], and a dish of anchovies, wine
of all sorts, and Northdown ale,' and they stayed until eleven
a.m. Pepys and his wife went to noonday dinner with his
cousin, 'a sorry, poor dinner, there being nothing but ordinary
meat in it.' Then, after doing a little financial business, he
took her to supper with another official in the Navy, 'where
we had a calf's head carboned [= grilled], but it was raw, we
could not eat it, and a good hen. But she [Mrs. Pierce, the
hostess] is such a slut that I do not love her victualls.' Then,
evidently elevated by all this entertaining and being enter-
tained, he sent his wife home by coach [= taxi], played cards
until midnight, and 'then to bed with Mr. Shepley.' Innocent
enough, no doubt, but tactless: or selfish.

Next year, 1662, he has been having his wife's portrait
painted, which is a sign of increasing prosperity. He is now
'worth about £500 clear in the world, and my goods of my
house [= furniture] my own, and what is coming to me from
Brampton [the family home in Huntingdonshire] when my
father dies, which God defer.' He has also 'taken a solemn oath
about abstaining from plays and wine, which I am resolved to
keep according to the letter of the oath which I keep by me.'
However, on the very next day he went to see *The Spanish
Curate* by Beaumont and Fletcher. On January 1st, 'waking
out of my sleep on a sudden, I did with my elbow hit my wife
a great blow over her face and nose, which waked her with
pain, at which I was sorry, and to sleep again.'

By the beginning of 1663 he has a home at the Office of the
Navy 'in good condition, furnished and made very convenient,'
and owns about £650 in cash. By now he has four servants
and is rising rapidly in the world. The young couple spent the
night at the house of the Earl of Sandwich. After getting up

Pepys went to Whitehall and spent some time 'walking among the courtiers, which I perceive I shall be able to do with great confidence, being now beginning to be pretty well known among them.' At the end of 1663 he is still more deeply engrossed in business, and spends the morning of December 31st at the office, listening to a bitter argument and coming home with a mighty headache. 'We had to dinner, my wife and I, a fine turkey and a mince pie, and dined in state, poor wretch, she and I, and have thus kept our Christmas together all alone almost, having not once been out'—because of his vow about shunning the theater. Next day, however, he took her to see Shakespeare's *Henry VIII*: 'which, though I went with resolution to like it, is so simple a thing made up of a great many patches that, besides the shows and processions in it, there is nothing in the world good or well done.'

December 31st, 1664, was very good. Pepys spent most of the day at the office, and after finishing the correspondence for the OUT basket, did his own personal accounts for the year, 'and was at it till past twelve at night, it being bitter cold.' (I don't know any other book which gives its readers so many twinges of sympathy as Pepys's Diary. How often have you and I worked hard over something like bank statements or income taxes and felt both sorry for ourselves and proud of our endurance, 'till past twelve at night, it being bitter cold'! But only Pepys, as far as I know, tells us this kind of thing frankly and habitually.) He is now, 'by the great blessing of God, worth £1,349.' So he went home to eat a little. 'Soon as ever the clock struck one, I kissed my wife in the kitchen by the fireside, wishing her a merry new yeare'—and then comes something strange: 'observing that I believe I was the first proper wisher of it this year, for I did it as soon as ever the clock struck one.' He would have been woundily surprised to hear the uproar in Times Square as soon as the clock strikes midnight.

On the same day he solemnly copies out a number of charms or spells to cure minor ailments. Here is one to prevent a thorn wound from swelling up and festering:

> Christ was of a Virgin born,
> And he was pricked of a thorn;
> And it did neither bell,* nor swell;
> And I trust in Jesus this never will.

1665 was the year of the plague in London. In the first week of September nearly seven thousand people died of it. Pepys went on working as hard as ever, although he worried about infection. In the last week of the year he was angry with Elizabeth because she wanted to engage a maid (who might carry contagion) before the plague was quite over. However, he did not catch the disease, and when he went over his accounts he found he had 'raised his estate from £1,300 in this year to £4,400' as well as acquiring two new government posts. Always fascinated by pretty actresses, he was just falling in love with Mrs. Knepp of the King's House players. On the 2nd of January 1666 he was enchanted by hearing her sing 'her little Scotch song of "Barbary Allen." ' So, he says, on the way home, 'I got into the coach where Mrs. Knepp was and got her upon my knee (the coach being full) and played with her breasts and sung, and at last set her at her house and so good night.' Mrs. Knepp with her surly husband came to a party at Pepys's next evening, but Mrs. Pepys developed toothache and went to bed, so that the party broke up.

1666 was the year of the fire; but again Pepys and his family survived and prospered. At the end of the twelvemonth he was 'worth in money, all good, above £6,200.' Britain was in a state of great misery because of the king's and the court's extravagance and incompetence. The Admiralty could not pay the sailors or send a fleet to sea, and people appeared not to be interested in rebuilding London after the fire. However, Pepys records with pride, whenever he gave a party he used only silver plates, having two dozen and a half pieces.

His interest in Mrs. Knepp continued in 1667 and began to affect his marriage. On New Year's Day 1668 he left Elizabeth to have a meal with the wife of a friend, while he dined with

---

* Cognate with *boil*.

Lord Crewe and talked about economics; then he went on to the theater, and finished at a gambling house, although he would not risk any precious money. His coldness seems surprising until we look back a few days in the diary. And there we find him visiting Mrs. Knepp several times. After meeting her and hearing her sing, Samuel went home and made the grave mistake of telling his wife where he had been. 'She was as mad as a devil, and nothing but ill words between us all the evening while we sat at cards [in front of the servants, too], even to gross ill words, which I was troubled for.'

By this time he was doing so well financially that he did not mention exact annual accounts any more. During 1668 he acquired a private coach, with horses, and a coachman in livery; and on New Year's Day 1669 he was more diplomatic. He took his wife (in the coach) to the King's Playhouse, paid for a box, and saw Dryden's *Maiden Queen*. 'Knepp looked upon us,' he remarks with an almost audible sigh, 'but I durst not shew her any countenance': in other words, he avoided her eyes. After a row with his wife next day, he agreed that she should have an allowance of £30 a year for her entire expenses, clothes and everything, 'which she was mightily pleased with, it being more than ever she asked or expected.' Only a week later she was so angry and jealous that she woke him up in bed and threatened him with a pair of red-hot fire tongs: he appeased her, but he says, 'I cannot blame her jealousy, though it do vex me to the heart.'

We can admire Samuel as a conscientious and efficient administrator, and, most of the time, we can enjoy his company as a bright observant versatile man. But we must be sorry for Mrs. Pepys: a foreigner, married young, perplexed (as the French are) by the phlegm and spleen of the English, and childless, and left much alone. Several times she made him terribly jealous. Once she took lessons from a dancing-master called Pembleton who called twice a day: Pepys wondered if they did anything else besides dance, and it put him 'into a great disorder.' Later she started wearing a pale blond wig. He accepted this for some time, and then became ready to burst with anger, no doubt because it was a fashion set by the naughty ladies of Charles's court. 'I discovered my trouble to my wife for her white locks, swearing by God, several times, which I pray God forgive me for, and bending my fist, that I would not endure it. She, poor wretch, was surprized with it, and made me no answer all the way home; but there we parted, and I to the office late, and then home, and without supper to bed, vexed.' Next day was Sunday. 'Up, and to my chamber, to settle some accounts there, and by and by down comes my wife to me in her night-gown [= dressing-gown], and we begun calmly, that upon having money to lace her gown for second mourning, she would promise to wear white locks no more in my sight, which I, like a severe fool, thinking not enough, begun to except against, and made her fly out to very high terms and cry, and in her heat told me of keeping company with Mrs. Knepp, saying, that if I would promise never to see her more—of whom she hath more reason to suspect than I had heretofore of Pembleton—she would never wear white locks more. This vexed me, but I restrained myself from saying anything, but do think never to see this woman—at least, to have her here more, but by and by I did give her money to buy lace, and she promised to wear no more white locks while I lived, and so all very good friends as ever, and I to my business, and she to dress herself.'

He was mean and treacherous to her. The only foul stain on his diary is the guilt, concealment, and hypocrisy which ooze out of his allusions to other women. Although he was using cipher, in these passages he usually breaks into a disgusting jargon made of French and Spanish words, partly as an additional concealment, partly from his own unwillingness to write his misdeeds down in plain English. He had an affair with the wife of a carpenter called Bagwell; and once, when he was prevented by the arrival of guests from going to her, he records it thus: 'This night je had agreed para aller at [à?] Deptford, there para avoir lain con the moher de Bagwell, but this company did hinder me.' There are far too many incidents of this kind. The most infuriating to Mrs. Pepys must have been his dalliances with the housemaids. She actually caught him embracing Deb. Willet, and made him discharge her. Yet Deb. stuck in his mind, and appears on the last page of his diary. He says good-bye to his journal. From now on it will be kept by his clerks in longhand, so that nothing can be written in it more than is fit for them and all the world to know; 'or, if there be any thing, which cannot be much, now my amours to Deb. are past, and my eyes hindering me in almost all other pleasures, I must endeavour to keep a margin open to add a note in shorthand.' This was written on May 31st, 1669. Less than six months later, his wife was dead.

If she had ever read Samuel's diary, would she have been more understanding and sympathetic? I doubt it. If she had kept a diary and Samuel had read it, what would he have felt? He would have clenched his fist, vowing that it made him almost mad. But would he have mended his ways?

Beer-bottle on the Pediment

The thought of what America would be like
If the Classics had a wide circulation
Troubles my sleep.

So, in one of those formless and arrogant utterances that he
called poems, wrote Ezra Pound. He meant it to be a hostile
criticism of his native country, as a land of materialistic boors.
But a thoughtful reader might interpret the sentence differently. If the classics of Greece and Rome really had a wide
circulation in the United States, Pound would long ago have
been not only detested as a traitor and pitied as a lunatic but
despised as a charlatan.

Born in 1885, Pound left the United States in 1908, and,
until he surfaced on the Italian radio in 1942, talking about
'the kikes who made the war,' was virtually forgotten by American readers and critics. But recently some scholars have been
treating him with sympathy: out of respect for his longevity,
sympathy for his sufferings in jail and madhouse, or admiration for his parade of exotic learning. There is a biography
by Charles Norman and an introduction to his poetry by M. L.

Rosenthal.* Only the latest biography, by Noel Stock (Pantheon, New York, 1970), is cool and sometimes negative in its attitude to his work as a poet. There is an *Annotated Index to the* [first eighty-four] *Cantos of Ezra Pound,* compiled with impressive self-sacrifice by J. H. Edwards and W. W. Vasse,† who observe in their prefatory note that 'the poem, like the mountain, was there.' However, Pound's *Cantos* are not Mount Everest. They are a dump, containing some beautiful fragments of antique and Oriental sculpture (often disfigured by careless handling), some outrageous fakes, loads of personal trivia, some gobs of filth, many promising but embryonic artistic sketches, and a huge scree of pure rubbish.

Pound always made a great show of learning and a bold claim to authority. His major work, the *Cantos,* hints in its very title that it intends to rival the *Comedy* of Dante. It is nearly as polyglot as Joyce's *Finnegans Wake.* It contains sentences and phrases not only in poetic English and slang both American and Cockney, but in Chinese, ancient Greek, classical Latin, medieval Latin, French, Italian, Provençal, German, and jargons of various origin. Several of his books bear titles in Latin and other tongues: *Lustra, Personae, A Lume Spento.* One makes him an admiring successor of a difficult Latin poet, *Homage to Sextus Propertius.* His *Literary Essays* contain several boldly magisterial pronouncements—'Early Translators of Homer,' 'Notes on Elizabethan Classicists'—which look at first sight like products of serious scholarship. He even published an arbitrary selection and discussion of Great Books, called *How To Read.*

His interest in Greek and Latin is not merely a pose. It is an essential part of his development as a poet. He really loved the classics and believed in them. But he would not take the trouble to understand them thoroughly. In the first of his *Cantos* he speaks through the mask of the far-traveled Odysseus, which he puts on at intervals thereafter. Mr. Rosenthal

* C. Norman, *Ezra Pound* (Macmillan, New York, 1960); M. L. Rosenthal, *A Primer of Ezra Pound* (Macmillan, New York, 1960).
† University of California Press, 1957.

explains that Pound enriched the Odysseus legend by crossing it with the myth of Dionysus, the god of ecstatic intoxication who was an adventurous traveler and a versatile lover and who (like Odysseus) often disguised himself; and Mr. Norman makes it clear that, as the first Canto comes from Homer, so the second refers back to Ovid's *Metamorphoses,* a Latin poem on Greek mythical themes.

Now, to most of Pound's public, all this is impressive: especially when he throws in a few words of Greek or paraphrases a Latin poem or says something unintelligible but vaguely 'classical,' like this from *Canto LXIV*:

SUBILLAM

> Cumis ego occulis meis
> sleeping under a window: pray for me,
> withered to skin and nerves *tu theleis* respondebat illa
> *apothanein*; pray for me gentlemen

An earnest reader, if he has no Greek and Latin himself, is pleasantly mystified and feels a vague admiration for a poet with so many languages and echoes ringing in his mind. Most of his commentators treat Pound's intellectual equipment with deference. Even if—like Mr. Norman—they decry his economic theorizing and detest his politics, they usually assume that, in poetry at least, he knows what he is talking about. They put in much hard work on tracing the sources of his allusions; and often—as do Messrs. Edwards and Vasse—they tacitly correct what they take to be mere misprints and they gently pass over the irrelevant and the inexplicable as though they were dark poetic mysteries instead of blunders and claptrap. Most readers seem to believe that Pound is a truly scholarly writer. How deeply, how accurately, and how sensitively he knows other languages I cannot tell; but although he shows off his Greek and his Latin, his Latin is poor and his Greek is contemptible.

What does this matter? Is it even true? Does not Pound's earlier biographer, Mr. Charles Norman, call the *Cantos* 'an anthology of many literatures, quoted in the original . . . or translated by Pound with his incomparable skill'?

Unfortunately for an ambitious and energetic poet, it is true. Pound never had more than a smattering of Greek, scarcely enough to enable him to spell Greek words correctly, either in the Greek alphabet or in our own. In Latin he knew enough to let him follow the general sense of a simple sentence, and to grasp some of the more obvious effects of sound and rhythm, but not nearly enough to permit him to understand or even to approach the greatest Roman poets, or to save him from making coarse and degrading blunders in interpreting Roman poetry. Worse than that, he would not learn. He would not admit his deficiencies and cure them through humility and industry. Nor would he shun those areas where a display of ignorance might be damaging. Where others would turn their eyes away from the sanctuary, or else enter with quiet step and bowed head, Ezra Pound charged in, shouting and singing and hiccuping, on roller skates, and rollicked around breaking the decorations and scrawling his name on the walls.

We see this in the very first pages of his most ambitious work. There he makes it clear that one of his chief personae, or masks, is to be Odysseus, and one of his chief themes a visit to the underworld. The first Canto is a translation (with a few omissions) of the first hundred and fifty lines of the eleventh book of Homer's *Odyssey*. It is not a rethinking of the *Odyssey* with its events and ideas and persons transmuted and rearranged, in the manner of Joyce's *Ulysses*. It is not even a loose paraphrase. It is a version which tries to be a close translation, sentence for sentence, sometimes even line for line.

Now, from time to time, this version becomes paradoxical or meaningless. If we are convinced that poetry, to be truly modern, must be paradoxical or meaningless, then we shall welcome certain passages. But if we remember that Pound was working with the straightforward narrative of a brilliantly lucid poet and trying to emulate it, we shall realize that he was not writing modern poetry, but simply putting down words without reflecting on their meaning.

Sailing from Circe's island, Odysseus reaches the fog-shrouded land of the Cimmerians (possibly modeled after travelers' tales of the dark gloomy North Sea countries). Pound describes the place thus:

> The Kimmerian lands, and peopled cities
> Covered with close-webbed mist, unpierced ever
> With glitter of sun-rays
> Nor with stars stretched, nor looking back from heaven
> Swartest night stretched over wretched men there.

You might puzzle long and long over 'Nor with stars stretched,' and then conclude that Homer meant the mist was never pierced by the rays of the sun or thinned by starlight. You would be wrong—although it would be a reasonable interpretation. But you could never discover the meaning of 'nor looking back from heaven,' because it is quite senseless. What Homer actually says is far more orderly and intelligible:

> The sun looks never through the canopy of cloud,
> either ascending up toward the starry heaven
> or else descending back from heaven toward the earth,
> but deadly darkness stretches over the wretched folk.

Pound missed the central idea, which is that, although the sun apparently travels from east to west and moves over the entire world, its rays never pierce the Cimmerian fogs from any angle; and so he wrote a sentence which was not only silly, but (with its repetition of 'stretched' in two different senses, and its unfortunate near-echo 'stretched . . . wretched') unpoetical.

The very next sentence defies explanation.

> The ocean flowing backward, came we then to the place
> Aforesaid by Circe.

If the ocean flowed backward—presumably in a gigantic tidal wave—why was Odysseus' ship unaffected? Or was this a sinister deviation in the current off the land of the dead? It was not. The Greeks believed that the ocean was a great salt stream flowing all round the world; Homer's Odysseus said 'We followed along the stream of Ocean' presumably into the cold north; and Pound got it wrong.

And so it goes throughout Canto I. The stream of meaning keeps flowing backward, because Pound is an inveterate guesser, and nearly always unlucky. For instance, Odysseus in the underworld meets the ghost of one of his sailors who died because he got drunk in Circe's palace, slept it off on the roof, and missed the ladder coming down. Pound makes him say, 'I slept in Circe's ingle.' 'Ingle' is a Scots word for the hearth fire, or by extension the cosy corner by the fireside, from which nobody could possibly fall down and break his neck.

You will wonder how a presumably sensitive writer could so grossly misrepresent the thoughts of a greater poet. If Pound had not so evidently been attempting to follow Homer *closely,* if he had been writing free variations on a set of Homeric themes, these alterations of tone and meaning would have been understandable. But he was obviously trying to put Homer exactly into his own style of English. Now, if a more modest or more dedicated poet did not know Greek and yet wished to use a passage from Homer in his poetry, he would take five or six versions of Homer in languages which he did understand—English and French and Italian, for example— and by combining them and extracting their essence, he might get fairly close to the original. Or—reflecting that art is long— he would set out to learn Greek. Pound did neither. He used a line-for-line word-for-word translation from Homer's poetic Greek into flat literal Latin prose which was published in 1538 by a hack named Andrea Divo. Whether he thought this was the best available translation, it is difficult to tell. If he did, he was quite wrong. And in any case the affectation of using a Renaissance Latin pony to help him understand a Greek poem caused him far more trouble than it was worth. Not only did Andrea Divo sometimes get Homer's meaning wrong, but Ezra Pound sometimes got Andrea Divo's meaning wrong. The result was a double layer of misunderstanding spread, like

Cimmerian mist, between the radiant sun of Homer and Pound's wretched readers, benighted beneath.

These are not trivial or pedantic criticisms. They go to the heart of Pound's poetic ambitions. He opens his central work by translating Homer: that is, by putting himself into competition, or into close connection, with one of the greatest poets in the world. If a French poet began his major poem with an extract from *Paradise Lost* turned into modern French, he would be asking for severe criticism. Dante himself, although following Vergil with loving devotion, nevertheless translates only a few short passages directly from Vergil, and those into a different style, simpler and more lucid.* But Pound takes Homer's brisk clear narrative and makes it into a halting monologue studded with wrongheaded and meaningless phrases, like the ramblings of a medium or an alcoholic.

And he finishes this, the exordium of his ambitious spiritual autobiography, with five lines of pure gibberish which have nothing to do with the subject, and are simply stuck on like a random collage because he cannot think how to conclude his first Canto. Leafing through the translation of the *Odyssey* he had been using, he found, following it, a line-for-line Latin prose version of the Homeric Hymns. His eye fell on the short second hymn, addressed to Aphrodite. From its opening he copied and translated a few disjointed words and phrases, and jammed them into this hotchpotch:

> Venerandam
> In the Cretan's phrase, with the golden crown, Aphrodite,
> Cypri munimenta sortita est, mirthful, oricalchi, with golden
> Girdles and breastbands, thou with dark eyelids
> Bearing the golden bough of Argicida.

This is not poetry but confetti. 'In the Cretan's phrase' means only that the man who did the hack Latin translation was a Greek from Crete. 'Girdles and breastbands' is rubbish, showing the cheapness of Pound's mind. The Graces would not

---

* Even he got one passage wrong: *Purgatory* 22.40–41, from *Aeneid* 3.56–57.

dress the new-born goddess Aphrodite in a girdle and bras-
sière; Aphrodite has no need of such things. They gave her 'a
crown and necklaces.' Nor were her radiant young eyelids
'dark.' The author of the Greek hymn said she had 'glancing
eyes,' moving quickly and softly like light on water. Then the
Renaissance translator called them 'liquid eyelids,' writing
enigras (a misspelling of a rare Greco-Latin word *enhygras*).
Of course Pound missed this: he read the word as *nigras*,
'black'; he ignored the original Greek; and he misconceived
the whole picture, making young Aphrodite into a vulgar
mascara-laden vamp. To top this off, he gave her a golden
bough, which she never carried, and then attributed it to
'Argicida,' the slayer of Argus—a title of the god Hermes
which he found in another hymn several pages earlier, and
which could scarcely be more out of place. But, most important
of all, Aphrodite, the bright goddess of love and beauty, is
logically and poetically irrelevant to Odysseus and his dark
visit to the world of the dead. This is pure fakery, a meager
pretense of learning, cynically manipulated to look like the
product of deep knowledge and intense poetic imagination.

Look back now at the quotation from Canto LXIV. Can it
be interpreted to make any sense?

SUBILLAM

Cumis ego occulis meis
sleeping under a window: pray for me,
withered to skin and nerves *tu theleis* respondebat illa
apothanein; pray for me gentlemen

Latin (misspelt), Greek (misspelt), and English. Let us try to
turn it into English:

UNDERHER

at Cumae I with my own eyyes
sleeping under a window: pray for me,
withered to skin and nerves *whit do you want* she answered
to die; pray for me gentlemen.

It makes very poor sense, even when all put into English. This is the poetry of fragments and of allusions, where you are supposed to know the original text which is in the poet's mind, or else look up the notes: like

> Why then Ile fit you. Hieronymos mad againe

at the end of Eliot's *Waste Land*. Here, in Pound, an observant reader might recognize fragments of the quotation which Eliot placed at the beginning of his poem. A classicist would see in it a distorted version of the sentence which concludes one of the vulgar millionaire's boastful speeches in the *Satyrica* of Petronius (48.8). Addressing a professor of literature, Trimalchio declares that he knows Greek poetry and Greek mythology,

> and in fact I saw with my own eyes the Sibyl hanging up in a bottle at Cumae, and when the children said to her, 'Sibyl, what do you want?', she answered, 'I want to die.'

The Sibyl was a prophetess who had been loved by the god Apollo. As the price of possession, he offered her any boon she wished to choose. She chose to live as many years as there were grains of sand in a handful (showing it); he granted the boon; then she refused him. He turned from her in anger and disdain. But she had forgotten to ask, not only for many years of life, but for youth and beauty also. As the centuries passed, she became like the Struldbrugs in Swift's horrible story, who shrank and shriveled and lost most of their faculties but still could not die. She is one of the two dominating figures in the sixth book of Vergil's *Aeneid,* where she conducts Aeneas through the world of the afterlife. That is why Trimalchio mentions having seen her, now apparently shrunk to the size of an insect, like the cicada into which Aurora's lover Tithonus dwindled after he too received longevity without rejuvenescence. The meaning of the strange declaration by Trimalchio, that he had actually seen the being supposed to be the Sibyl, has been much discussed, but does not concern us here. Why T. S. Eliot used it to announce his poem is clear. The major figure of *The Waste Land*—whether represented by Tiresias, another figure from Greek mythology, 'old man with wrinkled dugs,' or hinted at in phrases from other poems of Eliot, 'why should the agèd eagle stretch its wings?,' or felt throughout the poem in symbols of impotence and world-weariness—is old or feels old, so old as to wish for death and yet be incapable of finding its blessed release.

No doubt the connotation is the same in Pound's sixty-fourth Canto; but he has made it almost unintelligible by fracturing and distorting the sentence from Petronius. The misspellings (occulis for oculis and *tu theleis* for *ti theleis*) are not important, except that they make us distrust the writer. The word SUBILLAM is a little more treacherous, because it does mean something: sub illam = under her; but a few moments' thought shows us that Pound has miswritten SIBYLLAM. Then, what is so special about the poor ancient 'sleeping under a window'? Lots of people do that in hot countries. What Petronius says is 'in ampulla pendere' = 'hanging up in a bottle,' and apparently both the concept and the words were too hard for Pound to digest. His sole positive contribution to the curious little mythologem is making the Sibyl say 'pray for me gentlemen,' as though she were a Christian asking the attendants at her death to pray for the repose of her soul: the reverse of the real situation, which is that she *cannot* die.

It would be easy to expand these charges against Pound as a poet and an interpreter of poets. His *Homage to Sextus Propertius* is an insult both to poetry and to scholarship and to common sense. It consists of twelve free-verse poems which try to follow, *very closely,* the themes and wording of certain love elegies by Propertius. On every page Pound displays his ignorance: as though confident that, for scholars, his verse will be too subtle, and, for amateurs, his knowledge of foreign tongues will be overpowering. But he can grasp neither the significant little details nor the large essentials; and the suave delicate rhythms of Propertius' carefully styled poetry are quite beyond his grasp.

A simple instance. The Latin love-word for a sweetheart is

puella. Kinder than *domina* ('mistress' meaning one who commands), it can describe another man's wife or an unmarried woman or a courtesan, provided the poet is tenderly and passionately in love with her and she reciprocates or may soon reciprocate. The word is used in this sense only in love-poetry and similar genres: not in high poetry or dignified prose. It is a diminutive: so *mea puella* is 'my girl' in modern English. Yet even this simple central fact about Latin love poetry is hidden from Ezra Pound: so he makes *puella* now into 'woman,' which is insensitive, and now into 'young lady,' which is ridiculous.

As for his larger misinterpretations, one out of many will show their quality. In an important poem dealing with his own poetic mission, Propertius says that, being a poet of love, he cannot write an epic—although he would like, if possible, to have written an epic about the victories of Augustus Caesar (2.1). Those would have been his theme: not—and then he runs through other heroic subjects on which he would *not* have composed poetry—the Trojan war, Xerxes' invasion of Greece, the ambitions of Carthage, and 'the challenge of the Cimbrians and the good deeds of Marius.' By this he means the formidable attack upon Italy by the Germanic tribe of the Cimbrians, ending in their annihilation by the Roman general Marius.

What does Pound do with this? He makes Propertius say that he cannot write 'of Welsh coal-mines and the profit Marus had out of them.' This is really rubbish. The Romans did not mine coal and had not then penetrated into Wales. Like a sophomore, Pound wanted to give a bright answer quickly, without thinking too long. He remembered that the Welsh call themselves 'Cymry'; then he looked at the Latin again and saw *minas,* meaning 'challenges': so he took *Cimbrorum minas* to mean 'Welsh coal-mines,' and (not knowing the famous general Marius) he vulgarized 'the good deeds of Marius' into 'the profits of Marus.' The misinterpretation of Propertius' words is disgusting, but explicable to anyone who has ever read undergraduates' attempts at translation of a difficult poet; it is even, from certain points of view, amusing. What is much more truly disgusting is that Pound, although himself a poet, should have degraded the sensitive thoughts of another poet. Propertius had a high theme: they call it a 'refusal,' and it is a disguised compliment: for he is saying that although he would like to write heroic poetry about the deeds of Augustus Caesar, the subject is far above him . . . and also far above other noble themes, which he skillfully lists. But Pound made him say that he could not write about a mine-owner's dividends— a subject far from high poetry both in Roman and in modern times, and utterly irrelevant. This is not a mistake in language alone. It is a fundamental failure of taste.

Reflecting on Pound's incoherent and shallow work, reading the record of his wasted life, glancing through the respectful but impercipient commentaries on his poems, and looking with painful puzzlement through his collected letters, we can understand why many intelligent people —not only in the United States but elsewhere—turn away from him with pity and scorn. He ruined what might have been a viable talent, because he believed that he could be a great writer without humility, without knowledge, and without concentration. When he began to write, he possessed several of the qualities of a poet. His mistake was to believe that he was already complete, that he did not need to grow, and that his few inborn qualities were enough. We are surrounded, infested, by poets of this kind two generations later. In Canto LXXIV he quoted the Greek proverb 'Beauty is difficult'; but he did not remember it. He wrecked his mind with exhibition and competition and improvisation and opposition and destructive criticism and silly self-advertisement and pointless correspondence and a perpetual compulsive self-justificatory monologue which served as a substitute for thought.

Also, there was always a regrettable cheapness and crudity in Pound's talk and writing, which is politely alluded to in Mr. Norman's biography, and which makes several of his Cantos not only unreadable but unprintable. Once, recalling a conversation with a friend, he wrote:

> Beer-bottle on the statue's pediment!
> That, Fritz, is the era, today against the past.

In this he was unconsciously describing the effect of his own poetry on classical themes: a shiny brittle vulgarity, an irrelevance, posed near an immortal work of art. And in his version of Propertius he summed up his own chances of fame:

> I shall have, doubtless, a boom after my funeral,
> Seeing that long standing increases all things
> regardless of quality.

Love among the Romans

THE ROMANS wrote much about passionate love between men
and women, but it was usually stolen **or** unhappy love. In all
their hundreds of pages of poetry there are very few lines about
the love of a wife for her husband and a husband for his wife.
It is tempting therefore to assume that there was little real love
between married couples in old Rome; that there was, at best,
the companionship of two dumb working animals which happen to pull the same plow or share the same stall—a feeling too
crude and inarticulate to be worthy of the noble name of love.

However, there is some evidence on the other side, although
it is rather difficult to assemble. To find it, we must go not to
poetry, but to history, to biography, and to inscriptions carved
on stone.

One of the most moving of these inscriptions was put up by
a husband as a memorial to his dead wife, three or four years
before the birth of Jesus. It tells almost the entire story of their
lives together—an unusually exciting story, involving exile,
murder, and other adventures, once at least approaching close
to divorce, and ending, if not in happiness (because of the be-
reavement of one partner), at least in peace. The adventures

of the inscription itself are almost as strange as those of the couple whom it commemorates. It was carved in fine big letters on two marble slabs about seven feet high. They had a title running along the top, in very large capitals: when new, the whole thing must have looked rather like two gigantic pages from a marble book. Perhaps it was attached to the front of the dead woman's tomb. Where the tomb was, no one now can tell. Doubtless it was beside one of the highroads that ran out of the city of Rome: as you drive along the Appian Way today, you can still see some relics of such buildings, the final homes of the Roman dead. As Roman civilization began to decline into the Dark Age of ignorance and barbarism, the Romans and their half-savage invaders began to break up and pillage earlier sanctuaries. The marble slabs carrying this inscription were torn off the tomb and sawn into pieces. Seven of these pieces survived for many centuries, and four of them still exist. The two largest existing sections were cut down a bit and made into part of a coffin for one of the early Christians. They were discovered in the catacombs, and they are now in the Villa Torlonia, where it is almost impossible to see them. Another bit was carried off into a saloon and used as a gambling table; so we can tell from the lines scratched on its back. It was discovered a few miles outside Rome by workmen who were excavating for a new sewer: it is now in the museum that was constructed out of the baths built by the emperor Diocletian. One smaller piece was built into the wall of a Cistercian abbey; there it was seen and copied several times by antiquarians. A good thing, too; for now the abbey is gone, the wall is gone, and the inscription is gone; but the copies remain, in the Vatican Library. Two other pieces also survive only in copies made by devoted scholars. The last piece of all was discovered in January 1949 by Professor Arthur Gordon of the University of California. He has an exceptionally good memory, and a fine eye for Roman lettering. He and his wife were going through a Roman museum, looking at inscriptions which no one had yet managed to place, when he spotted a fragment which contained some words that seemed to him to be unusual: not the conventional list of official dignities, but far more personal phrasing and touches of genuine emotion. Also, the style of the carving belonged to 'the best period.' So he copied it out, and when he combined its words with the words remaining on the other fragments and copies, the sense was almost perfect. Now, with the existing fragments and the copies of lost pieces, we have rather more than two-thirds of the original inscription, including many interesting and moving passages. What we do not have, strangely enough, is the name of the man who put it up, and of his wife. On the face of one piece (the piece with the gambling-table scratches on it) there is carved, in extra large letters,

XORIS

—which, if we add the initial V, reads *uxoris* and means 'of my wife'; but that is all.

The inscription is a curious thing: unique in certain ways. Memorials usually say 'Here lies X, beloved wife of Y' and then go on to describe the deceased and her virtues. This does not. Instead, it is in the form of a speech, a farewell speech addressed by the husband to his wife just after her death. Some Roman monuments actually summon the public to read them: they say *siste, uiator,* 'stop, passerby,' and then go on to explain whom they are commemorating. But in this inscription no attention is paid to the public. They may read it if they wish. Indeed, they are invited to do so, by implication, for it was expensively carved and no doubt set up in a public place. But they are not asked to read it. Instead, they can, as it were, overhear the husband speaking to his wife. He may well have made this address to her while she lay on the funeral pyre, before he took the burning torch and said good-bye.*

* Friedrich Vollmer, in his notes on the inscription, conjectures that the opening of the speech (which is still missing) was directed to the public, and that thereafter the husband turned to address his dead wife; or that the whole speech was addressed to the public when spoken, and then altered when he prepared it for the stone carver. Possible; but there is much in the speech which sounds as though it were meant for one person, and one person alone.

He retells the whole story of their mutual trust and co-operation. They became engaged and were married in times as troublous as our own: in fact, more grievous, inasmuch as civil war, with its treacheries and unnatural hatreds, is worse than any foreign war. Before their marriage they were threatened with separation and impoverishment; after it, with the banishment or execution of the husband. The girl was born about 70 B.C., the man perhaps in 75. They became engaged about the year 51 or 50. Julius Caesar was just finishing the conquest of Gaul—which he had undertaken partly in order to extend the Roman Empire, but more emphatically to enrich himself and his supporters, and to train a private army loyal to himself personally, which he could use to dominate, and if necessary to invade and conquer, the hitherto free republic of Rome. Caesar kept making demands which his opponents found unacceptable, because, if granted, they would have built him swiftly into an irresistible dictator. The demands were refused; they were renewed with greater vehemence; the people of Rome were split into passionate supporters and passionate opponents of Caesar; a civil war was ready to break out.

In the first months of 49 B.C. Julius invaded Italy at the head of his army. There was no force in the peninsula capable of opposing him: so his opponents and the majority of the government left, to raise armies in the provinces. With them went the young fiancé, to fight along with the supporters of the republic. He left the girl living quietly in the country with her parents. Their house was attacked, and both her father and her mother were murdered. We are not told by whom; but no doubt the murders took place during the disorders of Caesar's invasion, when central authority had, for the time being, broken down. How the girl escaped we cannot tell either; but she escaped, and what she did thereafter was noteworthy. As soon as order was restored, she set up an investigation of the murders: she found witnesses and collected evidence and instigated a prosecution of the criminals, and (says the inscription) she 'took full vengeance on the guilty.' The man who later became her husband adds that, while the case was proceeding, she could not live alone in the home of her dead parents, because her life was not safe: she went to the home of her married sister, who had slaves and freedmen to protect them both. She was a courageous and strong-willed girl.

After that, she moved in with the mother of her fiancé, to wait for the outcome of the civil war. Two more dangers now appeared.

The first was that several years earlier her fiancé had bought the house from the estate of an extremist politician, Milo, who had been convicted of murder and had had his goods confiscated and sold by auction when he went into banishment. Now, in the disorder of the civil war, Milo returned to Italy: a gang of his armed supporters tried to break in, take over the house, and expel its occupants. The girl enlisted her servants, and, perhaps with help from the neighbors, drove off the gang in total defeat.

The second danger was that her fiancé had chosen the losing side in the war. He had fought against Julius Caesar; and Caesar issued an order prohibiting his opponents (for a time at least) from returning to Italy after his victory. During the period of this order, the young man was in effect an outlaw, and of course had no money. The girl sold all her jewelry, turned it into cash, and sent him the proceeds. Even that had to be done through clandestine routes. There always has been an underground working against totalitarian governments, and there always will be.

Now there was a pause, while Caesar consolidated his victory. At this juncture the girl was involved in a further problem. This was a lawsuit, so complicated that modern experts in Roman law can scarcely understand it. In outline, the case turned on the fact that Roman women were not considered to be capable of managing their own affairs. A girl who had any male blood-relatives living was assumed (if she was not married) to be the ward of the nearest of them. If she had no close male relatives, she could be treated as the ward of any distant relative. For instance, if a girl called Arria were left an

orphan with no uncles or brothers or cousins, anyone called
Arrius could come in and take over her property and admin-
ister it for her, provided he was a distant member of the same
family or clan. But this particular girl was certainly capable
of managing her own affairs. She had been through several
crises already, and she faced this new one with confidence.
Her murdered father had bequeathed his property by will to
her and her sister, her fiancé, and her sister's husband. Some
men bearing the same name as the family now turned up,
claiming that the father's will was invalid because he had made
a second marriage after signing it; therefore the girl, as his sole
unmarried child, was the heir to all his property; and since
they were members of the same family, they could take it all
over. The girl went to court. She proved that the people who
claimed to be her guardians because they bore the same name
as she did were in fact not related to her at all; and she won
the case.

By the time this crisis was over, Julius Caesar had conquered
the forces of the republic and had become virtually monarch
of Rome. He permitted his opponents to return home. Our
young friend came back with the rest, married his girl, and settled down. Time passed. In 44 B.C. Julius was killed by lovers
of the republic and of liberty. Another civil war broke out.
The young husband joined the forces of the republic, commanded by Brutus and Cassius. With them he was beaten; with
their supporters, he was outlawed—put on the list of men 'proscribed,' which meant that he was virtually condemned to
death without trial. (Shakespeare, with his wonderful gift for
seizing important moments, dramatized the creation of these
proscription lists, in a short scene of *Julius Caesar,* Act Four,
scene one. 'Your brother too must die; consent you, Lepidus?'
'I do consent.' 'Prick him down, Antony.')

His wife at once set out to have her husband's sentence an-
nulled. The empire was temporarily being run by three heirs
of Julius: Mark Antony, who was out in the East; Octavian,
who was to become the emperor Augustus; and a slight, un-
meritable man named Lepidus, who had been given Italy for

the moment. The young wife persuaded her brother-in-law to visit Octavian and intercede with him for her husband's life, while she herself appealed to Lepidus. So low had the Romans sunk then that she had to lie on the ground prostrate, begging for clemency; and so harsh had the heirs of Caesar become that she was brutally pulled away, kicked, and bruised. However, her brother-in-law was successful. He got a free pardon for the husband from Octavian (who was technically equal in authority to Lepidus, but in prestige stronger): so that the husband was saved, and could return to Italy as a free citizen, or (if he had been in hiding) emerge into the free air. But his wife did not rest. At this point in the inscription there is a touch which reminds us of her behavior after her parents were murdered. Evidently the husband had been denounced as an anti-Caesarian and 'enemy of the state' by one particular enemy; and now, he says, 'through your patient endurance the man responsible for my danger was detected and revealed; and thereafter your determination provied to be his undoing.'

There the story ends; or almost. The husband had been through two civil wars: Julius Caesar against the forces of the republic led by Pompey; and the heirs of Julius Caesar against the forces of the republic led by Brutus and Cassius. He seems to have taken no part in the third and last, Mark Antony and Octavian as heirs of Julius against each other. He and his wife settled down, accepted the rule of Octavian (later Augustus), and enjoyed the custom of peace which he spread over the Mediterranean world.

One further problem confronted them. They were unable to have children. (It looks as though the wife had suffered a miscarriage, for in the inscription he says, 'We prayed for children, and our hopes expected them, but fortune turned away and ended our hopes.' Did her mistreatment at the interview with Lepidus have something to do with this?) So she offered to give him a divorce, so that he could marry a young and fertile wife. She promised that she would not only share her property with the new family (the couple had always held their property in common) but treat the children of the new marriage as though they had been her own. At this point we can almost hear the husband's voice crying from the stone slab. 'I must confess,' he says passionately, 'that I was so distressed by your proposal that I almost lost my mind. To think that you could plan to leave me, when you, at a time when I myself was almost banished from life, remained wholeheatedly faithful!' The proposal was dropped. The couple remained together, childless and aging, until at last, after forty-one years of marriage, she died. Almost the final words on the inscription are: 'I know that you deserved everything, and yet I did not manage to give you all you deserved.' He is not really very eloquent; his language is sometimes awkward; but his simple frankness is more convincing than richer periods and more complex paragraphs. We know neither his name nor hers.* We do not know if any portrait of them is extant—although they may well be looking at us from one of those Roman funeral monuments which show a husband and wife, sober and thoughtful, gazing out as though from a window of their home, at the passerby. What we do know of them is the essential which the husband wished to communicate: that they risked their lives and fortunes for each other; that they lived together for over forty years; and that neither found those forty years enough to express and enjoy their love. In such men and women was the true strength of ancient Rome.

* So many men ran the risks of outlawry and death during the civil wars that there are several different possibilities: for instance, Q. Lucretius Vespillo, who was proscribed in 43 B.C. and was hidden by his wife between the rafters and roof of his own house, with only one maid in the secret, until the wife got him a pardon; later he rose to be consul in 19 B.C. But not one of the men so far suggested quite fits the facts given in this inscription.

The inscription is number 1527 in the sixth volume of the *Corpus Inscriptionum Latinarum*; F. Vollmer's notes come in his history of Roman funeral speeches with the texts (Leipzig, 1891); there is a special edition of this speech by M. Durry (Paris, 1950); and Professor Gordon describes his find in 'A new fragment of the *Laudatio Turiae*,' *American Journal of Archaeology* 54 (1950), 223–26.

Writing

How To Torture an Author

In MORE robust days than these, a hundred years ago or so, there were many heartily sadistic sports to enjoy. You could watch a bull being attacked by specially bred bulldogs whose jaws clamped fast on its nose; you could see fighting cocks trying to stab and rip each other to death; you could sit by while two men fought with bare fists for 150 rounds. That kind of thing is against the law nowadays, and the difficulty is to find a substitute for it. There is, however, one legal sport which has many variations and which produces many of the same pleasurable sensations as watching a badger fighting a pack of savage terriers. This is author-baiting.

The simplest way to torture an author is to get his name wrong and forget what books he has written. I once saw a woman cover John Steinbeck with flattery, and tell him that he well deserved to win the Nobel Prize for such a fine novel as *South Pacific*. A friend of mine achieved deathless fame among author-baiters when he was presented to a tall, brilliantly dressed lady of mature years who had an exotic headdress, a unique aquiline profile, long thin seaweed hands, and an air of intense though blasé distinction. 'Dame Edith,' said the introducer, 'may I present Mr. Geoffrey Winbucket?' The lady extended a fragile hand. Winbucket gazed at her with a wild surmise, and said, 'Please forgive me. I didn't catch your name. Do you write?'

Another vulnerable spot in writers is finance. Authors seldom make decent incomes, and they earn money very irregularly. Therefore they are more sensitive on that point than the members of any other profession, except the stage. You can make any writer yelp satisfyingly if you hit him in the pocket. There are at least four techniques for this.

The first is to tell him that you couldn't get hold of his new book for nearly six months after its publication, because there were so many people on the waiting list at the lending library. When he hears that you didn't think his book worth more than 15¢, and that you refused all temptations to take out your little moth-infested wallet and buy it, he will writhe.

The second method is to say that you bought a copy as soon as it came out, and that you have been lending it around to all your friends. 'I think twenty-five or thirty people must have read my copy of your marvelous book: it is almost coming to pieces.' It is a very strong-minded author who can think of twenty or thirty sales which you have sabotaged, deliberately sabotaged, without groaning and shaking his heavy head.

A third *suerte* (as we *aficionados* say) is to praise the author's new book highly, and then ask him to lead you a copy. 'I'm sure you must have one handy: I'll return it promptly, and keep it in a paper wrapper.' Some author-baiters even write to their victims saying that they have seen reviews of his book and would love to read it, could he send them an 'author's copy'? This implies that the author has a private store of 'author's copies,' three or four hundred extra volumes which fell out of the machine when the printer was not looking and are kept in a private warehouse like a wine-grower's personal stock. In fact, the author usually gets six copies free from the publisher. He keeps two for his files, and presents four to his nearest and dearest. If he gives any more copies away, he has to pay the publisher for them in his good scanty hard-earned dollars.

Perhaps the simplest variation of this type of torture is the fourth. If the author does know you personally and does send you a free copy of his book, don't thank him; don't write him about it; and when you do meet him next, make no reference to it whatever. Don't even mention the reviews. Contrive that he shall think it arrived, but was thrown into the garbage together with last week's newspapers.

By correspondence, one simple but effective method of tormenting an author is to write him a short letter saying that you know his reputation, and that you have heard he has recently published a book on a subject dear to you. Then ask, quite straightforwardly, 'How can I get hold of your book?' The author has spent the last eight or nine months in close contact with his publisher; he may also have talked with the salesmen and met the representatives of a dozen leading booksellers. He will read this question with his stomach writhing. He will think about it all day, and wonder what to reply. The obvious answer is, 'Go to a bookstore and buy it.' But that seems too simple. The author begins to worry. He starts to think that perhaps the publisher—or someone in the publisher's office—is deliberately smothering the book, so that no copies of it have ever been sent out to the bookstores; or else that, after reaching the bookstores, they have been dissolved by cosmic rays. If you write him from, say, West Virginia, he will worry about the possibility that his books may never have penetrated to the Panhandle State, and he will start pestering his publishers to put on a special West Virginian advertising campaign, and to get copies of his book into every store in every town and at every crossroads of West Virginia. This will improve the relationship between him and the publisher, and produce a handy, cheap, self-perpetuating type of author-torture.

Using a different technique, you can hit an author in a tender spot by treating your own literary work as far more important than his. Remember the definition of an actor, attributed to Marlon Brando: 'An actor is a guy who, if you ain't talking about him, he ain't listening.' The same often applies to authors. Therefore when you meet one it is an excellent idea to describe your own books or the books of someone else you know. I once saw T. S. Eliot stand for a long, long time in silence, while a plump elderly lady quoted stanza after stanza of her daughter's lyrical poems to him. Mr. Eliot's face habitually expressed a deep world-weariness, illuminated by a remote and saintly good humor; but on that day, minute by minute, its lines grew deeper.

> Between the idea
> And the reality
> Falls the Shadow.

Many, many people practice one of the most fiendish tortures which can be inflicted upon a working author. This is to send him your own unpublished work. Preferably it should be in a large heap of typescript on flimsy paper (third or fourth carbons are best), which collapses and flies out of order the moment the package is opened, so that the author must spend twenty minutes picking up the pages and getting them back into some sort of shape. There should be a covering letter, in which you write that you don't want money, but only a chance to say all that is in your heart; you *do* want detailed criticism of your writings from your victim; and you end by telling him to take steps to have your book published as soon as possible. In order to increase his agony, you should never on any account enclose a stamped addressed return envelope. He has nothing else to do, between writing and publishhing books, the lazy hound. Make him rummage around in his storage closet and find some brown paper and string and tie up your parcel properly for return to you: the exercise will do him good. Of course you will not have enclosed any stamps, and he has thrown out your original wrapping, so that he cannot guess how much the bundle weighs: therefore he will have to take it to the post office several miles away, and stand in line waiting to have it weighed and buy the stamps and see it dispatched, and then make his way home again. A whole morning's work will have been shot to blazes, but your author will have had some valuable exercise and a chance to develop his moral fiber.

To meet the author is even better. If he is meek and absent-minded, and if you catch him out of his *querencia* with his self-confidence down around his ankles, then corner him. Fix him with your glittering eye. Start reading your unpublished work to him, slowly and emphatically. This will give him the same pleasure as showing him the X-ray photographs of the baby your wife is expecting in four months. James Thurber has a splendid essay on this subject in *The Middle-Aged Man on the Flying Trapeze* (Harper, 1935), called 'How to Listen to a Play.' The best way to do it, he says, is to choose a comfortable chair, get into a relaxed position, resting your head on your hand, close your eyes in rapt attention, and pass into a kind of trance. Thurber says that he can remain motionless and cata-leptic for three whole acts, saying 'Fine, that's fine,' and 'Just swell,' at intervals, without taking in a single word. But the danger is that rest may pass into sleep and sleep into dream. 'For instance,' he says, 'this question occurred in the second act of a play a woman was reading to me recently: "How've you been, Jim?" "Fine!" I answered, coming out of my doze without quite knowing where I was, "How've *you* been?" That was a terrible moment for both of us.'

The principal form of author-baiting is called criticism. No writer really wants criticism after his book has come out. He merely wants to see it being bought steadily, so that he can re-lax for a few weeks before he starts thinking about the next one. He does not want to read other people's opinions of how he should have written it, or how they could have written it. Sometimes he wants to forget it altogether, because he is ab-sorbed in planning something quite new. If a writer wants criticism after publication, he will ask for it. He never does. Therefore an effective method of tormenting him is to offer him unsolicited criticism, to thrust it on him, to send it to him in long single-spaced letters, or to back him up against a wall in the smoke and wealth and noise of a cocktail party and shout it in his ear. To stand on your two tired feet after a long day's work, breathing in the pungent and nauseating odor of other people's cigarettes, to watch a comparative stranger's mouth opening and shutting and occasionally spraying out half-chewed fragments of chopped olive and anchovy spread, and, above the concerted squawking of thirty or forty human voices, to strain in order to catch the sentences in which the stranger is vivisecting your poor quivering book—this is one of the most refined agonies which any author, however unpretentious, can be called on to endure.

There are several exquisite variations of this particular technique.

Type 1. Tell your author that you enjoyed his book, such as it was, but that he ought to have written a totally different work. If he has spent five years writing a biography of Boccaccio, explain to him that you were grievously disappointed because you had hoped he would give the world what he was uniquely qualified to produce, a definitive study of Savonarola.

Type 2. Express the utmost admiration for the book. Then ask him whether he really wrote it. Did he have much *help* with it? How often did he (or she) consult his wife (or husband)? No doubt he must have an enormous research staff, with highly trained assistants? Make it perfectly clear that neither you nor anyone else believes the book is all his own work; and, if possible, imply that the best parts do not sound like him in the slightest degree.

Type 3. This needs a little research, but is satisfying. Praise the book highly, and go into some detail. Then ask him if he knows that the same field was covered last year rather more fully by a German writer who is expected to win the Nobel Prize.

Type 4 takes a great deal of trouble, but is frequently practiced, especially in the learned professions. Read the author's book several times, with a notebook beside you. Write down every misprint, however small—even a misplaced apostrophe.

Look up every citation and note every variant. Verify all the references. Collect contradictory evidence for every disputable statement. Supply extra information on every topic where your victim seems to be a little weak. Then send the whole thing to a periodical which he knows and respects, in the form of a 'review-article.' I know several men who have spent a happy and rewarding lifetime never by any means writing books themselves, but plunging poisoned daggers in the backs of colleagues who do; and after all, the Borgia family lived a rich and full and rewarding life, did they not?

Best of all inflictions is the simplest. Show your author that the whole business of writing books is merely silly, why bother, who reads them? If you are a millionaire, or a hereditary nobleman, or a powerful official, this is your most effective form of author-baiting. The miserable Russians got a lot of it under the late Joseph Vissarionovitch Djugashvili, and have had more under his successors. After the poet Ariosto presented his delightful romantic epic poem *The Madness of Roland* to his patron, the Cardinal Ippolito d'Este, the Cardinal looked through it and said, 'Where the devil did you dig up all this rubbish?' And one of the royal house of Hanover, William Henry, Duke of Gloucester (brother of George III), on hearing that the greatest living English historian had produced another volume, summed it up in an immortal piece of author-squelching: 'Another damned, thick, square book! Always scribble, scribble, scribble! Eh, Mr. Gibbon?'

Sense and Nonsense

IN OUR language there is quite a large collection of nonsense poetry and nonsense prose. I am not thinking of the *Cantos* of Ezra Pound; I do not mean the juicier pages of the *Congressional Record*; I did not even mention the name of William Burroughs: I mean open-and-above-board, custom-tailored, universally admitted nonsense.

But there are degrees and grades and species of nonsense.

> 'Twas brillig, and the slithy toves
> Did gyre and gimble in the wabe:
> All mimsy were the borogoves,
> And the mome raths outgrabe.

Most people, if you asked them for an example of nonsense writing, would mention that poem, Lewis Carroll's 'Jabberwocky': certainly it occurs in almost every modern anthology of nonsense verse. It is pretty good poetry, too, a lot better than much contemporary free verse 'lyrics.' But it is not complete nonsense. It has a meaning, and if the meaning is a little hard to elucidate, well, think of Dylan Thomas. Much of the meaning is allusive: it depends on the reader's knowing a tra-

SENSE AND NONSENSE / 275

dition and accepting wild variations on that tradition. Here is one of its normal representatives, the first stanza of the ballad *The Bonnie House o' Airlie*:

> It fell upon a bonny simmer day,
>   When the corn grew green and the barley,
> That there fell oot a great dispute
>   Atween Argyle and Airlie.

The rhythms and rhymes and syntax of 'Jabberwocky' tell us that the poem is not gibberish, but a distorted ballad in stately archaic phrasing: ''*t*was,' '*did* gyre,' '*all* mimsy.' As the tale proceeds, it becomes perfectly clear that it handles one of the most ancient heroic themes: the young man who faces a dangerous monster, kills it, and carries its head home in triumph. We hear him welcomed by his father in lofty language:

> 'And hast thou slain the Jabberwock?
>   Come to my arms, my beamish boy!
> O frabjous day! Callooh! Callay!'
>   He chortled in his joy.

'Jabberwocky' has a plot, it has three recognizable characters, it follows a well-known poetic pattern which is easily intelligible. We can understand everything that happens in it.

Or almost everything. It is full of incomprehensible words: incomprehensible at first sight, but not meaningless. We know they are not meaningless, because Humpty Dumpty, in Chapter six of *Through the Looking-Glass*, explained some of them and demonstrated the principle on which they are formed. Most of them are either recognizable English words with a slight twist in them or an unusual affix, or else pairs of English words telescoped into each other. For instance, the word 'beamish' suggests the brilliance of sunbeams and the radiance of victory, and must signify 'bright with glory.' 'Slithy' comes from 'lithe' and 'slimy.' 'O frabjous day!' obviously does not mean 'O miserable day!' or 'O boring tedious day!' The context shows that the old man is wildly, almost incoherently, happy: the ending '-jous' reminds us of 'gorgeous' and the beginning 'fra-' of 'frantic.' As for 'chortled'—coming just after 'Callooh!

Callay!' it must mean something like 'shouted and laughed
and made weird noises'; and it is now a recognized English
word, sanctified by the *Shorter Oxford English Dictionary,*
which observes that it is apparently a blend of 'chuckle' and
'snort.' Clearly 'Callooh' and 'Callay' are not English. 'Calloo'
is the name, and the characteristic utterance, of *Anas glacialis,*
an Arctic duck; Lewis Carroll liked odd birds such as the Dodo
and the Lory, and he was a bit of an odd bird himself, but
Anas glacialis is too far out even for him. But if you say 'Beautiful! Beautiful!' first in the masculine and then in the feminine, in ancient Greek, what comes out is 'Kalós! Kaláy!' and
there you have it, with the right stress on the last syllable, too.

Almost the whole poem is intelligible. This is proved by the
fact that it has been translated into Latin and ancient Greek.
The Greek version (in the style of a tragic messenger's speech)
is by Ronald Knox, and appears in his *In Three Tongues* (ed.
L. E. Eyres, Chapman & Hall, London, 1959). The Latin version which I have (there may well be others) is attributed to
A. A. Vansittart. It forms Latin neologisms exactly on the
model of Lewis Carroll's English inventions. *Brillig* is the time
when people start broiling and grilling things for dinner. In
Latin combine *cena,* dinner, and *uesper,* evening, and you get
cesper. The toves were *slithy* [= lithe + slimy]; in Latin they
are both *graciles* and *lubrici,* namely *lubriciles.* So the first
stanza goes:

> Cesper erat; tunc lubriciles ultrauia circum
>   urgebant gyros gimbiculosque tophi:
> maestenui uisae borogouides ire meatu,
>   et profugi gemitus exgrabuere rathae.

The English like crosswords, and complicated puzzles.

(By the way, 'Jabberwocky' has another relation to reality.
It is a parody. Many of Lewis Carroll's poems, although ridiculous and improbable on the surface, become more intelligible when it is seen that they are parodying famous poems or
famous poetic themes. ' 'Tis the voice of the lobster' is a parody
of a very serious poem beginning ' 'Tis the voice of the slug-
gard,' by the famous hymn-writer Isaac Watts—which was in-

spired by some verses of the Bible, Proverbs vi. 9–10. 'You are old, Father William' is a travesty of a serious poem called 'The Old Man's Comforts' by the ineffable Robert Southey. 'The Hunting of the Snark,' divided into 'fits' like a medieval poem, parodies that favorite mid-Victorian epic theme, the quest for the Holy Grail. The figure of the Jabberwock itself, as drawn by John Tenniel for *Through the Looking-Glass,* is a parody of the great devil in Callot's *Temptation of St. Anthony.*)

When Prince Pantagruel was at the University of Orleans, he met a spruce young student who belonged to the University of Paris, and who tried to cut him down by talking a learned jargon. 'How do you spend your time there?' asked Pantagruel. The student answered:

> We transfretate the Sequan at the dilucul and crepuscul; we deambulate the compites and quadrives of the Urb; we despumate the Latial verbocination; and if by fortune there be rarity or penury of pecune in our marsupies and they be exhausted of ferruginean metal, then for the shot we dimit our codices and oppignerat our vestiments, whilst we prestolate the coming of the Tabellaries from the Penates and patriotic Lares.

'Prut, tut,' said Pantagruel, 'what doth this fool mean to say? I think he is upon the forging of some diabolical tongue and means to bewitch us.' But one of his men interposed, 'This fellow would counterfeit the language of the Parisians, but he doth only flay the Latin, imagining that he is a great orator because he disdaineth the common manner of speaking.' And in fact all the queer words are Latin. What the youth said was:

> We cross the Seine at dawn and twilight; we traverse the crossways and crossroads of the City; we skim off the best of the Latin language; and if there is a lack of money in our purses and they are empty of dark metal, to pay our bills we give up our books and pawn our clothes, while we wait for letters from home.

But when Pantagruel heard that he was only a country boy from Limoges, he took him by the throat and shook him till he cried for mercy and crapped for terror.* The unfortunate Limousin died a few years later of the death Roland, in plain

* Rabelais, Book II, chapter 6, translation based on Urquhart's version.

English called thirst; but before that he had married a Limousine, and left one son, through whom he became the ancestor of the polysyllabic sesquipedalianist Samuel Johnson.

Such prose as the student talked, and such verse as 'Jabberwocky,' are not real nonsense. They contain continuous coherent meaning; only they veil it in enigmatic language. No bigger or better example of this technique exists than Joyce's *Finnegans Wake,* which is one gigantic series of multiple puns and portmanteau words. Even those who have never heard of Joyce get obfuscated by technical language. You ask a specialist whether he can fix your television set, and he answers that he can patch up the armauirumque, but the cano has been put too close to the primusaboris, and the entire Lauinaque litora has to be taken out and cleaned and then moliserated.

There is another group of poems and stories which are often called nonsensical, but are not. Take an early limerick by Edward Lear:

> There was an old man of Thermopylae
> Who never did anything properly.
>   So they said, 'If you choose
>   To boil eggs in your shoes,
> You cannot remain in Thermopylae.'

Or a newer limerick by Gelett Burgess:

> I wish that my room had a Floor;
> I don't so much care for a Door,
>   But this walking around
>   Without touching the ground
> Is getting to be quite a bore!

Both these poems are perfectly coherent. Therefore they are not nonsense. They are peculiar simply because they describe in straightforward language wildly extravagant behavior. And yet is the behavior so extravagant, at that? I can think of many people who have been penalized for offenses which now seem more trivial than boiling eggs in their shoes and never doing anything properly. As for walking around in a room without a floor, the poet might be describing one of the beat generation, who have no contact with the solid earth trodden on by other people and no visible means of support. Horace, the Roman laureate, wrote an ambitious poem in which he said he would soon be flying through the upper atmosphere and felt feathers growing on his fingers; it is a perfectly serious ode, and—although few readers admire it much—no one calls it nonsense verse. Poems like this therefore are not nonsensical either. We might rather call them eccentric, because what they describe is strictly improbable, or even impossible, but is set forth in calm logical terms. Many such eccentric tales are about animals acting as people. One of my favorites is a legend by Patrick Barrington about a duck-billed platypus (*Ornithorhynchus anatinus* to its friends). It was kept as a pet by a young man who was studying at Oxford. Inspired by his example, it started studying too, and tackled the examinations for entrance to the Foreign Office. (My son Keith had a friend whose Siamese cat used to sit on his shoulder while he typed, and reach down at the end of every line to push back the carriage, when the little bell rang.)

> I had a duck-billed platypus when I was up at Trinity,
> With whom I soon discovered a remarkable affinity.
> He used to live in lodgings with myself and Arthur Purvis,
> And we all went up together for the Diplomatic Service.

The author and his friend Purvis failed; but the platypus passed, and was given a series of increasingly important posts.

> The wisdom of the choice, it soon appeared, was undeniable.
> There never was a diplomat more thoroughly reliable.
> The creature never acted with undue precipitation O,
> But gave to every question his mature consideration O.

However, just as the platypus was approaching the climax of its career and looking forward to the rank of H. M. Minister (with a knighthood to follow), nature intervened.

> My friend was loved and honored from the Andes to Esthonia;
> He soon achieved a pact between Peru and Patagonia; . . .

No Minister has ever worked more cautiously or slowly O;
In fact, they had decided to award him a portfolio,
When, on the anniversary of Greek Emancipation,
Alas! he laid an egg in the Bulgarian Legation.

This gesture, perhaps inevitable but nevertheless hideously indiscreet, caused a serious international crisis and ruined the future of a promising foreign service officer.

This unexpected action caused unheard-of inconvenience.
A breach at once occurred between the Turks and the Armenians;
The Greeks poured ultimata, quite unhinged by the mishap, at him;
The Poles began to threaten and the Finns began to flap at him; . . .
My platypus, once thought to be more cautious and more tentative
Than any other living diplomatic representative,
Was now a sort of warning to all diplomatic students—
The perfect incarnation of the perils of imprudence.
Beset and persecuted by the forces of reaction O,
He reaped the consequences of his ill-considered action O,
And, branded in the Honours List as Platypus, Dame Vera,
Retired, a lonely figure, to lay eggs at Bordighera.*

All this is perfectly possible and reasonable, except that it is an animal which commits the diplomatic indiscretion instead of the usual fallible human diplomat. No doubt there is a special significance in the climax of the story, where a promising statesman turns out to be a sexual anomaly. And is it so absurd to think of a platypus at the conference table? In our own time we have seen worse beasts ranging over the field of international affairs: rabbits and weasels, rats and wolves.

One of the best tales and the least-known in *The Arabian Nights* is a story of lies and nonsense and competitive absurdity. It was told by Ali the Persian to cheer up Harun al-Rashid on a night when he was sleepless and melancholy.†

   Some years ago I left this my native city of Baghdad on a journey, having with me a lad who carried a light leathern bag.

* Quoted from 'I had a Duck-Billed Platypus,' in *Songs of a Sub-Man,* by kind permission of the author, Patrick Barrington.
† Two Hundred and Ninety-fifth and Two Hundred and Ninety-sixth Nights; Burton's translation.

Presently we came to a certain city, where, as I was buying and selling, behold, a rascally Kurd fell on me and seized my wallet perforce, saying, 'This is my bag, and all which is in it is my property.' Thereupon I cried aloud, 'Ho Moslems, one and all, deliver me from the hand of the vilest of oppressors!' But the folk said, 'Come, both of you, to the Kazi [the magistrate] and abide ye by his judgment with joint consent.' So I agreed to submit myself to such decision and we both presented ourselves before the Kazi, who said, 'What bringeth you hither and what is your case and your quarrel?' Quoth I, 'We are men at difference, who appeal to thee and make complaint and submit ourselves to thy judgment.' Asked the Kazi, 'Which of you is the complainant?'; so the Kurd came forward and said, 'Allah preserve our lord the Kazi! Verily this bag is my bag and all that is in it is my swag. It was lost from me and I found it with this man mine enemy.' The Kazi asked, 'When didst thou lose it?'; and the Kurd answered, 'But yesterday, and I passed a sleepless night by reason of its loss.'

'An it be thy bag,' quoth the Kazi, 'tell me what is in it.'

Quoth the Kurd, 'There were in my bag two silver styles for eye-powder and antimony for the eyes and a kerchief for the hands, wherein I had laid two gilt cups and two candlesticks. Moreover it contained two tents and two platters and two spoons and a cushion and two leather rugs and two ewers and a brass tray and two basins and a cooking-pot and two water-jars and a ladle and a sacking-needle and a she-cat and two bitches and a wooden trencher and two sacks and two saddles and a gown and two fur pelisses and a cow and two calves and a she-goat and two sheep and an ewe and two lambs and two green pavilions and a camel and two she-camels and a lioness and two lions and a she-bear and two jackals and a mattress and two sofas and an upper chamber and two saloons and a portico and two sitting-rooms and a kitchen with two doors and a company of Kurds who will bear witness that the bag is my bag.'

Then said the Kazi to me, 'And thou, sirrah, what sayest thou?'

So I came forward (and indeed the Kurd's speech had bewildered me) and said, 'Allah advance our lord the Kazi! Verily, there was naught in this my wallet, save a little ruined tenement and another without a door and a doghouse and a boys' school and youths playing dice and tents and tent-ropes and the cities of Bassorah and Baghdad and the palace of Shaddad bin Ad and an ironsmith's forge and a fishing-net and cudgels and pickets and girls and boys and a thousand pimps who will testify that the bag is my bag.'

Now when the Kurd heard my words, he wept and wailed and said, 'O my lord the Kazi, this my bag is known and what is in it is a matter of renown; for in this bag there be castles and citadels and cranes and beasts of prey and men playing chess and draughts. Furthermore, in this my bag is a brood-mare and two colts and a stallion and two blood-steeds and two long lances; and it containeth eke a lion and two hares and a city and two villages and a whore and two sharking panders and an hermaphrodite and two gallows-birds and a blind man and two wights with good sight and a limping cripple and two lameters and a Christian ecclesiastic and two deacons and a patriarch and two monks and a Kazi and two assessors, who will be evidence that the bag is my bag.'

Quoth the Kazi to me, 'And what sayst thou, O Ali?'

So, being filled with rage, I came forward and said, 'Allah keep our lord the Kazi! I had in this my wallet a coat of mail and a broadsword and armouries and a thousand fighting rams and a sheepfold with its pasturage and a thousand barking dogs and gardens and vines and flowers and sweet-smelling herbs and figs and apples and statues and pictures and flagons and goblets and fair-faced slave-girls and singing-women and marriage-feasts and tumult and clamour and great tracts of land and brothers of success, which are robbers, and a company of daybreak-raiders with swords and spears and bows and arrows and true friends and dear ones and intimates and comrades and men imprisoned for punishment and cup-companions and a drum and flutes and flags and banners and boys and girls and brides (in all their wedding bravery) and singing-girls and five Abyssinian women and three Hindi maidens and four damsels of Al-Medinah and a score of Greek girls and eighty Kurdish dames and seventy Georgian ladies and Tigris and Euphrates and a fowling net and a flint and steel and many-columned Iram and a thousand rogues and pimps and horse-courses and stables and mosques and baths and a builder and a carpenter and a plank and a nail and a black slave with his flageolet and a captain and a caravan-leader and towns and cities and an hundred thousand

dinars and Cufa and Anbár and twenty chests full of stuffs and
twenty storehouses for victual and Gaza and Askalon and from
Damietta to Aswan; and the palace of Kisra Anushirwán and
the kingdom of Solomon and from Wadi Nu'uman to the land
of Khorasán and Balkh and Ispahán and from India to the
Sudán. Therein also (may Allah prolong the life of our lord
the Kazi!) are doublets and cloths and a thousand sharp razors
to shave off the Kazi's beard, except he fear my resentment and
adjudge the bag to be my bag.'

Now when the Kazi heard what I and the Kurd avouched, he
was confounded and said, 'I see ye twain be none other than two
pestilent fellows, atheistical villains who make sport of Kazis and
magistrates and stand not in fear of reproach. Say, fellows, is
this bag a bottomless sea, or the Day of Resurrection that shall
gather together the just and the unjust?'

Then the Kazi bade them open the bag; so I opened it and
behold, there was in it bread and a lemon and cheese and
olives. So I threw the bag down before the Kurd and ganged
my gait.

This nonsense comes from the accumulation of illogicalities
and impossibilities. (In a curious way it inverts the usual pattern of the wonder-tales in *The Arabian Nights,* where a magical kerchief can be shaken out to become a huge pavilion or an
old bottle contains a demon hundreds of feet tall.) You might
wonder why Ali, the owner of the bag, did not state what was
really inside it right away. But (although born in Baghdad) he
is called Ali the Persian; his opponent is a Kurd; the Persians
and Kurds have hated one another for many centuries, and Ali
is determined not to be outdone in volubility and ingenuity
by one of those rascally highlanders.

A third type of writing which looks like nonsense is neither
a jargon of obscure words nor a tissue of improbabilities, but
a stream of incoherent thoughts driven by the rapid flow of
emotion and association, and not controlled by any process
of logical choice. In *Little Dorrit* Charles Dickens drew an
amusing caricature of one of his own former sweethearts who
had turned into a silly gushing widow. Here she is, asking a

caller for news of little Miss Dorrit, whose father has just become fabulously wealthy (Book II, chapter 9).

> And now pray tell me something all you know about the good dear quiet little thing and all the changes of her fortunes carriage people now no doubt and horses without number most romantic, a coat of arms of course and wild beasts on their hind legs showing it as if it was a copy they had done with mouths from ear to ear good gracious, and has she her health which is the first consideration after all for what is wealth without it Mr. F. himself so often saying when his twinges came that sixpence a day and find yourself and no gout so much preferable, not that he could have lived on anything like it being the last man or that the precious little thing though far too familiar an expression now had any tendency of that sort much too slight and small but looked so fragile bless her!

It is set down just as it comes out—a gush of what looks and sounds like rubbish, but, if it were properly punctuated and the parenthetical remarks played down or even omitted, would make perfectly good sense touched with genuine emotion. The only additional difficulties in understanding it are the lady's allusiveness (Mr. F. is her husband, now deceased) and the obscurity of some of the social phrases which were quite clear in Dickens's day. 'Carriage people' are a family rich enough to own a carriage and horses and employ a coachman and footman—like having a private aircraft and pilot today. On the door of such a carriage there would be the family coat of arms: a shield held up by two supporting heraldic animals gazing at the beholder, like good school children showing a neatly copied lesson to the teacher. 'Sixpence a day and find yourself' means that your wages are sixpence a day and that you supply your own food, clothes, and lodging out of them: an encouragement to frugality and a prophylactic against the gout.

A modern masterpiece ends with a long unspoken monologue which also might be nonsense at first sight, since for page after page it has no punctuation and no structure and no central core of meaning. Read it slowly, and it comes clear.

Let me see if I can doze off 1 2 3 4 5 what kind of flowers are those they invented like the stars the wallpaper in Lombard street was much nicer the apron he gave me was like that something only I only wore it twice better lower this lamp and try again so as I can get up early Ill go to Lambes there beside Findlaters and get them to send us some flowers to put about the place in case he brings him home tomorrow today I mean no no Fridays an unlucky day first I want to do the place up someway the dust grows in it I think while Im asleep then we can have music and cigarettes I can accompany him first I must clean the keys of the piano with milk whatll I wear shall I wear a white rose or those fairy cakes in Liptons I love the smell of a rich big shop at 7½d a lb

That is Molly Bloom in *Ulysses* trying to get to sleep but also musing about a possible future visitor to her home, in a continuous flow of lightly non-logically linked, but not incoherent, thought. It looks avant-garde and difficult, a monologue printed in forty-odd pages of almost continuous type without punctuation and with only the occasional paragraph indentation to show a slight pause. But much modern poetry and prose which its authors have thought unworthy of the artificial aids of punctuation would turn out to be much clearer, and sometimes shallower, if punctuated. A continuous stream of tape-recorded words is not a book. Let us try running this tape again.

Let me see if I can doze off: one, two, three, four, five. . . . What kind of flowers are those they invented [the designers of the bedroom wallpaper which she is gazing at with sleepless eyes]? The wallpaper in Lombard Street [an earlier home of the Blooms] was much nicer. The apron he [Mr. Bloom?] gave me was like that, something; only, I only wore it twice. [In colloquial Irish-English 'only' is used as an adversative conjunction: 'I was going in to have a jar of Guinness, only [= but] I didn't have the price of it on me.'] Better lower this lamp and try again, so as [= so that] I can get up early. I'll go to Lambe's [shop] there beside Findlater's, and get them to send us some flowers, to put about the place, in case he [her husband] brings him [the stranger] home tomorrow. Today, I mean [because it is after midnight]. No, no. Friday's an unlucky day. First I want to do the place up, someway [= somehow]: the dust grows in it, I think, while I'm asleep. Then we can have music and cigarettes. I can accompany him. First I must clean the keys of the piano with milk. . . . What'll I wear? Shall I wear a white rose? Or [as well as, or instead of, flowers] those fairy cakes in Lipton's [the famous grocer's]—I love the smell of a rich big shop—at sevenpence halfpenny a pound. . . .

The smooth sleepy rhythm of somnolence is broken by punctuation, but the connections of Molly's ideas are now much clearer; and the reader finds the whole thing simpler, and more banal, and less of a deliberate mystification mystification he says and who knows what he means perhaps at the heel of the hunt he might mean it is a big fake musha is that any word in the world to use of a masterpiece written about a great old menstrual monologue O patience above its pouring out of me like the sea

A long uninterrupted flow of words gabbled by Flora or ruminated by Molly can be dissolved into separate sentences and clauses, each understandable in itself: it is the connections that are difficult to trace. Is it possible to write a text in which each separate sentence is apparently meaningless? and in which the connections between the clauses and sentences are utterly obscure? It is. Certain types of lyric poetry contain such texts. The surrealist poets of the Twenties and Thirties believed that true poetry should be composed by the subconscious mind without any interference from the faculty of reason; and furthermore they held that life was so complex and inexplicable and irrational that no ordinary combinations of words and images could represent it. But their compositions were usually failures.

Crushed against the basaltic dumbness of the ibises hanging from the
    bridles of underground rivers a prey to mad forests of hydras

where the thick summers' sermons gargle dreamy rivalries night swal-
    lows us up and casts us out to the other end of the lair

moving beings whom the eyes' grammar has not yet defined upon the
area of tomorrow. . . .*

And yet a really fine poet can compose lyrics which are almost
equally unintelligible.

> A grief ago,
> She who was who I hold, the fats and flower,
> Or, water-lammed, from the scythe-sided thorn,
> Hell wind and sea,
> A stem cementing, wrestled up the tower,
> Rose maid and male,
> Or, masted venus, through the paddler's bowl
> Sailed up the sun. . . .†

Without much study I could not venture to explain this stanza
or the poem which it opens, even to myself. Yet, partly because
of the clear beauty of the first phrase, and partly because other
poems by Dylan Thomas, almost as obscure, have yielded me
much meaning and deep aesthetic satisfaction, I know this is
not rubbish, but metasense, worth learning and meditating.

To write pure incoherence deliberately is difficult. One attempt was made in the Age of Reason. Two eminent actors of
the eighteenth century were discussing one of the central problems of their profession: how to remember difficult speeches.
Charles Macklin said that he would guarantee to remember
anything he read, and repeat it after only one or two readings.
To test him, Samuel Foote wrote this:

> So she went into the garden to cut a cabbage-leaf to make an
> apple-pie; and at the same time a great she-bear, coming up the
> street, pops its head into the shop. 'What! no soap?' So he died,
> and she very imprudently married the barber; and there were
> present the Picninnies, and the Joblillies, and the Garyalies, and
> the grand Panjandrum himself, with the little round button at
> top, and they all fell to playing the game of catch as catch can,
> till the gunpowder ran out at the heels of their boots.

---

* Tristan Tzara, 'The Approximate Man,' translated by David Gascoyne
in his *Short Survey of Surrealism* (London, 1935).
  † Dylan Thomas, 'A grief ago.'

It is full of little incongruities, but it is not totally incoherent. A skilled memorizer would start with the fact that most of it concerns a wedding, and lists the guests and describes the festivities. Also, it is easy to memorize, if not to understand, because it is pleasant: it has a sort of charm, something between *The Wizard of Oz* and *The Love for Three Oranges*.

In such puzzles the man who is speaking or writing has some idea of what he is doing, even though his audience or his readers may not. But there are some kinds of nonsense where nobody really knows what is going on.

Here is a ceremonial song which accompanies the composition of an emetic.

> Yo-owo hahaye . . . holagai . . . o-o-ha-yai it is you, to this one I come, piñon nut, to the next home I usually go, piñon nut yoye he ai yeye . . . Weasel do-dja-ne ha-ye you it is . . . You it is, my! to it I come . . . to the next home I usually go . . . piñon nuts yo-ye-aiyee . . . wrapping cord do-djan haye you it is.*

It is part of a ceremony performed by the Navaho Indians, and called Beautyway. We are tempted, of course, to suggest that it loses something in translation; but the trouble is that the Navahos have forgotten what some of the ritual signifies and what some of the words mean. Because it is traditional, they go on singing and dancing, but they are singing what is at least in part pure nonsense. By a curious chance, one of the very earliest specimens of the Latin language was carved upon a wall nearly a thousand years after it was composed. It is the song of the Brothers of the Grainfields; they sang it at an annual festival, and danced as they sang, but they had to read the words out of written texts, and they could not interpret them all: nor can we. Languages change, and their changes obliterate meaning.

Some years ago a letter came to me at Columbia, signed by

* *Beautyway: a Navaho Ceremonial,* translated by Father Berard Haile, edited by Leland C. Wyman (Bollingen Books no. 53, New York, 1957), p. 87.

the sender and mailed in New York City. I still have it, and it is still a puzzle. It begins:

> Cenderma Chempra candra durasority entra orekentra bulolo-
> marsity gecineemorsatity boradie junorara darasie tilala alterie
> slowma shlam jumpru crutue sermordy

and continues like that for about 160 lines. It is expertly typed, with perfect spacing and regular impressions. If you were shown the sheets and told they were a chapter from a language which was known to have existed but was still untranslated, you would be inclined to believe it. Possibly a brilliant linguistic analyst who knew much about psychiatry might be able to make a diagnosis from the document; but for all other readers it is devoid of sense. There is too much of it to be a practical joke. It is headed 'Superior Latin,' but it has no relation to Latin or to any other language I know; and it closes with the ominous words 'Thus ends this message i received.' This is the most painful kind of nonsense, a product of someone who has lost control over his mind. Such writing and talk are the results of mental disturbance, or of injuries to the speech centers of the brain. Many men and women suffering from extreme religious excitement have spoken loudly and vehemently in unintelligible verbiage, sometimes losing control of their bodies at the same time, writhing and rolling on the ground. The phenomenon has often appeared in the Christian churches. It has usually been connected with the miracle of Pentecost, when the twelve apostles—simple Galilaean Jews—preached the wonderful works of God in many foreign languages (Acts ii. 1–41): except that there the message was understood by all the visitors from abroad ('how hear we every man in our own tongue, wherein we were born?'), while in most such cases no one can understand what the visionary is saying. St. Paul warned the Corinthians that they should have an interpreter standing by to make sure that the ecstatic was not merely babbling and jabbering: 'if there be no interpreter, let him keep silence in the church' (I Cor. xiv. 27–28). Glossolalia, 'speaking in tongues,' is the name of this activity; and I fear that the missive addressed to me at Columbia was typoglossolalia. The distressing thing about it is that the unhappy creature who composed it, line by line, page by page, knowing with part of his or her mind that it was senseless, was still able to type clearly and neatly. Part of that troubled brain still functioned. The machine worked, but the human being was damaged.

Is it possible for people who are not mentally sick to talk and write gibberish? and why should they do so?

> Grim glim gnim bimbim
> grim glim gnim bimbim
> grim glim gnim bimbim . . .
> bum bimbim bam bimbim
> bum bimbim bam bimbim . . .
> grim glim gnim bimbim
> grim glim gnim bimbim
>
> Tata tata tui E tui E
> tata tata tui E tui E . . .
> Tillalala tillala
> tillalala tillalala . . .

These are two movements of a sonata published in 1925 by one of the most extreme of the Dadaists, Kurt Schwitters.* Among his other activities he used to compose works of art out of broken glass and pieces of junk. You may say that he, and most of the Dadaists, were mentally afflicted; but I believe rather that they were visionaries with a genuine message consisting of non-sense. Founded in 1917 during the direst chaos of the first world war, Dadaism was an unsystematic assertion that the world had no meaning; that the only kind of art worth producing was a denial of all noble aspirations and formal excellences; that a scream meant more than a symphony. Schwitters was trying to blend two different types of simplistic art: the kind of poetry which is based on repetitious sound with

---

* *Sonate* by Kurt Schwitters (slightly abbreviated), reproduced on p. 274 of *The Dada Painters and Poets: an Anthology,* edited by Robert Motherwell and published in 1951 by Wittenborn, Schulz, Inc., New York.

the minimum of meaning and is much favored by primitive peoples, and the simpler kind of music which is dominated by percussion rhythms. Even in that grim time he may have had some glimmerings of the cheerful energies of jazz.

How about baby talk? Sentimental grandparents sometimes look at the baby and say 'Oojie, koojie, poojie.' But they are not trying to make the helpless infant throw up its last meal. They are endeavoring to talk to it in its own language: that is, to say something which is not burdened with meaning, but will sound to the baby like its own first babblings—which are usually nonsense noises with vowel patterns and intonation of the same general type as the language of its parents.

If we talk nonsense without a baby to talk to, what are we doing—assuming that we are not insane? I tried this on my wife. I said, 'Listen. Oogalalla woogalalla hagallala ha. Is that gibberish?' She thought, and said, 'Not exactly. First of all, it sounds like a counting-out rhythm: the kind of thing children say when they are choosing sides or playing hide-and-seek: "eenie, meenie, minie, mo," "one potato, two potato, three potato, four." So it has a pattern. Also, you are thinking of an Indian chant—Ogalala is the name of one tribe of Dakota Indians. You've been seeing too many westerns; or perhaps we ought to go out to New Mexico again, and watch the Gallup Indian Festival.'

The Final Words

———————————

I<small>N THE WRITING</small> of every book or poem or play there are two crucial moments. One comes when the author puts down the first few words, and the other when he starts the last page. The tone of the concluding sentences is even more important than the beginning, for it will surely help to determine his readers' judgment of the whole, and sometimes these words are among those which remain most clearly in their memory. Many authors seem to have devoted particular attention to their final words.

Sometimes a writer cannot make up his mind to stop without saying something directly to the men and women who are going to read his book—even if this means breaking the illusion of impersonality which he has been trying to establish throughout. So Mr. Gibbon, after an eloquent final chapter about the ruins of the city of Rome, finishes his history with a summary of the main points of interest in it, and then closes on a dignified personal note:

The historian may applaud the importance and variety of his subject; but, while he is conscious of his own imperfections, he must often accuse the deficiency of his materials.* It was among the ruins of the Capitol that I first conceived the idea of a work which has amused and exercised near twenty years of my life, and which, however inadequate to my own wishes, I finally deliver to the curiosity and candour of the public.

After more than twelve hundred pages of *War and Peace*, Leo Tolstoy brought his story to an end just as his hero was about to marry his heroine, the delightful Natasha: or rather, not to an end, but hanging in mid-air, with Natasha day-dreaming and chatting with a friend:

> 'It won't be just yet—some day. Think what fun it will be when I am his wife and you marry Nicholas!'
> 'Natasha, I have asked you not to speak of that. Let us talk about you.'
> They were silent awhile.
> 'But why go to Petersburg?' Natasha suddenly asked, and hastily replied to her own question. 'But no, no, he must. . . . Yes, Mary. He must. . . .'

And then Tolstoy could not shut up. He added a long Epilogue, containing a lecture on the career of Napoleon I and a description of his hero and heroine some time after their marriage, stout and domestic and a little bit dull; and then a second Epilogue on historical determinism, which is both tedious and wrong-headed.† Seldom has there been a more deadening last page for a work of fiction than that which ends:

> In the first case [the Copernican revolution in astronomy] it was necessary to renounce the consciousness of an unreal immobility in space and to recognize a motion we did not feel; in the present case [when abandoning the idea of free will in history] it is similarly necessary to renounce a freedom that does not

* An elegant method of saying 'I have done as well as I could; but have the goodness to remember that the historical evidence for the fall of the Roman Empire is often very thin and untrustworthy.'

† The translation is by Constance Garnett. Comments on Tolstoy's view of history will be found in Isaiah Berlin, *The Hedgehog and the Fox* (Simon & Schuster, New York, 1953) and Karl Popper, *The Poverty of Historicism* (Harper, New York, 1964) pp. 147–49.

exist, and to recognize a dependence of which we are not conscious.

It is only the narrative genius, sustained through so many vivid and varied chapters, and the psychical sensibility of Tolstoy that keep these long dissonant final chords from ruining the book.

Many distinguished authors have chosen at the end of their story to carry the reader's imagination further on, and thus to make him believe in the living reality of their characters. After the exciting last chapter of Dostoievski's *Crime and Punishment,* which ends with the long-postponed confession of the criminal, there is an epilogue taking him to prison in Siberia and describing how, instead of being crushed, he was transformed.

> But that is the beginning of a new story, the story of the gradual renewal of a man, of his gradual regeneration, of his slow progress from one world to another, of how he learned to know a hitherto undreamed-of reality. All that might be the subject of a new tale, but our present one is ended.

Dickens usually left his characters at the end of their story, the good ones happy and looking to further happiness, the evil ones punished or dead. Once, however, he ended a novel with bitter disillusionment, separation, and sorrow. This was *Great Expectations.* The hero, having expected to be left a great inheritance and become an independent Man of Property, learned that he had been living on chimeras, and had nothing. Even the cold beautiful Estella whom his false patroness had used in order to torment him was still unflinchingly, unmeltingly cold. Dickens originally ended the book with a page or two on his hero's loneliness and despair. (Dickens himself was engaged in an unhappy love affair with a beautiful but recalcitrant girl at the time, and transferred some of her character and some of his feelings into the novel.) Bulwer-Lytton, after reading the proofs, persuaded him to change the ending, and make it at least potentially a happy one. Dickens did so

—perhaps, as Mr. Edgar Johnson suggests in his biography, because he himself hoped for a happier outcome in his own love. The final sentences as he revised them are sensitive and touching.

> 'Tell me we are friends.'
> 'We are friends,' said I, rising and bending over her as she rose from the bench.
> 'And will continue friends apart,' said Estella.
> I took her hand in mine, and we went out of the ruined place; and, as the morning mists had risen long ago when I first left the forge, so the evening mists were rising now, and in all the broad expanse of tranquil light they showed to me, I saw no shadow of another parting from her.

The endings of two famous American novels carry the reader forward into durable misery, unquenchable despair.

> It wasn't any good. It was like saying good-bye to a statue. After a while I went out and left the hospital and walked back to the hotel in the rain.

That is Hemingway's reticence at its best and purest. The symbolism of rain, so natural and poignant, is used again in the close of Faulkner's *Sanctuary,* where the ruined girl sits with her old father listening to the band in the gardens of the Luxembourg, and longing to die.

> From beneath her smart new hat she seemed to follow with her eyes the waves of music, to dissolve into the dying brasses, across the pool and the opposite semicircle of trees where at sombre intervals the dead tranquil queens in stained marble mused, and on into the sky lying prone and vanquished in the embrace of the season of rain and death.

In several famous poems the close is designed to carry the mind upward from suffering into tranquillity. Each of the three sections, Hell, Purgatory, Paradise, which make up Dante's *Comedy* ends with the thought and sight of the stars: the third sums up the vision of God in one of the noblest final lines ever written:

l'amor che move il sole e l'altre stelle.
[Love, which moves the sun and the other stars.]

Towards the end of Milton's *Paradise Lost* there is a terrible glimpse of paradise occupied by warrior angels and guarded by the flaming sword, 'the Gate with dreadful faces thronged, and fiery arms.' But then, as Adam and Eve together journey into exile, sinners but together, and reconciled to the painful present by the hope of redemption in the future, there is a lightening of tension and a calmer close.

> Some natural tears they dropped, but wiped them soon;
> The world was all before them, where to choose
> Their place of rest, and Providence their guide:
> They, hand in hand, with wandering steps and slow,
> Through Eden took their solitary way.

So in Matthew Arnold's heroic poem *Sohrab and Rustum,* after the painful account of a duel between a father and his unknown son, the tragic recognition and farewell, and the son's death, we leave the father mourning beside the corpse; but, rather than close on this note of anguish, the poet turns our gaze to the great river of central Asia, Oxus, beside which the duel has been fought, and carries us into a vast and peaceful panorama in which there is no room for human sorrow.

> But the majestic River floated on,
> Out of the mist and hum of that low land,
> Into the frosty starlight, and there moved,
> Rejoicing, through the hushed Chorasmian waste,
> Under the solitary moon: he flowed
> Right for the Polar Star, past Orgunjè,
> Brimming, and bright, and large: then sands begin
> To hem his watery march, and dam his streams,
> And split his currents; that for many a league
> The shorn and parcelled Oxus strains along
> Through beds of sand and matted rushy isles—
> Oxus, forgetting the bright speed he had
> In his high mountain cradle in Pamere,
> A foiled circuitous wanderer:—till at last
> The longed-for dash of waves is heard, and wide

His luminous home of waters opens, bright
And tranquil, from whose floor the new-bathed stars
Emerge, and shine upon the Aral Sea.

Not all endings are so serene. Many famous books and poems end in something regrettably like an anticlimax. Plays often have to be brought to a close not with a dramatic final speech, but with some words which will be enough to get the actors off the stage and out of sight. This is of course the commonest thing in ancient Greek drama and in the drama of Shakespeare's time, where there was no drop curtain which could cut the stage and its occupants abruptly away from the audience. The *Prometheus Bound* of Aeschylus closes in unequaled terror and magnificence, as the earth quakes, thunder and lightning sweep through the atmosphere, and the crucified Titan sinks downward to an aeon of torture, calling to earth and the light of heaven to witness the injustice done to him. But many Greek tragedies end with a brief sententious comment, perilously close to a platitude, to be sung by the chorus as it moved off the stage: such is the end of Sophocles' *Ajax*:

> Much can be known by mortal men
> after they see; none can foretell,
> before he sees it, his future fate.

At the conclusion of Shakespeare's tragedies the corpses must be carried off the stage. The last words therefore are usually spoken by a secondary personage, and prepare for the funeral. Always intent on characterization, Shakespeare makes the final words fit their speaker—and also, like a closing chord of music, define the tone of the play.*

In *Hamlet* the warlike prince Fortinbras says that the palace looks like a battlefield, and orders it cleaned up.

---

* Dvořák's symphony *From the New World* does not end with the conventional fortissimo chords; but with a strong *tutti*, which, instead of stopping with a downbeat, dissolves into a long calm chord sustained by the woodwinds and brass alone—as though the composer were thinking of the limitless plains and the indefinite future of the New World where his Czech friends had settled.

> Take up the bodies: such a sight as this
> Becomes the field, but here shows much amiss.
> Go, bid the soldiers shoot.

A funeral march is played as the corpses are carried off, and the play closes with a burst of cannon fire. The stronger, simpler prince survives to claim the realm of Hamlet.

Antony and Cleopatra were deadly enemies of Julius Caesar's heir Octavian, who became Augustus. After Antony's death and Cleopatra's suicide the new ruler represented him as the puppet of a wily Oriental houri: the war which ended with their deaths was not a civil war for the mastery of the empire, but the defense of Rome and Italy against corrupt foreign invaders. Such was the Augustan propaganda line (see, for instance, Vergil's *Aeneid* 8.696–713). But since Shakespeare admired Antony and Cleopatra, he made Octavian end the play by praising and honoring them. Looking at the body of Cleopatra with admiration, the conqueror says

> Take up her bed,
> And bear her women from the monument.
> She shall be buried by her Antony.
> No grave upon the earth shall clip* in it
> A pair so famous. . . . Our army shall
> In solemn show attend this funeral.

Macbeth ends with no such generous tribute, but with Macduff displaying the severed head of Macbeth and hailing Malcolm his rightful successor as ruler of Scotland; then with a short kingly speech by Malcolm, who promises to root out

> the cruel ministers
> Of this dead butcher and his fiend-like queen

and invites his supporters to see him crowned at Scone. (*Flourish of trumpets.*) Shakespeare's most unpleasant and bitter work, the savage satire *Troilus and Cressida,* closes with a strain of heroic tragedy ('Hector is dead; there is no more to say') followed by a foul mocking speech spoken to the syphi-

* embrace.

litic bawds and pimps in the audience by the Trojan prince
Pandar, first of their line.

That was a deliberate anticlimax. But what are we to say
of the very last words of Goethe's *Faust*?

> Das Ewig-Weibliche
> Zieht uns hinan.
> [The Eternal Feminine
> Draws us onward.]

These are words which have nothing whatever in common
with the Christian faith—of which *Faust,* judging by its closing scene, is supposed to be an assertion—and very little to do
with the career of the hero Faust as related in the play. Was
Goethe thinking of the end of Dante's *Comedy*—in which the
immortal beloved, Beatrice, leads the poet Dante onward and
upward to see the ultimate vision of God—and then repeating it without God? Perhaps; but if so, the conclusion is
false. Neither Faust nor Goethe was led onward and upward
by any noble influence emanating from the eternal feminine.
A big Faustian poem written in our own days, Nikos Kazant-
zakis's *Odyssey,* brings the hero to the ends of the earth and
into a defiant confrontation with death itself, his only impulse
being life, that unconquerable Yes.

Much of T. S. Eliot's *Waste Land* is poignant, much is
mysteriously memorable, like fragments of a melody once
half-heard and always recalled with regret; but the ending—
which can be understood at first reading only by someone who
knows both Elizabethan tragedy and Sanskrit hymnology—is
disappointing: by its affection it destroys much of the reader's
sympathy for the tortured spirit who speaks in the rest of the
poem.

> Why then Ile fit you. Hieronymo's mad againe.
> Datta. Dayadhvam. Damyata.
>   Shantih   shantih   shantih

If, instead of Sanskrit hymnology, one happens to know some

of the popular Irish songs of the nineteenth century, one will be comically reminded of

> Here's a health to you, Father O'Flynn!
> Slainte and slainte and slainte agin!

There is one particular anticlimactic ending which I have never understood, because it was written by a careful stylist who usually got such things right. If you have read Stevenson's *Treasure Island* you will recall the superb last paragraph:

> The bar silver and the arms still lie, for all that I know, where Flint buried them; and certainly they shall lie there for me.* Oxen and wain-ropes would not bring me back again to that accursed island; and the worst dreams that ever I have are when I hear the surf booming about its coasts, or start upright in bed, with the sharp voice of Captain Flint [the parrot] still ringing in my ears: 'Pieces of eight! pieces of eight!'

How remarkable it is that the man who wrote like that could end another story, the exciting yarn called *Kidnapped,* with one of the flattest sentences imaginable:

> The hand of Providence brought me in my drifting [through Edinburgh] to the very doors of the British Linen Company's bank.

I remember that when I first read that story and came to that end (I was a schoolboy of twelve or thirteen) I was convinced that a page must have been lost out of the book, and insisted on looking into a couple of library copies before I could accept the association of the hand of Providence with the British Linen Company's bank.

It is difficult to finish off a long novel with a climactic page. Readers want to know what happened to all the characters. Few stories can be devised which will dispose of them all in a few moments or a single catastrophe. But this has been accom-

---

* Strange how quickly language alters. This idiom, 'they shall lie there for me,' meaning not 'for my benefit,' but 'as far as I am concerned,' 'for all I care,' sounds quite obsolete nowadays.

plished once, at the end of Melville's *Moby Dick.* I have never been able to give full credence to the last event described; but it makes a striking picture, it is filled with sharp symbolism, and it is narrated in prose that surges like the sea.

> As the last whelmings poured themselves over the sunken head of the Indian at the mainmast, leaving a few inches of the erect spar yet visible, together with long streaming yards of the flag, which calmly waved over the destroying billows they almost touched;—at that instant, a red arm and a hammer hovered backwardly, uplifted in the open air, in the act of nailing the flag faster and yet faster to the subsiding spar. A sky hawk that had followed, pecking at the flag and incommoding Tashtego there, now chanced to intercept its broad fluttering wing between the hammer and the wood, and simultaneously feeling that ethereal thrill, the submerged savage beneath, in his death-gasp, kept the hammer frozen there; and so the bird of heaven, with unearthly shrieks, and his imperial beak thrust upwards, and his whole captive form folded in the flag of Ahab, went down with his ship, which, like Satan, would not sink to hell till she had dragged a living part of heaven along with her.
>
> Now small fowls flew screaming over the yet yawning gulf, a sullen white surf beat against its steep sides, then all collapsed, and the great shroud of the sea rolled on as it rolled five thousand years ago.

Of all book endings the most peculiar were of course created by Joyce. *Ulysses* closes (not a minute too soon) with the long dreamy interior monologue of Molly Bloom, and the repeated Yes, her acceptance of love and life. But *Finnegans Wake* drifts away like a dream merging more and more faintly into sleep, as Anna Livia Plurabelle, the girl who is a river, moves toward the sea in little phrases like the blinks of dream-consciousness dissolving and like a faint laplap of ripples in moving water.

> We pass through grass behush the bush to. Whish! A gull. Gulls. Far calls. Coming, far! End here. Us then. Finn, again! Take. Bussoftlhee, mememormee! Till thousendsthee. Lps. The keys to. Given! A way a lone a last a loved a long the

And there it does not end. The final half-sentence connects with the first half-sentence in the book and brings us back into the eternal cycle of history and life:

> riverrun, past Eve and Adam's, from swerve of shore to bend of bay, brings us by a commodius vicus of recirculation back to Howth Castle and Environs.

It is a magical book. I would read more of it more often, were I not afraid of being bewitched.

Most conclusive of all conclusions is one which forcibly summarizes the central theme of a book. So, after many hundreds of pages, Oswald Spengler approaches the close of his massive *Decline [and Fall] of the West*. He has foretold what he calls the clash between money and blood, and the overthrow of capitalism and democracy by Caesarism [= dictatorship]; he wishes to emphasize his belief that the laws of historical change are as immutable and as irresistible as the laws of physics: so he concludes thus:

> For us . . . whom a Destiny has placed in this Culture and at this moment of its development—the moment when money is celebrating its last victories, and the Caesarism that is to succeed approaches with quiet, firm step—our direction, willed and obligatory at once, is set for us within narrow limits, and on any other terms life is not worth living. We have not the freedom to reach to this or to that, but the freedom to do the necessary or to do nothing. And a task that historic necessity has set *will* be accomplished with the individual or against him.
> *Ducunt Fata uolentem, nolentem trahunt.*

It is claptrap; but it is splendidly sonorous claptrap.*

* The Latin line means 'He who wills is led by the Fates; the unwilling man is dragged by them.' It comes from Seneca, *Letters* 107.11, a free translation of two lines of Cleanthes the great Stoic (Epictetus, *Enchiridion* 53). Spengler had a tin ear, and misquoted it so that its iambic meter is destroyed: it should be *ducunt uolentem Fata. . . .* On the whole concept, 'our direction . . . is set for us within narrow limits,' see Isaiah Berlin, *Historical Inevitability* (Oxford University Press, London, 1954).

Of another important book, Marcel Proust's *In Search of Time Past*, the main theme is the perpetual flux of time and change. The last sentence of the entire work is a complex and obscure utterance, in which the word Time occurs thrice, like the tolling of a bell through the mist. Majestic though this is, I prefer the lighter and more poetic handling of the same motif in the final words of his first novel, *Swann's Way*:

> Places which once we knew now belong only to the world of space where we situate them for our own convenience. None of them was more than a thin layer among a mass of neighboring impressions which made our former life. Memory of a special image is nothing but regret for a special moment; and houses, roads, avenues, are fugitive, alas, like the years.

How To Write an Essay

───────────────

At school they tried to teach me how to write an essay, and how to draw a large brass pot full of zinnias. I grieve to say that they failed in both these laudable aims. I am not sure why I could never draw a brass pot full of zinnias, but I know why my schoolmasters could not teach me to write an essay. The first reason was that they gave us rather unattractive models to study and emulate: Charles Lamb, who is a great deal too quaint and old-fashioned for modern youngsters; Robert Louis Stevenson, whose style is often affected and artificial;* and E. F. Benson, whose essays *From a College Window* are mild and flaccid and middle-aged and uninspiring. The other reason was that they never explained to us what an essay was, and what purpose we were attempting to achieve when we wrote one.

But there are other ways of learning how to write an essay —by trial and error, observation and meditation. There are plenty of good stimulating contemporary models. A news-

───────────────

* In a memorable but unfortunate phrase, Stevenson said he had formed his own style by imitating many earlier writers, and making himself a 'sedulous ape.'

paper editorial is only a short essay; so is a review of a new book, a play, or a concert; so are the articles of newspaper columnists. Some of the columnists write well, some of them atrociously, but they all try to obey the first law of the essayist: *Be interested and you will be interesting.*

Also, I now know what an essay is. One good way to get a clear idea of any literary form is to look at its origins, and see what the men who first practiced it thought they were doing. The first man in modern times to write essays was the eccentric and charming Montaigne, who apparently invented the name as well as the pattern: essay = attempt, that is, an exploration, something tentative and incomplete, but suggestive and stimulating. He was quickly followed by the English statesman and philosopher Francis Bacon. These men both thought in print: they mused on subjects they considered to be important, and they allowed the public to share their thoughts by overhearing. They were not trying to teach systematically and completely, but rather to stir and interest their readers' minds and to give some instruction while doing so. In shape and method many of these early essays derive from the letters written on philosophical subjects in ancient Greece and Rome. The letters of Epicurus to his pupils and of Seneca to his friend Lucilius are really philosophical essays; some of the letters of St. Paul are religious essays; and Montaigne's essay on the education of children is set out as a letter to a lady.

An essay is a fairly short and fairly informal discussion—of what? Of any subject in the world, any topic whatever which can be discussed in public. It has two purposes—to interest its readers, and to inform them; but it is far more important that it should interest them. One of William Hazlitt's finest essays is about a champion player of handball, or fives. There are few subjects nowadays about which I care less than handball; I gave the game up when I got a heart warning thirty years ago; and I should not normally turn a single page of print in order to get information about the game and its champions. But Hazlitt writes so warmly and with such conviction that I have read his essay ('The Death of John Cavanagh') thirty or forty

times, always with delight. One of G. K. Chesterton's wittiest
essays is simply 'On Running after One's Hat': now, there is a
topic on which most people would not even waste a couple of
sentences, and on which nobody (except perhaps a heart
specialist) could give us any useful data; but in less than four
pages Chesterton takes this piece of trivia and builds it into
a fanciful little philosophical system. Essays are intended not
to exhaust the subject—which usually means exhausting the
reader—but rather to say a few good things about it, and to
give readers the pleasure of continuing the author's thought
along their own channels.

It is not hard to write an essay, if you can write decently
and think a little. The first essential is to choose a subject
which is clear and precise in your mind and which interests
you personally—so that you really enjoy thinking and talking
and writing about it. Now that it comes to mind, that was a
third reason why I never learned to write essays in school: the
master was inclined to choose vague and tepid subjects. For
instance, 'Scenery.' Very few boys and girls can really appreciate scenery; and only an aesthetically trained mind can have
anything rich and challenging to say about scenery in general.
Scenery: the word fell on our minds like a thick coating of
mud, chill and stifling. I remember that I once escaped from it,
and infuriated my unfortunate preceptor, by writing about the
unique scenic qualities of the industrial city of Glasgow, with
ironically rhapsodical paragraphs about the view of the gas-
works from the slag heaps, and the superb assemblage of
factory chimneys, some of which (Dixon's Blazes) resembled the
divine guardian of the Children of Israel in the Exodus, a
pillar of smoke by day and a pillar of fire by night. At least I
felt that aspect of the subject, and I knew it precisely.

The next thing is to devise a form for your essay. This, which
ought to be obvious, is not. I learned it for the first time from
an experienced newspaperman. When I was at college I earned
extra pocket- and book-money by writing several weekly
columns for a newspaper. They were usually topical, they were

always carefully varied, they tried hard to be witty, and (an essential) they never missed a deadline. But once, when I brought in the product, a copy editor stopped me. He said, 'Our readers seem to like your stuff all right; but we think it's a bit amateurish.' With due humility I replied, 'Well, I am an amateur. What should I do with it?' He said, 'Your pieces are not coherent; they are only sentences and epigrams strung together; they look like a heap of clothespins in a basket. Every article ought to have a shape. Like this' (and he drew a big letter S on his pad) 'or this' (he drew a descending line which turned abruptly upward again) 'or this' (and he sketched a solid central core with five or six lines pushing outward from it) 'or even this' (and he outlined two big arrows coming into collision). I never saw the man again, but I have never ceased to be grateful to him for his wisdom and for his kindness. Every essay must have a shape. You can ask a question in the first paragraph, discussing several different answers to it till you reach one you think is convincing. You can give a curious fact and offer an explanation of it. You can take a topic that interests you and do a descriptive analysis of it: a man's character (as Hazlitt did with his fives champion), a building, a book, a striking adventure, a peculiar custom. There are many other shapes which essays can take; but the principle laid down by the copy editor was right. Before you start you must have a form in your mind; and it ought to be a form felt in paragraphs or sections, not in words or sentences—so that, if necessary, you could summarize each paragraph in a single line and put the entire essay on a postcard.

No. Perhaps that is going too far. Reading through some of the most brilliant essays of Virginia Woolf and E. M. Forster, we realize that they have no obvious form: they often try to break away from patterns and abstract outlines. But they are held together by two factors which not all of us can use. Neither Virginia Woolf nor E. M. Forster was capable of writing a dull commonplace obvious sentence; and both of them—in spite of, and indeed because of, their eccentricities—had minds which were organic wholes, so that whatever they wrote, although sometimes apparently discontinuous, reflected the activity of a single imagination, as the same light is caught in many broken reflections from the surface of a pool. Virginia Woolf's talk and some of her novels were slightly incoherent in rather the same way; but they formed spiritual unities. However, others who cannot claim to possess minds so intense and so deeply penetrated with harmonious impulses might find it dangerous to write without a preconceived form; and their readers might find the result tedious. Never forget the immortal remark of Richard Brinsley Sheridan:

> Easy writing's vile hard reading.

When you plan the shape of your essay, should you also plan its length? Yes, and no. You should always realize that whatever you write as an essay is going to be incomplete: a Sunday afternoon drive is not the Mille Miglia race. You will therefore say to yourself, thinking over the topic, that this particular subject demands forty pages or so—because you have not only to discuss the character of the man but to describe his friends and enemies and lovers; while this one—for instance, the new pleasure of aqualung diving—can have enough said about it in ten pages. But when writing (as in conversation, and even, if you are smart, in making a speech) you will always leave room for new ideas, fresh insights, 'ad libs': you can cut them out later if they seem forced or extraneous. But think often of conversation and of letter writing. No one says to himself, 'I am now going to talk to this attractive woman for exactly twelve minutes'; no one thinks, 'I want to tell my sister about our trip to Japan: I shall take exactly four pages.' An essay is a conversation between oneself and an unseen friend.

One more hint from the newspaper and magazine world. Find a good lead sentence. The opening words are important. They are far too often bungled. If they are effective, they will catch the reader's interest and start to mold his feelings. They should therefore be rather vivid, even dramatic, and contain a certain emotional charge; or else be hard and bright and factual, so that the reader knows at once what is to be discussed. There are a large number of critics writing on political and social problems, literature, music, and art, who habitually begin their essays with a sentence so long, so precious, so involved, so obscure, so filled with scholastic allusions and in-jokes and ripostes to unknown opponents that they repel every reader who is not already initiated into the clique and prepared to be impressed. Turn to the good essayists: what do you find? Bacon opens his essay on 'Gardens' with the remarkable but true statement:

> God Almighty first planted a garden.

George Orwell begins a touching essay on the Moroccan city of Marrakesh with a drastic but significant sentence: 'As the corpse went past the flies left the restaurant table in a cloud and rushed after it, but they came back a few minutes later.' Another of Orwell's essays, written during the second world war, starts even more dramatically: 'As I write, highly civilized human beings are flying overhead, trying to kill me.' Once you have read such an opening, hard must be your heart and busy (or empty) your brain if you do not wish to read on. But here is the opening of an essay which, like bad antipasto, kills the appetite for anything else:

> The imbecility with which Verecundulus complains that the presence of a numerous assembly freezes his faculties, is particularly incident to the studious part of mankind, whose education necessarily secludes them in their earlier years from mingled converse, till, at their dismission from schools and academies [= universities], they plunge at once into the tumult of the world, and, coming forth from the gloom of solitude, are overpowered by the blaze of public life.

The subject of this essay is 'Bashfulness.' The author is Samuel Johnson. The idea is good. Intellectuals are often uncomfortable in large groups of people. They have spent most of their time thinking, reading, and talking with other specialists —or making scientific experiments which cannot be discussed in general language; and they have few subjects of social conversation. (In a way, this essay is a remote precursor of C. P. Snow's *Two Cultures*.) But what a way to start discussing the idea! The first sentence contains seventy-one words and is made up of one principal clause with at least six subordinate clauses and phrases hanging onto it like lampreys on a lake trout. And apart from that, who is Verecundulus? Who has heard his complaints? Not I. Not you. Only Samuel Johnson. His essay is in fact a reply to an imaginary letter asking for sympathy and perhaps advice; but he might have invented a few sentences of the letter itself, to lead into the essay. As for the name Verecundulus, that is really pedantic. No one who does not know a reasonable amount of Latin will understand the word; and in Latin the word does not exist in this form: Johnson invented it. It means only 'Shy little man.' Addison or Steele would have produced a delightful essay on the same subject, built around a character called 'Mr. Modest,' or 'Dr. Diffident'; but Johnson had to take the Latin *uerecundus* [= shy] and build a diminutive out of it, Verecundulus, which sounds not like a shy man but like a new kind of orchid.

I hope this does not make you feel that it is necessarily hard work to write, or even to read, an essay. If I have, then either I have mistaken the technique of writing this pleasant form of literature, or I have failed to show you how delightful it is to read a good essay. Would you like to receive an interesting letter from someone who once met you and who wants to tell you something you did not know and would like to learn? If so, you can either read or write an essay, or both.

The Ancient Mariners' Association, Inc.

————————

It is always embarrassing to have to apologize, especially to
an old friend, but it is sometimes inevitable. I have been
writing a letter of regret to Mrs. Boggles because I missed the
wedding of her only daughter. The trouble is that I do not
quite know how to explain what happened.

The reception was held at the River Club in New York City.
I live not far from there, so I walked over. Two blocks from
the Club a man stopped me—a fellow wearing a navy blue
turtleneck sweater, a heavy duffle coat, and a sailor's cap, old
and hard-worn. He looked rather like Alan Arkin in *The Russians Are Coming the Russians Are Coming*, but he wasn't. I
took him for a seaman temporarily on the beach, looking for
a ship, and I was quite ready to give him a small handout.
He was polite about that, but firm. 'No, sir,' he said, 'I don't
want any money: I don't need any. I simply want to explain
to you about the bird.' I said, 'What bird?' And he went on,
'*The* bird, and what it did to me. We sailed on the 31st of
September from Pier 189 in Hoboken with a cargo of nitrous
trioxide for the port of Valparaiso.' 'Just a minute,' I said,
'I'm on my way to a wedding: in fact I can hear the music

playing now.' 'Never mind that,' said the sailor, 'you must hear my story. The weather took a turn for the worse after we rounded Cape Horn, and for some reason we missed Valparaiso altogether. I thought it was sloppy navigation on the captain's part: he never cleaned out his chronometer, he kept forgetting to wind up the sextant, and when he couldn't sight the Pole Star he cried for two days. But the crew blamed me. They called me a jinx, a Jonah. There was a big bird that used to follow the ship hunting for garbage, an alcatraz or an albacore or an abalone or something, anyhow, one of the order *Tubinares*. I thought it was a filthy creature, and I was awful tired of cleaning up the deck, so I took out my .38 and shot it. You should have heard the crew! You would have thought I had shot the cook, and sometimes I wish I had.'

The seaman sighed gloomily and gazed at the ground. I looked at my watch and made another effort to get away; but he held me with his glittering eye, and went relentlessly on.

'They took the corpse of that dirty stinking bird—you won't believe this, but I swear it's true—they took that bird's dead corpse and they hung it round my neck like some sort of a bloody decoration. The next thing was that the engines broke down altogether, just off the Galapagos Islands, the radio went on the blink, and we drifted until the water ran out. All the crew died of thirst except me. I was saved when Typhoon Teresa struck the ship, plenty of rain, and there was some canned food in the galley, so I just steered straight ahead due north till I ran her into Fisherman's Wharf at San Francisco. Damaged the jetty and sank the ship, but I didn't care. The bird had fallen off my neck during the typhoon, and now I was home at last! What do you think of that?'

By this time I had missed the wedding reception altogether, and I could see the guests beginning to drive away from the River Club. I said, 'I never heard such an incredible story in my life: absolute poppycock! Do you want me to believe that rubbish?' 'Believe it or not as you like,' said the sailor, 'I don't care, I just wanted you to listen to my story, for I had to explain about the bird.' And off he went along East 52nd Street, looking for another victim.

Long ago, in 1797, he met Samuel Taylor Coleridge and told him the same story. Coleridge did not understand it much better than I did; but he thought it over, and filled it up with details from his omnivorous reading,* and added a moral—that if you love water snakes you can love anything and so your soul will be saved. Then he made it all into a famous poem, 'The Rime of the Ancient Mariner.' How many other unfortunate people the sailor has stopped and forced to listen to his yarn, I know not; but there must have been thousands. In Coleridge's poem, the very moment the sailor stepped ashore he was asked by a hermit who he was; and immediately, under a severe compulsion, he felt he had to tell the entire tale.

> Forthwith this frame of mine was wrenched
> With a woful agony,
> Which forced me to begin my tale;
> And then it left me free.

Not only that, but he was compelled to go on repeating the yarn, always roaming over the world reiterating the same rigmarole about albatrosses and death ships and water snakes.

> Since then, at an uncertain hour,
> That agony returns:
> And till my ghastly tale is told,
> This heart within me burns.
> I pass, like night, from land to land;
> I have strange power of speech;
> That moment that his face I see,
> I know the man that must hear me;
> To him my tale I teach.

Notice, he does not expect his audience to believe him: he

---

* Details in *The Road to Xanadu* by John Livingston Lowes (Houghton, Mifflin, Boston, 1930 ²).

simply wants to get his history off his mind, whenever he finds an audience he can dominate.

Now, is the Ancient Mariner entirely alone in suffering from this compulsion? Of course he is not. Take any trip lasting over two hours by train or ship or airplane, and if you do not stay incognito in a private compartment, some total stranger will start telling you at least part of the story of his life. My friends who give lectures to culture clubs tell me that it is comparatively easy to deliver the lecture itself. The real exhaustion, they say, comes afterward, when dozens of men and women come up to shake hands with the lecturer and say a few words to him. They do not want to hear him talk any more; instead, *they* want to talk to *him,* as though in retaliation for his lecture; and, whether he is tired or not, they usually give him a chapter of their own autobiography.

Instead of telling them to the casual wedding guest, such compulsive storytellers sometimes print their stories. They type them out, and slice them up into chapters, and publish them. If you read many modern novels, you must have noticed that some of them are written in order to tell a coherent story which expresses a certain emotional or rational view of the human condition; some again are written as pure entertainment. But there are some which are only half coherent. The story line is broken like a badly spliced tape recording: sometimes it is neglected, while all sorts of insignificant details are put in with loving care, loving and disproportionate care; logical development of character and rational motives for action are almost entirely lacking; conversations which have little to do with the plot are reprinted word for word—not as a dramatic novelist would phrase them, but with the same dutiful accuracy as a recording tape plays what has been imprinted on it. The Canadian physician Wilder Penfield discovered that if he electrically stimulated a certain area of the brain, his patient would remember and repeat a flood of memories, some of which in his conscious life he had not commanded. The patient could not control or select those memories: they rushed out of his mind like a cataract through a broken dam. He was *compelled* to repeat what he had experienced—like the Ancient Mariner, and like some modern writers. Many so-called novels are not works of fiction. They are not stories which the author has invented and offers to the public for its entertainment and instruction, but confessions which he is forced to utter.

Most such confessions deal with sexual adventure. It is common nowadays to read an amateurishly written and vaguely plotted tale, without even an attempt at achieving some of the graces of style, which contains vivid and detailed pictures of the author and his or her friends engaged in sexual divagations. Frequently, the disguise of fiction is made as thin as possible, so that the reader will know he is reading, not invention, but truth. For instance, the story is laid in a fictional town called Sharp Angles, Maine; and on the jacket you are told that the author hails from Hard Corners, Vermont. The heroine, that inexhaustible heroine, is named Jacynth Stargazer; on the jacket the authoress smiles over her portrait as Jemima Steugerblinken; you can draw your own conclusions. Once there was a young Catholic priest who was nervous about hearing his first confessions: so he asked an older and more experienced colleague to sit with him in the confessional and criticize his technique. The first customer was the prettiest and most alluring, and perhaps the frailest, girl in the parish. She had a long and detailed confession, punctuated by sighs and sobs. The young priest listened, gave her a short serious admonition, imposed a penance, and dismissed her. 'How did I do, Father?' he asked. 'Fine, my boy, fine. The penance was even too severe. But next time, while you are listening, you should put in a lot more *Tch, tch, tch,* and not so much *Whee-oo!*' It is the reverse when we are not hearing but reading confessions. 'Breathing heavily, he started to tear the clothes from her unresisting body. . . .' We are expected to utter, not a disgusted *tch, tch, tch,* but an admiring *whee-oo.* Did you actually let him do *that* to you? You must be truly extraordinary—even if you can't write a single paragraph without stylistic blunders. In the sexual field, you must be *something*. The answer is never spoken or printed, but is always implied: YES, I AM!

Another rich mine for these self-revelations is madness, with its subspecies drug-taking and alcoholism. Many men and women who have recovered from these maladies feel that they are absolutely bound to describe all that happened to them. Occasionally this is interesting, when the author happens to be an interesting man or woman: for instance, Cocteau's diary of his treatment for opium addiction; and, rarely, it can be made into a minor work of art like Charles Jackson's *Lost Weekend*. Some of the books about madness and drink and drugs do inform us and manage to make us sympathetic through both understanding and sorrow. But there are far too many which seem to be merely prolonged boasts, loud cries for sympathy, or compulsive repetitions of a degrading tale better forgotten.

One of the oldest and basest of human passions is cruelty. It can be exercised on other human beings and on animals. It can also be inflicted, directly or with the co-operation of others, on oneself. The two sides of the emotion are closely connected: more closely than most people ever realize. Often a man or woman who feels a special delight in making others suffer will also be devoted to some form of self-degradation and self-torment.

A high dignitary of the Roman Catholic church gave up much of his life to destroying heresies and heretics. Often his victims perished in hideous pain, having been imprisoned and starved and tortured and at last burned to death. When he himself died, those who prepared his corpse for interment found that he wore, beneath his priestly robes, a shirt of haircloth which constantly irritated his skin, and a belt with spikes turned inward on his flesh, which jagged and bit him at every movement, at every moment. Some Gothic sculptures show men of this kind, portrayed with startling accuracy.

The bishop lies supine, with hands clasped, upon his tomb, awaiting the last day and the resurrection. His episcopal vestments are ornate, carefully disposed. His tall mitre is on his head. But the large sunken eyes, the hollow fleshless cheeks, the tight lipless mouth, the deeply cut vertical folds in the face, the brow furrowed with anxiety (or with grief so deep as to resemble anxiety), the skeleton clarity of jawline and cheekbones beneath the skin, the concave temples in which a troubled vein still seems to throb, portray a man profoundly and incurably miserable, with a misery which he made himself. As Housman said, his sickness was his soul.

At the other extreme is the extremist after whom his own speciality was named, Count Donatien Alphonse François de Sade. When he was at liberty he loved inflicting degradation and pain on people whom he controlled or duped or persuaded or bought or otherwise dominated. When he was in prison he wrote fantastic, impossible, illogical stories about powerful men who inflicted degradation and pain on people whom they virtually owned as slaves—and that without fearing retaliation from their victims, revenge from their kinsfolk, or punishment from society acting through the law. His tales were his own dreams. Sometimes, but only sometimes, he was able to realize them on a small scale. But others have done so much more fully, both before and after de Sade's time. Most of us think that Bluebeard and Dracula are imaginary [= impossible] characters out of horror stories: like the evil sorcerer Kastchei in *The Fire Bird*. Yet there was a real person behind Bluebeard: Gilles de Rais, Marshal of France, who was executed in 1440 after confessing himself guilty of innumerable atrocious crimes committed on the bodies of kidnapped children. (One of the grimmest novels ever written traces his abominable career, counterpointing it with the sinful degeneration of his biographer, a French intellectual who was plumbing depths almost as low as his: *Là-Bas*, by J.-K. Huysmans.) And behind Dracula stands the real figure of a Rumanian ruler called Vlad IV (1455–62 and 1476–77). His nickname was the Impaler, because his favorite method of killing his victims was to stick them alive on pointed stakes—a method more ingeniously cruel than crucifixion. He would hold banquets in the courtyard of his castle, surrounded by stakes on which there writhed his moaning and screaming victims.

Sade wrote several stories describing actions almost as cruel as these, inflicted on helpless victims by powerful despots such as he wished to be. They do not read like police reports factually reconstructing brutal murders. The author sides with the torturer. He gloats with pleasure on the sufferings of the victim. He always makes the subject spiritually as well as physically helpless: weaker and softer than the tormentor; able to scream and squirm and die, no more. In history it has not always been like this. In Persia (now styled Iran) there used to be a special penalty for enemies of the Shah. The criminal was splayed open and hung up by the feet, and then vertically chopped into two pieces. However, the punishment was discontinued after one victim retained enough strength and courage to shout out (doubtless after every blow) unendurable and unforgettable insults against the mother of the Shah. His blood was soon licked up by the dogs who ate his mutilated body. But his words left on the imperial family an all but indelible stain.*

However, in Sade's writings the chief tormentor is as powerful as God. Indeed, since in Sade's world there is no God, he has taken over. (C. S. Lewis would have remarked that he was in fact representing the Devil, in our temporarily devil-occupied silent planet.) And yet, from time to time, the torturer hurts and defiles *himself.* At the end of a magnificent banquet where the table has been supported by naked girls leaning on spikes so that their groans serve as dinner music, the tyrant finishes his last dish and drains a glass of the finest Burgundy.

---

* The polymorphous Sir Richard Burton was so taken with this atrocity that he brought it several times into his gossipy notes on his translation of *The Arabian Nights* (Bassorah edition, vol. 1, p. 246; 4, p. 72; 6, p. 250; supplementary volume 6, p. 96; and supplementary volume 7, p. 194). The name of the punishment sounds just right: *shakk.* Burton credits Fath Ali Shah (1797–1834) with it, and adds that he would not issue an order for its infliction until he had donned a scarlet costume.

Then he eats a hot, fresh, steaming plateful of human excrement. His guest is astonished, disgusted. The tyrant—or rather Sade—tries to justify the act with a grandiose speech; but the speech is unconvincing. At that point, the sadist had (as quickly as Jekyll metamorphosed into Hyde) become a masochist, showing how he could humiliate himself and degrade himself as vilely as he degraded his victims.

Sade himself operated through books much more than through flesh and blood, simply because he spent so much time in prison. He wished to accomplish through his writings what he was prohibited from carrying out on human bodies. (He spent many pages on describing how his own relatives and enemies, lightly disguised, were brutally humiliated: for instance, his mother-in-law, Mme. de Montreuil, who had him arrested and imprisoned for thirteen years [see *Justine*], and a provincial magistrate who tried him on charges of poisoning and sodomy [see *The Puzzled President*].)

But further, when he described a petty dictator carrying out revolting tortures, and very often boasting of his own ingenuity and ruthlessness to a horrified but duly impressed onlooker, he wished to make us, his readers, into his accomplices (like the onlooker). He even wished to make us into his victims. By converting us into witnesses of his foul and bold fantasies, he degrades us, saying by implication, 'See, you cannot even imagine the horrible things *I* have planned and will do when they release me from this unjust and impossible incarceration. Let me teach you. You are out, I am in. I can only imagine the crimes: you may commit them. Go on!' And then, quite unexpectedly, he will picture his hero degrading himself by eating excrement. 'Could you do that?' he seems to say. 'Can you even think of it? No? Why not? I can think of it,' he says; and he implies that he has done it; and that you might. His books were meant to humiliate and torment their readers, just as their heroes humiliated and tormented their submissive victims, and later themselves. This is one reason why they are not widely read. Many other books about cruelty, often interwoven with sex, have been written. The *Satyrica* of Petronius, for instance, has many perversions, some floggings, and a touch of cannibalism; but it is gay, bright, witty: its author (if conjectures are right) was an intelligent and charming man, in spite of having to live at the court of Nero. But Sade's novels have no wit, no charm, nothing but the fiendish inventiveness of a maniac, who, hating both mankind and himself, has determined to degrade every living person in the world.

He was the first of many such writers. They are compulsive sadists and masochists. They feel they must affront every reader of their books, by telling him how low they have sunk (in imagination or in fact) and then by pulling him down to the same level, in imagination: perhaps later even in fact.

The psychologist Jung is said to have read James Joyce's *Ulysses* and commented, 'Good: if he hadn't been able to write that, he might have gone mad.' The same is true of many modern novels and plays. They are the substitute for confessions made to a priest and explanatory monologues entrusted to a psychiatrist; and in some ways they are more satisfying. It is more exciting for their authors to have a captive audience which can be dominated, puzzled, disgusted, horrified, perhaps converted. Until their ghastly tale is told, their heart within them burns.

G. Gorer, *The Life and Ideas of the Marquis de Sade* (Peter Owen, London, 1953 ²).

M. Praz, *The Romantic Agony,* translated by A. Davidson (Meridian Books, New York, 1956).

The Songs of the States

THE RICH and populous state of New York has existed since 1776. It contains, reading from left to right, Niagara Falls, Howard Hanson (leading the Eastman-Rochester Symphony Orchestra), 149 species of trees, Lake Placid (shrine of fonetik speling), Schenectady (scene of the 1690 massacre), Governor and Mrs. Nelson Rockefeller (surrounded by antique furniture, contemporary art, and future ambitions), the Hudson River, stiff skyscrapers, flexible commuters, blue jeans, white ducks, and—like an unexpected shiny pimple on the end of a long thin nose—Montauk. It has people. It has variety. It has scenery. It has wealth. It has a grand past and a glorious future. It has a state motto, *Excelsior*. I don't know who chose it, but he hoped that it meant *Ever Upward* or *Higher Yet*. Unfortunately it does not. It means *Rather Tall*, applying to a man, or a masculine object such as a mast. Longfellow wrote his poem without realizing this, and was upset when he found out. Yet there is something delightful about the picture of a man bearing, 'mid snow and ice, a banner with the strange device, *Rather Tall*.

But New York has never had a state song.

This has worried many inhabitants of New York State, but only one of them has done anything about it. Mrs. Bessie A. Buchanan, a member of the New York State Assembly, sat down and wrote a set of lyrics; and in 1962 she introduced a bill which, if approved, would have made her poem the official song of the Empire State. Senator John Marchi sponsored the bill in the Senate.

The chief difficulty confronting any poet who attempts to write such a song is the name of the state itself. Short and clear, but far from euphonious, the two syllables *New York* do not lend themselves to the rhythms of exalted lyricism. They sound too much like a hoarse two-toot taxi horn, or an inarticulate roar from a traffic cop. Furthermore, the name *New York* will scarcely rhyme with anything worth mentioning in a serious poem: what can you do with *cork, fork,* and *stork? Pork* contains a slightly different vowel, and anyhow it is not kosher. But Mrs. Bessie A. Buchanan solved this problem with confident ease. Not many modern poets would have thought of breaking down the barrier of rhyme in the very first couplet, but she did so. Her song begins

> In all the world there's no place like New York,
> Where dreams come true and happy hearts are taught. . . .

That is bold, indeed. That is direct, energetic, unconventional, like New York itself. To rhyme *York* to *taught*—that is really cutting the Gordian knauck. A few contemporary poets (for instance, W. H. Auden, an adopted New Yorker) have used assonance all through individual poems. Mrs. Buchanan did not. In the rest of her lyric she employed conventional rhymes: *light ~ might; revere ~ dear.* But as the opening of this important poem she clearly felt it was necessary to produce a sound-effect as daring and challenging as New York itself.

Here is the text as published in *The New York Times.*

> In all the world there's no place like New York,
> Where dreams come true and happy hearts are taught
> To walk and work together in freedom and in light,

To make our state the greatest in progress and in might.
In every way we honor and revere
The sight and sound of all we hold so dear,
From the beauty of the mountains to the magic of [the] streams,
And our buildings reaching high unto the sky.
In God we trust that peace will ever reign
O'er New York State, our home and proud domain.

The ten lines are grouped into five couplets. The first couplet contains the new breakthrough rhyme *York* ~ *taught*. The second and third are regular. The fourth suddenly surges upward into a fountain of lyricism which interrupts the sequence. Bold though she may be, not even Mrs. Buchanan could ask us to rhyme *streams* to *sky*. She left *streams* without a rhyming equal (and indeed what could rival the Niagara and Hudson Rivers?), while *sky* is partnered by the companionable word within its own line, *high*.

A carping critic might make one objection to the style of Mrs. Buchanan's poem: that, if read by itself, without the music which it was designed to inspire, it concentrates rather too closely on one single rhetorical device, the repetition of closely allied ideas in pairs: *walk* and *work, freedom* and *light, progress* and *might, honor* and *revere, sight* and *sound, home* and *domain*. But this is doubtless meant to image the structure of New York State, which is composed partly of a city of nine million people (including their suburban dormitories) voting to spend money, and partly of a farming and industrial area containing nine million people voting to save money. A poem often reflects the structure of its theme.

As for the problem of rhythm, that is one which the composer of the music must settle with the poet. Surely a lyric such as this demands music fit to be sung and played by myriads of New York Staters. On the whole, it is in march tempo: except for one couplet which seems to be in waltz rhythm:

From the beaúty of the moúntains to the mágic of [the] stréams
And our buíldings reaching hígh —————— unto the ský.

But perhaps that couplet is a sort of scherzo, meant for the drum majorettes to sing while turning somersaults in front of the marching bands.

The anthem closes with a noble heroic couplet embodying a quotation of a famous American slogan:

> In God we trust that peace will ever reign
> O'er New York State, our home and proud domain.

This shows that the problem of fitting the three hard monosyllables *Néw Yórk Státe* into an iambic line has at last been solved. Mrs. Bessie Buchanan has hammered them in, and they will stay in.

With this stirring composition Mrs. Buchanan endeavored to put New York on the same level as many other states, some of them less populous, less ambitious, and less plentifully supplied with literary talent. A few states have resisted the temptation—or, we might say, have been deprived of the opportunity—of having their own song. For example, Massachusetts faces a virtually insoluble problem. If it is ever to have its name introduced into poetry, either the traditional rhyme-schemes of Anglo-American poetry will have to be abandoned, or the poem will have to be written in Algonquian. Vermont has been too thrifty, New Jersey too busy, and North Dakota too cold to have acquired state songs. Some of the southern states have contented themselves with famous traditional lyrics: *My Old K Home, Carry Me Back to Old V,* and so forth. Mississippi has no state song; but it has a state ode, which ends in phrases worthy of William Faulkner's necrophilic Miss Emily:

> Here, my life, ebb thou away;
> Here, my bones, turn back to clay—
> I love thee, Mississippi.

Other states have had their own songs written and officially approved long ago. One of the most moving is the Alabama song, by Julia S. Tutwiler:

Broad the Stream whose name thou bearest;
Grand thy Bigbee rolls along;
Fair thy Coosa—Tallapoosa
Bold thy Warrior, dark and strong,
Goodlier than the land that Moses
Climbed lone Nebo's Mount to see,
Alabama, Alabama,
We will aye be true to thee!

With its combination of Southern scenery and Biblical tradition, this hymn would be difficult to surpass. In a young state, sentiments are naturally franker and simpler:

Montana, Montana, Glory of the West
Of all the states from coast to coast
You're easily the best—
Montana, Montana,
Where skies are always blue
M-O-N-T-A-N-A, Mon-ta-na, I love you.

West Virginia, on the other hand, found in Mrs. Ellen King a poet who could not only eulogize the principal features of its landscape, but actually image them in the antiphonal setting of the state hymn:

O the hills   beautiful hills
      beautiful hills   beautiful hills
How I love those West Virginia hills.
If o'er sea or land I roam
Still I'll think of happy home,
And the friends among the West Virginia hills.

Mrs. Harriet Parker Camden of Oklahoma could hardly foresee, in 1905, that her state would be definitively glorified thirty-eight years later by two native New Yorkers. She did her best in a sort of Student Prince chorus:

We have often sung her praises,
But we have not told the half,
So I give you 'Oklahoma,'
'Tis a toast we all can quaff.

But this was perhaps too sophisticated for a state which was nominally dry until 1959, and it has surely been superseded by the simple song in which the entire audience faces the company and the entire company faces the audience and both join in a big locomotive, O-O-O-O-O-Oklahoma! More recently, in 1932, Roger Vinton Snow created a song for the State of Maine, which contains a group of sovereign clichés aged in the wood:

> Oh Pine Tree State
> Your woods, fields and hills
> Your lakes, streams and rock-bound coast
> Will ever fill our hearts with thrills
> And tho' we seek far and wide our search will be in vain
> To find a fairer spot on earth than
>   (cresc.) Maine!
>   (in strict tempo) Maine! Maine!

Here is a suggestion for the bicentennial celebration of the United States in 1976, for which plans are already being made. Wouldn't it be a fine thing if the separate states all sent delegations to Washington, to vie with one another in singing their official state anthems? Full many a flower, said the poet Gray sadly, is born to blush unseen and waste its sweetness on the desert air. The whole country ought to know and relish such lyrics as the hymn of Idaho:

> And here we have I-da-ho
> Winning her way to fame
> Silver and gold in the sunlight blaze,
> And romance lies in her name.

There is many a gem of purest ray serene in *Iowa*—'*Beautiful Land,*' composed by a poet delightfully named Tacitus Hussey, from Des Moines; and the song of Wyoming may be poor in grammar, but in sentiment it is unimpeachable:

> Wyoming, Wyoming, Precious art thou and thine;
> Wyoming, Wyoming, Beloved state of mine!

It will sadden all patriotic New York Staters to learn that

Mrs. Bessie A. Buchanan's proposal to make her poem the official state song was defeated in both houses of the legislature, and so far has not been reintroduced. Yet the year 1976 is fast approaching. It is not too late for some indigenous poet to produce a lyric which will at least put New York on the same level as some of the other great states of the Union. Allen Ginsberg might be approached; but he is not a native New Yorker, and he lives largely out of this world. Lowell is a New Englander with his roots elsewhere. Auden looks pretty tired. Perhaps the best thing to do would be to call on Betty Comden and Adolf Green. In their lyrics for Leonard Bernstein's *On the Town* they summed up New York City very well. A few trips on the Thruway, a visit to beautiful downtown Albany, and a helicopter flight over teeming Long Island ought to inspire them to something which would equal

> New York, New York, a hell-uv-a town
> The Bronx is up but the Battery's down
> And people ride in a hole in the ground.*

Eighteen million New Yorkers are looking to our poets for a state song, in time for 1976. Must they be disappointed?

---

* New York, New York, © MCMXLV by M. Witmark & Sons. Used by permission of Warner Bros. Music. All rights reserved.

Useless Speeches

ANYONE whose voice is heard in public or who has written a book or two receives many invitations to make speeches. Those which come to me fall into two different groups. To one of these groups I usually say Yes, right away, depending on how much time and energy I have. To the other I always say No. On my desk now are four invitations. One I am considering quite seriously. The other three have a big red NO written in my firmest hand in the top corner, and my secretary will send a polite letter explaining that pressure of work, an exacting schedule of research and teaching, &c., &c., &c. . . . The first is from the chairman of a group of people interested in the classics. I spent some time in Greece recently, and they would like me to tell them something of what I saw. But the other three are all of the same vague and general type, full of lofty abstract words which contain rather more sound than meaning. One is an invitation to take part in a WORKSHOP ON THE ARTS IN A DEMOCRACY; one asks me to attend a SYMPOSIUM ON TRADITION AND EXPERIMENT IN EDUCATION; and the last suggests that I should be the 'keynote speaker' at a CONVOCATION

ON HUMAN VALUES IN AN INDUSTRIAL SOCIETY. Now, about Greece I have something to say, I can give facts and suggest interpretations and put something at least partly new into the minds of the audience. But the other three are nothing but invitations to deliver useless speeches.

For one thing, the topics are far too large to be handled properly in a single speech, or even in a small group of speeches. THE ARTS IN A DEMOCRACY: it is a fine theme for an extended course of lectures, and could easily grow into a large book with a copious apparatus of learning. Anyone who undertook it ought to do some hard thinking about the various arts, as practiced in the Greek democracies, the Roman republic, the Italian city-states, the French republic in the various phases of its existence, the United States of America, and other regions; necessarily he would say something about the arts that flourished in very anti-democratic regimes such as the France of Louis XIV and in places which have never known democracy at all, such as Persia; surely he would also discuss the curious fact that the ideal democracy, Switzerland, has produced very little art, and that some intensely democratic places such as Australia appear to be positively hostile to the fine arts. It would make a valuable book, THE ARTS IN A DEMOCRACY; but as the subject for a speech it is hopeless. The same applies to the other topics: TRADITION AND EXPERIMENT IN EDUCATION and HUMAN VALUES IN AN INDUSTRIAL SOCIETY. There must be a few geniuses who, in fifty minutes and eight thousand words, could say all that needs to be said about these exalted themes, but I am emphatically not one of them.

There is something else wrong with these ambitious enterprises. Consider the names chosen for the various meetings. One is a WORKSHOP. Yes, but what work will be done there? What will be made, what tools will be employed, and who will direct the work? Another is called a SYMPOSIUM, a name which always amuses me, for it means a drinking party. In ancient Greece people always took wine with their dinner, and then, on ordinary evenings, went to bed. But on special occasions, after the food was eaten and (more or less) cleared away, they would open some fresh bottles of good wine and settle down to several hours of music and singing and conversation, jokes and party-games. This evening of drinking and domestic entertainment was called a symposium: *syn* means 'together' and *posis* means 'drink.' Once, at a very special party given by a clever young Greek playwright, the guests agreed, instead of singing and chatting, to make speeches on a single central topic which interested them all: the passion of love. Socrates was at the party. His pupil Plato wrote a description of it, recording the principal speeches and the other adventures of the evening, and he called it *Symposium*. From that one superb book the name has spread widely; but I am sure that the gentleman who invited me to take part in a SYMPOSIUM ON TRADITION AND EXPERIMENT IN EDUCATION would be surprised and even shocked if I arrived wearing a garland of flowers on my head and carrying a bottle of the wine of Hymettus. The third group is given a name which sounds even grander (something like 'coronation') but means even less: a CONVOCATION is simply an assembly called together by somebody: *con* means 'together' and *uoco* means 'call.' So of these three associations, one is a workshop where no work will be done, one is a drinking party where no drinking will be expected, and one is simply a meeting with a pompous name.

This indicates that the organizers have no real purpose in mind. They do not expect that, as the result of these assemblies, anything will be done. When twelve jurymen sit in a box listening and then talk among themselves in the jury room, their meeting usually ends in a very definite consequence: a man is disgraced and sent to jail, or liberated and vindicated. When the Congress of the United States listens to speeches and carries out its deliberations, its meetings can have profound effects on the lives of all American citizens and sometimes on millions of other people. But after the Workshop has been broken up, after the Symposium has run dry, after the Convocation has been dissolved, what result will remain? A few memories, perhaps, and possibly a printed summary which nobody will read. Nothing else; all the speeches and the meetings themselves will be essentially ineffectual.

The Greeks, who knew far more about speechmaking than we do, observed that there were three types of speeches, and only three. One is the speech made in a law court by any of the parties or their legal representatives. The second is the speech made in a meeting which has come together to take some collective action: a trade union's executive committee, a board of directors, a session of Congress, a meeting of the PTA. The third is the speech which is made without any definite purpose other than to give emotional and aesthetic pleasure to the audience. This the Greeks called a display speech, because in it the orator, instead of striving to conceal his skill, as he sometimes does in other types of oratory, shows it off like a virtuoso musician giving a solo recital. Such, for instance, is a commencement address, the proposal of a toast at a banquet, a Fourth of July oration. Legal speeches are meant to convince a court and win a case. Policy-making (or 'deliberative') speeches are intended to produce collective action. Display speeches are simply meant to please the audience.

All display speeches are useless in the sense that they are not intended to produce any effect in action. Does this mean that they are bad? No, not necessarily. If they are well done and appropriate to the occasion, they can give a great deal of pleasure. I have delivered a certain number of them in my time, and I expect to deliver more. Why then should anyone object to the speeches planned for the Workshop, the Symposium, and the Convocation? It is because they are mistakenly conceived and falsely represented. The meetings are masquerading as policy-making bodies. In the very names of the assemblies it is implied that those who attend and listen will go away and do something which otherwise would not have been done. They will make democracy more artistic, perhaps, or art more democratic; they will combine and balance tradition and experiment in education; and as for human values in an industrial society, they will emphasize them strongly. But you know, and I know, and the speakers know, and perhaps even the organizers might be induced to admit, that nothing positive will happen. Nothing at all.

Yet something can be achieved at a meeting which is openly intended not to evoke policy proposals but to provide an audience for display speeches. Such speeches are not directly effectual in changing the world, but they have their functions. One of these functions can be fulfilled only if the speaker really enjoys publicity. This is contact between speaker and audience. Many people who have read a book want to see the author with their own eyes, hear him speak, even touch him (shaking his hand or getting his signature), as though this gave them a closer appreciation of his mind. It may not be logical, but it is emotionally justifiable. Most people would rather sit in a concert hall and watch Horowitz play on a visible and audible piano than stay at home and hear him play exactly the same works through a phonograph recording. And so it is with speeches made by men and women who are known through their books but become more alive when they stand up and talk.

The second purpose can be achieved only if the speaker is truly distinguished. If he is, he can give his hearers the intellectual pleasure of hearing him utter some thoughts he has not committed to paper. Thus, in one single lecture, Robert Lowell could not possibly tell his admirers much about the art of writing poetry, yet he might well utter a few observations which would be profoundly illuminating, the result of his own thinking about his craft. Such minds are few, few indeed; and, wisely, they husband their words.

Last, and most important although frequently forgotten, a display speech should give its hearers aesthetic and emotional pleasure. If it contains platitudes, they should be gracefully put; if paradoxes, they should be elegant. It should be filled with memorable phrases, vivid descriptions, bright anecdotes, and (to add one charm of style often neglected) unusual and moving quotations from great prose and poetry. It should be an exercise in that much abused and sadly decayed art, the art of style; and more than that, it should be inspired by a genuine emotion which it can communicate to its audience, saying something more intense than they themselves have felt, awaking them to perceptions they have not yet experienced. Such a speech is truly difficult to write and to deliver: usually it cannot be delivered in a Workshop, or in any Symposium which is not on a level with that of Socrates and his friends. It is through power of style and depth or refinement of emotion that the display speech can become essentially valuable and memorable, and even if it produces no visible concrete result, it can still give both those who hear it and those who read it long afterward a deep gratification. When Mr. Lincoln, at the end of an exhausting flow of oratory from a much more distinguished speaker, stood up to read a short address of his own, he declared that it was useless. 'The world will little note, nor long remember, what we say here,' he asserted. In fact his address at Gettysburg had scarcely any direct historical result. But the sincerity of its emotion and the nobility of its harmonies have made it into one of the great speeches of the world and one of the permanent artistic achievements of the American spirit.

The Prose of the Law

'WHO IS THAT interesting-looking man with the strong shrewd face?' you say to your friend in a crowded room: 'some distinguished writer?' 'Oh no,' your friend replies, 'he isn't a writer; he's a lawyer.' You accept the distinction, and so does most of the world; but it is a false distinction. Many lawyers *are* writers, and a very important class of writers. They use language almost as constantly as poets, historians, philosophers, critics, or novelists. Some of them are orators, and speak with eloquence and precision—more precisely and sometimes more eloquently than priests and politicians. They depend on language: they write it, read it, analyze it, live by it. Among the lawyers whom I count as my friends there is one optimistic and versatile man who seems to take life very easily, and whose face, even in the hottest discussion, is seldom without a calm pleasant smile. But once I asked him to look over a document which I had been trying to draft. He put it on his desk under a lamp, and began to read. At once the carefree geniality of his manner disappeared; his eyes became as grave and his face as intent as a surgeon's during an operation; he appeared to read every sentence phrase by phrase and then word by word; when he had finished and given me his criticism, the whole document had been submitted to a dissection of its thought and language far more searching and serious than most philosophers give to the words of their opponents and most literary men give to the novels and poems which they try to appraise. The law is a profession which demands, as well as will-power, integrity, and learning, an intimate understanding of language.

There are not too many collections of writings about lawyers and writings by lawyers—perhaps because most lawyers have more than enough to read during their working hours (although there was an English judge who took a treatise on Contingent Remainders to read on his honeymoon) and also because most laymen are afraid of the technical parts of legal language. But I can recommend one large anthology of the prose of the law: a fat book called *Voices in Court: a Treasury of the Bench, the Bar, and the Courtroom,* compiled by W. H. Davenport of the University of Southern California and published by Macmillan, New York, in 1958. It has its faults, as all anthologies have. There are far too many cases from English law, and too many *fictional* trials; and I should gladly have exchanged the absurd trial of Sir Walter Raleigh and the libel suit concerning the alleged sexual escapades of Mr. Gladstone for the Dred Scott opinions and for famous American trials such as the impeachment of President Andrew Johnson and the prosecution of Al Capone. However, it is full of good meat, and is worth reading by every lawyer, every young man or woman who thinks of taking up the law as a profession, and every layman either interested in the law as a mode of thought or concerned with writing clear precise prose.

Until you read this anthology or something like it, you can scarcely imagine (unless you are a trained lawyer) how many different types of legal prose there are, and how vivifying their variety can be. That is, of course, quite apart from the mere formulae of laws and contracts and other instruments, which are meant to be precise but could almost be replaced by a series of conventional symbols like signs in mathematical logic.

First, there are the written opinions given by judges. These must be exact and definite; but they can also be elegant, and they ought to be convincing. Some of the best of them are almost speeches of persuasion meant to be heard by the inner ear. Some of the worst are masterpieces of obfuscation: in this volume Justice Frankfurter says that the voluble opinions of Chief Justice Edward Douglass White were 'models of how not to write a legal opinion. He made three words grow, usually, where there was room for only one.' All opinions are difficult to write. As Cardozo put it, 'Write an opinion, and read it a few years later when it is dissected in the briefs of counsel. You will learn . . . the limitations of the power of speech, or, if not those of speech in general, at all events [those of] your own.' Cardozo himself cites with unfeigned admiration part of an opinion by Lord Blackburn on a fraudulent stock market offering:

> If with intent to lead the plaintiff to act upon it, they put forth a statement which they know may bear two meanings, one of which is false to their knowledge, and thereby the plaintiff, putting that meaning on it, is misled, I do not think they can escape by saying he ought to have put the other. If they palter with him in a double sense,* it may be that they lie like truth, but I think they lie, and it is a fraud.

Cardozo also quotes a splendid sentence from an opinion written by Oliver Wendell Holmes, a sentence that ought to be inscribed in every school, college, and city hall today:

> A strong public desire to improve the public condition is not enough to warrant achieving the desire by a shorter cut than the constitutional way of paying for the change.

Mr. Davenport's anthology also gives in its complete form the opinion of the late Judge John Woolsey pronouncing Joyce's *Ulysses* to be emetic but not aphrodisiac: this is a piece of

---

* As an additional touch of elegance here, note the quotation from Macbeth's contemptuous dismissal of the witches,
those juggling fiends,
Who palter with us in a double sense.

writing to which that rare word of praise could justly be applied, 'luminous.'

There is also much good prose and good sense in certain essays and addresses written by lawyers for their colleagues and pupils, in order to explain the law as a profession, the law as a life's work, and the law as a major activity of society. The book opens with an admirably clear and frank discussion of a very awkward problem, the morality of the lawyer. Mr. Charles Curtis asks whether a lawyer may ever legitimately tell a lie for the sake of his client, or keep silence when he hears others (even the judge) making statements which may benefit his client but which he knows to be untrue. Mr. Curtis has been concerned with this question before. In 1957 he published *A Commonplace Book* (Simon & Schuster, New York), a stimulating collection of short quotations from books, illuminated by his own comments and occasionally by his own silence. One of these is a quotation from Trollope's *Orley Farm*: 'No amount of eloquence will make an English lawyer think that loyalty to truth should come before loyalty to his client.' Another is a brief passage from an English novel unknown to me, *Friends at Court*, by Henry Cecil.

> Mr. Glacier met Roger [the barrister] and Mr. Plumb in the Law Courts and thanked them for their help. 'But what a lot of time and money,' he said, 'it has cost to arrive at the truth.'
>
> 'The truth?' said Roger. 'No one in Court said anything about arriving at the truth.'

By way of comment on this Mr. Curtis quotes Professor Edmund M. Morgan of Vanderbilt University:

> A law suit is not a scientific investigation for the discovery of truth, but a proceeding to determine the basis for, and to arrive at a settlement of, a dispute between litigants.

And he adds that

> truth, that is, the true facts, is only an ingredient of justice, which is something larger than truth and far more difficult to attain.

Above discussions of these hard questions lie expositions of
the great principles which are the essence of law itself. In this
sphere few have ever excelled the great American jurists Oliver
Wendell Holmes and Learned Hand. It is Learned Hand who
writes:

> A law is . . . a prophecy . . . because it attempts to forecast
> what will be its effects, whom it will benefit and in what ways;
> on whom its impact will prove a burden; how much friction and
> discontent will arise from the adjustments that conformity to
> it will require; how completely it can be enforced; what enforce-
> ment will cost; how far it will interfere with other projects or
> existing activities; and, in general, the whole manifold of its
> indirect consequences.

When you say, 'There ought to be a law—!' do you ever think
of all these corollaries? And do they not explain many of the
most important problems of our own society—for instance,
the failure of the Eighteenth Amendment to the Constitution
of the United States, and current difficulties in enforcing the
Fourteenth and Fifteenth Amendments?

Law is much concerned with the conflict of opinions; and
it is moving to see, in this anthology, cheek by jowl with each
other, the opinion of a notable judge and the opinion of a
notable lawbreaker. Henry Thoreau in his essay on Civil
Disobedience, tells how he was put in jail for refusing to pay
poll tax. It was, he says, perfectly ridiculous of the state to act
in this way toward him, since it could imprison his body but
not his thought; and he goes on to emit the noble paradox:
'I do not hear of *men* being *forced* to live this way or that by
masses of men.' Did Thoreau really believe his own words?
This was 1849, when slavery still existed in the United States,
most of the Russians were still serfs, and the Turks were tyran-
nizing southeastern Europe. But apart from the question of
fact, consider the principle, as stated by Mr. Justice Holmes:
'You can see very plainly that a bad man has as much reason
as a good one for wishing to avoid an encounter with the public force, and therefore you can see the practical importance
of the distinction between morality and law. A man who cares

nothing for an ethical rule which is believed and practiced by his neighbors is likely nevertheless to care a good deal to avoid being made to pay money, and will want to keep out of jail if he can.'

In the literature of the law there are some magnificent examples of apparently irreconcilable conflicting opinions. This book contains one set of such opinions which was written as a pure fantasy—unreal in fact, yet demonstrating with classical purity some of the fundamental principles of law and government: it is by Professor Lon Fuller of Harvard, whose speciality is jurisprudence. The case supposed to be at issue is placed in the far distant future. The facts are clear, and are not disputed. Five men were trapped by the collapse of the mouth of a cave which they had been exploring. After three weeks they were starving to death. Making the decision by throwing dice, four of them killed the fifth and ate his body. After being rescued, they were tried for murder and found guilty. They appealed. Now the five members of the court of appeals give their divergent opinions. I shall not spoil this brilliant intellectual exercise by attempting to summarize it; but I must say that, intelligently produced, it would make a powerful drama for radio or television: for, although the judges are fictional, their diverse and yet typical characters come out very clearly in their words and in the ethos of their speeches.

Personalities are an important element in the administration of the law, although it is often imagined, ideally, to be quite impersonal. Mr. Davenport devotes two entire sections of his anthology to personalities: first, to biographical and autobiographical sketches of eminent lawyers and judges— Lincoln, Holmes, Marshall, and others (there is a fascinating set of portraits of five Chief Justices of the Supreme Court by Felix Frankfurter, who knew them all); and second, to personal exchanges in court, where—as at the trial of Oscar Wilde —everything may depend on the strength of the opposing characters, and the power of the prosecuting lawyer to undermine and finally to overthrow a clever, self-possessed, and conscienceless criminal. The strangest of all these court scenes is the conclusion of the trial of Frederick Seddon for poisoning. The accused was found guilty. Justice Bucknill was about to pronounce sentence of death, when Seddon made a short speech reminding the judge that they were both Freemasons. With the guilty prisoner in the dock before him, with the black cap actually upon his head, the judge broke down; and for a minute nothing could be heard but the ticking of the courtroom clock and the loud sobs of the judge who was torn between his oath of brotherhood and his sense of justice.

There is much more in this fine collection. There are some quotations from works of fiction, which are good enough in themselves but might have been omitted, particularly since the book concludes with a useful list of one hundred novels concerning the law. There are several penetrating technical studies, especially on that most difficult and sensitive art, the examination and cross-examination of witnesses. And there is a small but choice selection of essays on the relation between law and language. A quotation from Walter Scott (himself both a lawyer and an author) given in one of them is the best explanation of the purpose of this anthology:

'These,' said [the lawyer] Pleydell, showing his fine collection of classical authors, 'are my tools of trade. A lawyer without history or literature is a mechanic, a mere working mason; if he possesses some knowledge of these he may venture to call himself an architect.'

The Written Past:
Loss, Destruction, and Survival

THE OTHER DAY I met a friend of mine, an author who is successful and ambitious. Asking him about his work, I found him profoundly depressed. In a few years, he said somberly, there won't be any books: they will all be destroyed, and there will be nobody left to read them. It is difficult to argue with anyone who thinks he foresees the imminent end of civilization, but I tried to console him. Mankind has endeavored to kill itself off before this, and its books have nearly all been destroyed. Yet as long as there was someone who wanted to read, books and records have been saved.

It still strikes me with amazement when I open a book of speeches by Demosthenes and begin to hear the voice, the very syllables and cadences, of a man who died some twenty-three centuries ago. Surely it is almost miraculous that we can take up the *Aeneid* of Vergil, reproduced by machinery that would have astounded Vergil, on a material he had never seen, in a format he could scarcely have imagined, and after two millennia find that, undimmed by time and change, his poetry still sings, his mystical visions still transport us as they did his first readers, and the subtleties of his poetic architecture still hold secrets only half discovered.

The miracle of the preservation of thought through marks on a smooth surface is commemorated every week by one of the most impressive little religious ceremonies in the world. Every Sabbath in every Jewish synagogue, a handwritten copy of the Torah, the first five books of the Bible, is taken out of its palace. After a reading, the book is carried through the congregation before it is returned to the ark, and every pious Jew kisses it. It is always handwritten with a quill pen. It is always in the form of a parchment roll. Its text is always exactly the same as that of its predecessor, from which it was copied: the very letters are counted so that they may never vary by a jot, any more than the law of God Almighty can vary. By doing homage to the Book in this way, the Jews express their devotion to the name of the Creator contained in the Torah; but they also, by implication, express reverence for one of man's greatest inventions, the written book.

The Jews, like the Moslems, have always carried their sacred writings with them: the Book and the people have sustained each other. But among the Greek and Latin classics there are no sacred books of this kind; the nations for whom they were composed have disappeared; the very languages in which their authors thought and spoke have assumed new shapes and sounds—remote, although not wholly different, from the original tongues. How have the great books of the Greek and Latin past survived through so many centuries?

First, we must sadly admit that many, very many, of them have been lost. In Greece and the Greek-speaking world, and later in the Roman world, there were many libraries and many hundreds of thousands of books. Literacy was more widespread in the second century of our era than it was in the eighteenth. The walls of Pompeii, covered with public announcements and private scribbles in three languages (Latin, Greek, and Oscan), show how natural and commonplace was the use of writing. Nearly all townsfolk could read, free men and slaves alike. Only on the farms and ranches were many people illiterate. In Egypt today, excavators dig up large private book collections in ancient Greek, buried under the sand near villages where today few of the fellahin own a single book, or could read it if they did.

While some authors of antiquity (such as Vergil) composed only a few books—to which they gave all their life's energy— there were many who produced an amazing quantity of work. The comedian Aristophanes left fifty-four plays. Aeschylus, first of the great tragic dramatists, wrote at least eighty. Livy's history of Rome ran into one hundred and forty-two volumes; and such polygraphs were not exceptional. Yet of many of the most famous authors, we have only a few scanty though precious relics. It is as though we had the titles of all Shakespeare's plays, with some fragments quoted from most of them, but possessed complete only *Hamlet, Henry V, A Midsummer-Night's Dream,* and *As You Like It.* Of Aristophanes' half a hundred comedies, we have just eleven. Of Aeschylus' fourscore plays, only seven survive. We possess a summary of virtually all of Livy's Roman history, so that we know what he covered in each volume; but only thirty-five of his one hundred and forty-two volumes remain.

And while these great writers have survived, in however meager a proportion, dozens of others have vanished almost without a trace. Aristophanes was only one of a large school of competing comic dramatists. From quotations and allusions we know the names of about a hundred and seventy poets of the 'Old Comedy' with 1,483 titles of their plays. Except Aristophanes, not one survives. Where is his great rival, boozy old Cratinus? Where is the energetic Eupolis, whom Horace linked with the other two in a gay triad? Gone: except for a few jokes, some famous passages preserved in quotation, and many play titles. It is delightful to look through the titles, and read the quotations, and reflect how much fun the Athenians had in the fifth century before Christ; but it is painful to remember how much of it has disappeared.

Yet not all.

It would scarcely be worth studying classical literature if it were a heap of insignificant debris. It is not. It is like a city which has been bombed and shelled and partially burned, so that whole sections are in ruins and some streets with their houses and palaces are irrecoverable; but at its heart many of the most important and noble public buildings stand unscathed, full of statues and pictures and memories, while others, although damaged, retain a magnificent wing or a lofty tower. The two epics of Homer (or of the two Homers?) are safe. All Vergil's poetry is intact. The works of Plato are complete, and have even acquired some 'Platonic' forgeries in the meantime. All that Horace ever published, we have. We can read virtually all of Lucretius and Terence and Catullus in Latin, virtually all of Demosthenes and Thucydides and Herodotus in Greek. Besides these, we have the complete works of a number of authors who, although not 'classics,' i.e. first class, either in their time or now, are amusing, shocking, informative, or creatively eccentric. We do not have too many of the classical books from Greece and Rome, but we have many of the best.

They were written down between 800 B.C. and A.D. 450. They were first printed and disseminated to modern readers between A.D. 1450 and A.D. 1550. Once printed, they were likely to survive: because they were so good, or because there were now so many copies of them: duplication helps preservation. But between the distant centuries when the classics were composed and the comparatively recent era when they were reproduced by men with machines, grave obstacles and recurrent perils often threatened to obliterate them.

First and chiefest came the danger that haunts us all. Anyone born since 1900 has grown up with it always in his mind. It is the great destroyer, the waster, the terrible simplifier, the barbarizer: war. It is always more violent than anyone, even the warrior, expects. It is capricious. In the harsh conflict of human wills, deliberation and choice and purposive action are often sacrificed to sheer destructive energy. When the Crusaders were sacking Constantinople in 1204, a drunken soldier was seen tearing up the sacred books of the Hagia Sophia church.

King Matthias Corvinus of Hungary (1440–90) collected a magnificent library of manuscripts of the classics, some written for him by Italian calligraphers and some bought by his agents in Greece and Asia Minor. Part of this library was captured by the Turks in 1541 during their advance into central Europe; some specimens were sent back to Istanbul. The others were left in storage, damaged by fire and carelessness, recaptured in 1688 when the Turks were beaten, and divided up among the conquerors. And yet a few manuscripts from the original library still remained together—at least until the end of the nineteenth century—in the Grand Seraglio at Istanbul, after the drums and tramplings of four centuries.

The most famous of all libraries in ancient times was the collection at Alexandria, the Greek city in Egypt. In the western world it was the first large public library; it was the cradle of literary scholarship and of responsible publishing; it was part of the earliest university. In one form or another it seems to have lived for seven hundred years, although many doubtful legends have grown up around it. Its final destruction is wrapped in silence almost total. It was founded as part of the Shrine of the Muses (= Museum) by Ptolemy I, Alexander the Great's marshal and his successor as king of Egypt. Its administrators strove to have the best, the most authoritative, copies of all important books collated and catalogued with the utmost care. After two hundred and fifty years, it was burned during Julius Caesar's struggle to displace the twelfth Ptolemy and to set up his mistress Cleopatra as monarch of Egypt. Then Mark Antony, who succeeded Caesar both as de facto ruler of Egypt and as Cleopatra's lover, gave her as a replacement two hundred thousand books from the rival library of Pergamum in Asia Minor (it sounds just like Napoleon filching manuscripts from the Vatican Library). These were stored in the sanctuary of Serapis, and survived as a library until the empire went Christian. Pagan sanctuaries were turned into churches; Christians and pagans fought a cultural and religious war in the streets; a shrine of the pagan deity Serapis filled with books containing pagan poetry and learning could scarcely hope to survive the revolution. By A.D. 414 the Christian historian Orosius wrote that the stacks of the great library 'were emptied by our own men in our own time.' If anything survived for the Moslem Caliph Omar to condemn as fuel to heat the public baths in A.D. 640 (according to a late legend), it was only a group of departmental libraries.

In an even more turbulent city, the imperial library of Constantinople had still more brutal adventures. Its founder, the emperor Constantine, intended it to contain both Christian and pagan works: his city was the New Rome, and would have the best of both worlds. Its administrators collected many treasures of art and literature. Revolt, civil strife, and the turmoils of invasion struck the library again and again, but it was constantly restored by the Greek passion for culture. A rebellion and a fire in the fifth century A.D. destroyed it, with over a hundred thousand books—including one monstrous curio, a copy of Homer's epics written in gold letters on a snake's gut one hundred and twenty feet long. In the same blaze perished three of the most famous Greek statues. Rebuilt, refilled, reopened, the library was closed again for almost a century during the religious conflict within the Eastern Orthodox Church over the worship of images and holy pictures. Later it was burned and looted, at least in part, by the Fourth Crusaders in 1203–4. Restored once again, it was still in existence when Constantinople fell to the Turks in 1453. The Archbishop of Kiev, who witnessed the assault and capture, said that more than 120,000 books were destroyed. And yet many precious manuscripts survived in private collections. Lost in the outbuildings or substructures of some old mosque, deserted church, or disused barracks, there still may lie, in sealed jars or dust-covered chests, priceless relics of the Greek and Roman past, more precious (at least to us) than the Hebrew manuscripts found not long ago in the Genizah, or dead-storage room, of a synagogue near Cairo. One of our foundations, which seem to find it difficult to spend all their money, might make its name world-famous by financing a successful document-hunt in the chief cities of the former Ottoman Empire.

The invading barbarians from the north and east, after many attacks, at last split the Greco-Roman world into two parts, one eastern, the other western. In the West, those who were the heirs of the Roman Empire spoke Latin, and tried to teach it to their conquerors. In the East, the language was Greek. For some centuries the civilized Mediterranean world had been bilingual by practice and by sympathy; but from A.D. 500 or so, for a good five or six centuries, not many in the western world could speak or read Greek, and few in the East could speak or write Latin. Neither Pope Vigilius (537–555) nor Pope Gregory the Great (590–604) knew any Greek, although both of them had served as papal envoys in Constantinople. True, the Greek-speaking Eastern church was always in touch with the Latin-speaking Roman Catholic church, although doctrinal disputes often made their relations awkward; Greek Constantinople had strong military and political claims to suzerainty over Italy and exercised them when it could; and there were Greek monasteries (some of them with fine libraries) in the heel of Italy.* But among western Europeans generally, whose mother tongue was a Gaelic or Germanic or Latin-derived patois and who used Latin as the language of learning, the knowledge of Greek was—until the twelfth century—confined to a few lonely geniuses such as John Scotus Eriugena. For example, in A.D. 947–48 the Byzantine emperor made a diplomatic gesture to the magnificent Caliph Abd-al-Rahman III, who ruled southern Spain. He sent ambassadors to Cordova, where they received a brilliant welcome. Among the gifts they brought was a beautiful Greek book on medicine, probably Dioscorides' manual of medicinal plants. But none of the Caliph's Arab subjects knew Greek, and no Christian could be found in his dominions who knew

* For a learned and lucid description of the many links between Byzantium and the West during the Dark and Middle Ages, see K. M. Setton, 'The Byzantine Background to the Italian Renaissance,' *Proceedings of the American Philosophical Society* 100 (1956), 1–76.

Greek, so that the manuscript remained in his library untranslated. Not a single Greek manuscript which has come down to us was copied during those centuries in the Western World. The tradition of reading, understanding, teaching, explaining, and transmitting the Greek tongue—even although it was the language in which the Gospels and the Acts and the Epistles were written—virtually died out for six hundred years. Really ancient Greek manuscripts are very rare in the West; really ancient Latin manuscripts are very rare in the East. Therefore the important books had less chance of surviving. The invasions and wars of the Dark Age had split and fragmented Greco-Roman civilization and culture.

The second danger that confronted the Greek and Roman classics was not violent destruction, but peaceful change. Nowadays it is very difficult to purchase the piano works of Alexander Scriabin or to find scores of the music of Lully. Scriabin died in 1915, and since then most of his compositions have been allowed to go out of print. Much of Lully still remains in manuscript, unpublished, unperformed, unknown. In the same way, those books which ceased to interest the general Greek and Roman reading public ceased to be copied, and were therefore not transmitted through the generations. Thus, after Vergil's *Aeneid* was published, it was accepted at once as *the* great epic poem in the Latin language. It was read for pleasure, it was learned at school, it was studied and imitated and copied. Naturally it displaced all earlier epic poems in Latin, even the *Annals* of Vergil's most eminent predecessor, Ennius. For some time thereafter, Ennius was respected, but little read. Then he was forgotten. His poem vanished. Nothing is left of it now, except fragments quoted by Roman scholars to illustrate oddities of archaic style or to show how Vergil adapted and improved them: five hundred and fifty lines in all, no fragment larger than a page. Only four poets of the early Roman republic have survived entire, or almost entire: Lucretius, the philosophical missionary; the brilliant and versatile Catullus; and the comic playwrights Plautus and

Terence. All the others were neglected and eventually disappeared. No doubt some of them were trivial and others crude; yet there were several masterful writers among them—such as the satirist Lucilius—and several lively works in minor genres, such as the Atellan farce, which we should dearly love to be able to read.

There was another habit of taste that tended to make books obsolete in the ancient world: a habit which still persists among us. This was sheer laziness. Partly to cater to lazy adult readers and partly to create handy texts for use in schools, editors in later Greece and later Rome reduced the complete works of many distinguished authors to small neat anthologies, assimilable with little effort and easily portable. Thus, out of the eighty-odd plays by Aeschylus, the Seven Best were selected; out of more than a hundred by Sophocles, the Seven Best—or, if not the seven best, then the Seven Standard most suitable for studying. Soon fewer and fewer readers tackled the complete works; these selections ousted them; and they vanished. With Euripides we are luckier because we also have part of one set of Complete Works. But aside from these three playwrights (and aside from fragments recently found on papyri in Egypt) we have no Greek tragedies at all. Many of the lost books of Greece and Rome were not destroyed. They were allowed to slip into oblivion.

There were two further hazards that the classics had to survive before they could reach the age of printing. One was a change of format, the other was a change of script. The two changes sound unimportant, but they drastically affected our intellectual history.

Suppose that in 1980 all our publishers decided to give up publishing books in their present form, and began to issue them only on microfilm; and suppose that we all accepted this, rearranging our homes around microfilm readers and microfilm storage cabinets. In some ways it would be extremely convenient. All the important old books and all the standard

books would be transferred to microfilm: the Bible, the en-
cyclopaedias, the law books, the scientific and medical and
technical manuals; and Shakespeare, Milton, Pope, Shelley,
Keats . . . but who else? At once the question becomes complex. Should Langland's Piers Plowman be microfilmed, which
nobody reads except specialists? and Cowley's epic on King
David, which nobody reads at all? The change in the format
of books has created a selective grid, through which any book
in the English language must pass if it is to reach the post-
microfilm future. The books which do not pass it, without
being reproduced, will remain in storage for a while, will be
forgotten, and in a few generations will fall into dust or be
pulped. In our own lifetime some of us have seen a similar set
of changes in recorded music: first the old phonograph cylin-
ders, then the heavy 78 rpm discs (I still have the splendid
Glyndebourne *Figaro* on 78 rpm records in the basement), then
the lighter and more durable 33 rpm discs, and now tape,
which is threatening to make all discs obsolete.

Suppose also that we were to introduce a new phonetic
alphabet in 1980. All the important books would have to be
transcribed into the new simplifaid speliŋ. Every new book
published would be printed in simplifaid speliŋ. Within a
couple of generations nobody, except a few experts and professionals, would be able to read the older script. Therefore all
the books that remained in our present spelling would be
neglected, difficult, remote. Soon they would be unread, and
would decay into limbo.

Now, changes similar to these actually took place during the
centuries after the Greek and Latin classics were composed and
while they were being transmitted to us. The format and material of books changed. The scripts in which books were
written changed. Any book which did not survive the changes
was very likely to perish.

First, format. In the flourishing days of Greece and Rome
nearly all books were written on long narrow strips of papyrus,
in parallel columns arranged from left to right. When not
being read, the strip was rolled up around a central rod, and

(although its material was thinner and its dimensions generally smaller) looked something like the scrolls of the law kept in Jewish synagogues today. Although brittle, papyrus is quite a good material for books: if it does not get damp, it will remain firm and legible for a long time. The poem, *The Persians,* by Timotheus can easily be read today although it was written on papyrus three hundred years before the birth of Jesus.

However, the specially treated leather called parchment (named after Pergamum in western Asia Minor, where it was perfected about 170 B.C.) is far more durable. Also, since it has a finer, smoother surface than papyrus, it will take smaller and clearer letters. Furthermore, the book form which has separate pages sewn together at one edge is far easier to use than the long continuous strip which must be laboriously unrolled in order to find and read any single column of writing.

Therefore the Greeks and Romans gradually stopped using papyrus and began to use parchment. And they gradually stopped using the roll format and changed to the book form with separate pages, whose correct name is *codex.* The change-over was not at first encouraged by the government; it was spontaneous, and took quite a long time. But the Roman lawyers liked the codex shape because it was so easy to consult: two conflicting laws, for instance, could be located on pages 18 and 47 and scanned at the same time if the pages were held open. The Christians, who wished to read parallel passages in the four different Gospel narratives, and to compare the prophecies of the Old Testament with their fulfillments in the New Testament, came to prefer the large book which could be opened out flat. And scribes, both pagan and Christian, found that a parchment page would take graceful script and elaborate decorations far more readily than papyrus. The eminent British papyrologist C. H. Roberts suggests that the change in format was connected (as far as the Christians were concerned) with the first written versions of the life of Jesus. Saint Mark was the author of the earliest gospel. He wrote it in Rome, in the handy format of a parchment notebook with pages. This he took to Alexandria, and there (although they continued to use the cheap local material, papyrus) the early Christians grew accustomed to having their sacred writings in the form of a flat-paged book. After Christianity had become the official religion the emperor Constantine ordered fifty copies of the Bible for the churches of Constantinople, specifying that they should be written on parchment, that is, in the form of the book with pages.

By A.D. 400 the roll was obsolescent, whether in papyrus or in parchment. Any books that had not been recopied in the new format could survive only by exceptional good luck. Some Greek and Roman classics now lack their beginnings because the outside of the papyrus roll, with the first few columns of writing on it, had perished before it could be transcribed. Others are part of a once larger set, once written on several different rolls kept together in the same case but then mutilated when one or more rolls were lost. Aristotle's *Poetics* was a two-volume work, one part dealing with tragedy and the second with comedy; but the second was lost before it could be transcribed into the codex form, and now it will never be known unless it turns up in an Egyptian papyrus.

All Greek and Roman books were of course written by hand. Now, great changes took place in Greek and Roman script between the fourth and the eighth centuries of the Christian era. At the height of classical times, the Greeks wrote most of their books in what we call capital letters, with little punctuation and often with no spaces between words. The Romans, after hesitating for some time, followed them. However, after many experiments both in the Greek world of Eastern Europe and Asia Minor and Egypt, and in the Roman West, a radical change to a script much more like our own was carried through: a script in which the words are separated from one another and most of the letters are unemphatic, curved, and small (hence called 'minuscule') while only the important letters beginning sentences, lines of verse, and proper names are capitals, or majuscules.

Thereafter all the books written like this

ARMAVIRVMQVECANOTROIAEQVIPRIMVSABORIS

had to be rewritten in the newfangled script, with its word divisions and assertive capitals:

Arma uirumque cano, Troiae qui primus ab oris

But the work of transcription from one form of writing to another was specialized and difficult. A scribe who was accustomed to reading and writing

Italiam fato profugus Lauinaque uenit

would sometimes make mistakes in reading and transcribing

ITALIAMFATOPROFVGVSLAVINAQVEVENIT.

Therefore when a scholar today sits down to edit or analyze a Greek or Roman book, one of his most important tasks is to reconstruct the various phases of copying and recopying through which it has been transmitted, and to determine just what types of error were liable to be introduced at each transition. When a sentence in a Greek or Roman book looks doubtful or senseless, one of the first devices that scholars try is to write it out INTHEOLDVNDIVIDEDCAPITALS, and then see whether the misreading of one or two letters, or the failure to separate the words correctly, led to the error.

One amusing mistake of this kind is a matter of word separation. At the vulgar millionaire's dinner party in Petronius' *Satyrica* the guests are discussing a friend who has just died. 'Ah, he had a good life,' they say, 'the abbot isolated him, and he died a millionaire.' There were no abbots in the days of Petronius, and anyhow the phrase about the abbot is meaningless. In majuscules the phrase reads ABBASSECREVIT. Divide the words differently, drop one superfluous letter, and you get *ab asse creuit,* 'he started with a nickel.'

These particular ordeals—the transference of books from one type of script to another and from one format to another —were mechanical hazards to the survival of classical literature. There was another, far more destructive, which depended on the will of men. This was censorship. In pagan Greece we hear very little of censorship: although the emissaries of Antipater brought Demosthenes to his death, they made no effort to destroy his speeches. The emperors of Rome were more touchy. Even the clement Augustus felt himself compelled to exile the orator Cassius Severus and to burn his books, which were full of personal attacks on the Roman aristocracy and the imperial court. Labienus' history of the civil war, which treated Julius Caesar as a traitor to the republic, was destroyed; and, rather than survive his work, the historian killed himself. Although they were considered an antisocial group by the authorities, the Christians were at first not held to possess any books worth destroying. But in the last of the pagan persecutions (A.D. 303) Diocletian ordered the Scriptures to be burned. That persecution, however, soon ended; and we know of no Christian books which were irrevocably lost in it.

A generation later the Christians came to power. Soon they were destroying the books of the pagans. Because of this policy, although we possess a good deal of Christian propaganda from the early centuries, no pagan counterpropaganda is preserved intact. For instance, the great Neo-Platonic philosopher Porphyry wrote a destructive analysis of the Christian doctrine and the Christian Scriptures in fifteen volumes. It was burned by imperial order, and only a few fragments (quoted by his Christian opponents) now remain. In the Christian church there was always a sharp division between those who thought all pagan literature vicious and dangerous and would gladly have consigned it to annihilation, and those who believed that much of it was potentially good, so that under proper guidance it could be used for teaching and study. Christians of the first type were responsible for much wholesale abolition of the Greek and Roman classics. Christians of the second type selected most of the books we now possess, copied them, taught them in schools, and so preserved them for the age of printing. Of the many thousands of plays enjoyed by Greeks and

Romans, all were allowed to rot away except eighty-one: forty-three tragedies (thirty-three Greek and ten Roman) and thirty-eight comedies (eleven Greek and twenty-seven Roman). Three more Greek comedies and large fragments of others have been found in the last seventy years: these were not, however, transmitted through the ages by copying, but preserved as though in a time capsule. Drama was particularly repellent to the early Christians, for many reasons. They banned plays. The professional theater ceased to exist: for a thousand years men forgot the full power and meaning of drama, and the few plays that were permitted to survive were preserved mainly as models of fine Greek and Latin poetic and conversational style. The pagan Greeks and Romans also loved lyric poetry, which embodies or evokes song and the dance. Many of their lyric poems were loving glorifications of carnal experience: an invitation to drink ('the snow is deep outside and life is short') or rapturous desire for a beautiful body ('my eyes dazzle, a delicate flame runs through my limbs'). Others again were hymns to pagan deities. Such poems were particularly hateful to devout Christians, so that the vast majority of them were allowed to perish. In Latin we have four books of songs by Horace and half a book by Catullus and a few other trifles. In Greek almost all nondramatic lyric poetry has vanished (or had vanished until the recent discoveries began): only Pindar survived in any large quantity, and only his Victory Odes. The rest disappeared, and even the Victory Odes came through the Dark Age in one manuscript alone.

There was one curious way of survival for classical books, though it led through apparent destruction. For the sake of economy, scribes used to scrape or wash off the ink from a surface on which a book had already been written, and inscribe another book upon it. This could be done with papyrus, but it was both easier and more profitable with parchment, which is tougher. Often it was a pagan book which was erased. The Bible or a work of Christian doctrine was written on the palimpsest, or cleaned-off, pages. Yet traces of the old writing would still remain faintly legible underneath. For instance:

one of the best books by Cicero was his dialogue *On the State,* in which he discussed the rival claims of democracy, aristocracy, monarchy, and a mixed constitution in which the powers would balance one another. It was much admired and long read; but during the Dark Age it vanished. Some medieval writers quote *On the State* as though they had actually handled a copy; but such citations are very flimsy evidence, for they might be secondhand or thirdhand. The great book hunters of the Renaissance were never able to find a copy, although it was on their list of the Most Wanted Books. However, in 1819 Angelo Mai, an expert in detecting old books beneath later books on a palimpsest surface, was appointed head of the Vatican Library. There he discovered a commentary on the Psalms by St. Augustine, which had been written in the letters of the late seventh century over a manuscript of Cicero's *On the State* inscribed in the taller capitals of an earlier era. Cicero's words could still be read, and Father Mai published them in 1822. The book was incomplete, but at least a quarter of it was there. How many libraries still contain forgotten copies of forgotten works of doctrine, beneath which there sleep important classical masterpieces?

If you wish information to survive for many centuries, cut it on stone or bake it in clay; you can even paint it, if the surface is durable and protected from weather. Do not try casting it in metal, for someone will almost certainly melt it down.

The emperor Augustus wrote his own autobiography, listing his chief honors, benefactions, victories, and other exploits. It was deposited at the Home Hearth of Rome, with the Vestal Virgins, and a version of it in bronze was set upon his mausoleum in Rome. Both the original and the metal transcript are gone. But a stone-carved copy was found in 1555 on the walls of a mosque in Ankara (formerly the temple of Rome and Augustus); and since then, two more copies, fragmentary but helpful, have turned up in southern Turkey. Only through these bits of stone do we know what one of the greatest rulers in history considered to be his major achievements.

Two hundred years after Augustus, another public bene-factor (on a smaller scale) went to a stonecutter with a document to be perpetuated. He was an elderly gentleman who lived in the small Greek-speaking city of Oenoanda in Lycia. Now it is a lonely heap of ruins in Turkey; then it was prosperous, civilized, but (the old gentleman thought) not quite happy enough. He was a devoted adherent of Epicurus. Epicurus had taught him that the blessed gods have no interest in this troublesome little earth; that terrifying phenomena such as illness and earthquakes and comets are all explicable, not through divine malevolence, but through the processes of nature; and that the duty of man is to cultivate his garden, keep calm and quiet, and be happy. Old Diogenes, as he was called, had had a heart attack. He determined to use some of his money and energy in showing his fellow citizens and their descendants the road to happiness. So he had a huge inscription cut and set up in the central square of the little city, explaining the chief tenets of the Epicurean doctrine. All the voluminous works written by Epicurus himself have perished; we have nothing from his own hand except three letters and some fragments and apophthegms. But the inscription set up by Diogenes of Oenoanda, rediscovered by explorers and read by scholars in the nineteenth century, is one of the chief witnesses to an important philosophical creed that is not yet dead.

Laws and state announcements were often displayed on stone, for publicity and permanence. One of the most important pieces of early Greek legislation is the code of Gortyn: it was incised on the curving stone wall of the odeum, and still stands, perfectly legible, among the ruins of that city in central Crete. The names of Roman magistrates (some of them unrecorded in history books) appear on tablets of stone; so do the sums paid by the subject-allies of Athens to her imperial treasury; and so, too, the last effort of Roman bureaucratic government, the gigantic edict of Diocletian, which fixed the price of virtually every object of commerce throughout the western world.

Records cut on stone or cast in metal were intended to survive as long as possible. Books passed from hand to hand and deliberately recopied were kept alive for many generations. But there is a huge and steadily growing assemblage of documents that were, in the eyes of those who wrote them and used them, quite temporary. Many of them were actually thrown out as rubbish. Yet by a combination of good luck and crazy chance they have survived and become valuable. These are things written on ephemeral substances more frail than stone or metal: papyrus, potsherds, and clay.

The records found in Mycenaean palaces and deciphered by Michael Ventris in 1952 were scratched on clay tablets that were not even fired: they became permanent only when the palaces were burned down. Almost all the papyri written in Greek or Roman lettering that we now possess were found literally in rubbish dumps or in the ruins of abandoned houses. Since it scarcely ever rains in Egypt, they lay quite comfortably under the dry earth until modern searchers dug them up. In a single day's work at Oxyrhynchus (120 miles south of Cairo) Bernard Grenfell and A. S. Hunt got thirty-six basketfuls of papyrus rolls out of one mound alone. They had apparently been discarded as worthless.

Some papyri, on the other hand, have been preserved because they were deliberately buried. One of the oldest Greek literary manuscripts, containing the only known copy of Timotheus' *Persians,* was rescued in this way. It is an absurdly bad poem (although interesting to literary connoisseurs); but someone prized it, for it was discovered in a leather pouch, laid carefully in the coffin of a Greek soldier buried in Egypt. A truly magnificent copy of Book II of Homer's *Iliad,* now in the Bodleian Library at Oxford, was set in a coffin as a sort of pillow under the head of a young woman, whose fine skull bones, small regular teeth, and black hair make us believe she was a beauty: certainly she was beloved. Other papyri again— mainly letters, accounts, and official documents, although in- cluding a few treasures of literature—were found glued to- gether or squeezed tight with water to make cheap mummy- cases molded to the shape of the corpse. Out of one of these cases came part of the lost tragedy *Antiope* by Euripides. Even stranger were the finds at Tebtunis, where Grenfell and Hunt came upon a cemetery of sacred crocodiles. One dead sacred crocodile is very much like another, and the job of excavating these saurian mummies soon palled. Eventually a workman lost his temper and smashed one of them to pieces. Then it ap- peared that the crocodiles were encased in molded papyri, while some even had papyrus rolls stuffed into their mouths 'and other cavities.' From such absurd hiding places do we re- cover the records of the past.

We have as yet no idea of the treasures that may be hidden in the dry ground of Egypt and the neighboring countries. The oldest Latin papyrus ever found and the oldest text of Cicero (part of his most famous set of speeches), written down not long after his death, is now in Leipzig. It was bought in 1926 from Egyptian dealers in the Fayum—and where did *they* get it? In 1945 a Gnostic library of thirteen volumes was found in Upper Egypt, containing among other things a Gospel in Coptic, adapted from a Christian work written in Greek, which evidently preserved some beautiful traditional sayings of Jesus. An Oxford expert once told me, with affliction in his eyes, that among a pile of papyrus fragments he was classifying he had found a book label bearing (in Greek) the simple words COMPLETE PINDAR. Eagerly but vainly I besought him to go back to the collection and look through it again. 'No,' he said gloomily, 'it isn't there. The Complete Pindar must have been on the site in Egypt. But perhaps the excavators missed it when they were digging, or it had already been found and lost again or burned or used for "medicine," or someone stole it and sold it in Cairo. It may turn up tomorrow. It may turn up in thirty years. It may be lying at the back of a drawer forgotten.'

Last, most absurd, and yet most natural of all the hazards through which the classics had to pass was the barrier of human stupidity. When barbarism comes to outweigh culture —through foreign invasion, or social revolution, or deliberately nurtured sloth and ignorance—works of art and literature are frequently taken to be 'useless' or 'irrelevant' and destroyed. In waves of materialism and in times of social unrest, everything old is apt to be judged obsolete. It is a barrier to 'progress'; or it is lumber; or it is a memento of the old corrupt regime; or it is reactionary; or at the lowest level it cannot be eaten or drunk or sold or bartered: away with it! Only a few years ago the brilliant commissioner of antiquities in modern Greece, Spyridon Marinatos, told a sad story of the second world war. A farmer in the western Peloponnesus was digging a new well. Twenty feet down he came upon a stone box. He broke in its lid. Inside there was a big object 'like a bundle,' dark in color and crumbly in texture. He thought he saw letters written on it. He informed the police, who notified the local director of antiquities; but for some time they could not get out to the man's farm. This was 1944–45 and the Communist squads were trying to control all the roads. When at last the director of antiquities was able to reach the place, the 'bundle' was gone. The farmer had thrown it on the dunghill 'because it was not a treasure': he saw that it was not gold or silver or studded with jewels. Anyhow, he added, 'it looked like dung, and it fell to pieces quite soon.' Others had seen 'many letters' on it, and said that, although fragile, it held together on the dunghill for some days. Clearly it was a book roll: papyrus, or more probably parchment; clearly it was very precious to the man who had buried it in the stone casket; certainly it would have been precious to us. But the farmer could not eat it or drink it, and he was too stupid to realize he might sell it; and it is gone.

Destruction of this kind, senseless destruction perpetrated

by ignorant people, happens constantly. 'Foreign' books are particularly liable to be destroyed. A Spanish historian named Pascual Gayangos, traveling through Spain in the 1830's, called on an acquaintance who had been appointed librarian for a noble family with a house in Valladolid. He found his friend rearranging the library: picking out useless old books, ripping off the vellum bindings, and burning the pages in a brazier. Gayangos picked up one of the books waiting to be annihilated. It was a collection of the plays of William Shakespeare, published in 1623—which means that it was the First Folio. An inscription showed that it had belonged to the subtle Spanish diplomat, Diego, Count Gondomar, who had been ambassador to Britain, and had been so close to King James I that the British public forced him to withdraw. Gayangos noticed that the margins were full of hand-written notes in seventeenth-century script. Perhaps these were the notes made by Gondomar or members of his staff on the plays of Shakespeare which they had seen performed. Agreed, Shakespeare's last important drama, *The Tempest,* was produced in 1611, before Count Gondomar took up his post. Yet surely the notes must have had something to do with Shakespeare's plays, as seen or read by an intelligent contemporary. (The only known drawing of an Elizabethan theater made in the Elizabethan age is a sketch of the Swan done by a Dutch visitor, Johann de Witt, in 1596.) Gayangos at that time did not know much about the history of English literature, or he would have tried to save the book. But later, when he got to England, he mentioned the matter to the great bibliophile Sir Thomas Phillipps, and was sent back to Valladolid post-haste. But the library was now neatly arranged and modernized; the First Folio had gone up in smoke.*

And so it has always been. Boccaccio, who was a great booklover and book finder, once visited the monastery of Monte Cassino. He was particularly keen to see the library, with all its treasures of ancient handwritten books. Very humbly he

* Mrs. Humphry Ward, *A Writer's Recollections* (Harper & Brothers, New York, 1918), vol. 2, pp. 100–104.

asked one of the monks for admission to it. 'Walk up,' said
the monk, 'it's open.' And so it was. It had no door; grass was
growing on the windowsills; the shelves, the benches, and the
books themselves were shrouded in thick dust. Some of them,
he found, had lost pages or even whole quires, others had their
margins cut off. Boccaccio wept. He cried tears of pity 'that the
work and study of so many illustrious geniuses should have
fallen into the hands of scoundrels.' After he left he asked a
monk how such valuable books could have been so odiously
mutilated. 'Well,' said the monk, 'some of the brothers wanted
to earn a few pennies: so they took a page here and there and
scraped off the writing and made little psalters to sell to
children; and from the page-margins they made gospels and
breviaries and sold them to women.'

When a bibliophile sees good books neglected and on the
road to destruction, his first impulse is to rescue them. Say not
'steal.' ' "Convey" the wise it call,' as Pistol says in *The Merry
Wives*. Some splendid books from Monte Cassino are now in
Florence. If it was not Boccaccio who 'conveyed' them there,
it was an even more fanatical booklover. Niccolò Niccoli, or
an agent of his and of the house of Medici. One of these manuscripts—bless the hand that saved it—is the only surviving
book that contains Tacitus' account of the reigns of Claudius
and Nero and of the civil war after Nero's suicide. It also
contains Apuleius' wonderful romance, *The Metamorphoses*
(sometimes mistakenly called *The Golden Ass*). This magnificent codex, written in the eleventh century, now rests peacefully in the Laurentian Library, above the cloister of the
Church of San Lorenzo. Near it is the only surviving manuscript of the first six books of another work by Tacitus, the
Annals, found in Germany. Had these two manuscripts not
been 'conveyed,' they might well have been cut up into amulets
or used to bind later books, and we should have lost one of the
greatest historians who ever wrote of absolutism and the
degeneracy of despotic power.

In 1844 a young Biblical scholar, Lobegott Friedrich Kon-
stantin von Tischendorf, visited the remote monastery of St.

Catherine on Mount Sinai. There he found a great old book reduced almost to the same state as those which Boccaccio discovered in Cassino. It was a manuscript of the Bible, written in beautiful clear script between A.D. 330 and 400, and carefully corrected at or near that time. The book is now one of the chief treasures of the British Museum, which bought it from the Soviet Government in 1933 for a hundred thousand pounds. But when Tischendorf first saw it, nobody had paid any attention to it for seven hundred years. The latest intelligent markings on it, comments by readers, had been made in the twelfth century. Since then it had been brutally neglected and was considered waste material. Fortunately, Tischendorf, whose speciality was the history of the Bible text, realized its value. He copied out some of it; and he got the monks to give him forty-three pages, which he took back to Europe and published. Fifteen years later, backed by funds from the Czar of Russia, he returned to the monastery. This time he obtained the remainder of the poor battered Bible. (Notable that the Jews and the Moslems are much more respectful to their Scriptures: the Koran must not be held below the waist-level, and a worn-out Torah must not be thrown away, but put into dead storage or ceremonially buried.) Tischendorf carried it away in triumph and published it. In exchange the monks received nine thousand rubles. They were disappointed: they said Tischendorf had promised to get them a steamboat.

Stupidity; censorship; changes in format and changes in taste; war; and of course the inevitable accidents, especially flood and fire—such are the hazards to the frail life of books. How did the great classics ever survive them?

Ultimately, they were kept alive by men who loved books and who knew that books are an essential element in civilization. The biography of one single written book might fill many chapters. The British Museum owns a copy of the Gospels in Latin, together with some writings of the early Christian Fathers. It has outlived storm and fire, savagery and greed. A big book, over a foot high, with two hundred and fifty-eight stout vellum pages, it was inscribed about A.D. 700 by Bishop Eadfrith in the monastery of Lindisfarne, now Holy Island, off the northern English coast. His successor, Bishop Aethelwald, bound it; and an anchorite living on the island made a protective case for it, which he decorated with metalwork and jewels. A century or so later the Danish pagans invaded England and settled down to conquer and dominate as much of it as they could. Their power grew and spread. In A.D. 875 the bishop of Lindisfarne was forced to flee westward, carrying the sacred relics of St. Cuthbert and this precious book. In a storm on the Irish Sea it was lost, but it was recovered at low tide as though by a miracle. For seven years it wandered in exile; it survived more moves and invasions, and returned to its home at Lindisfarne, where it was catalogued (the simple boring work of librarians, which they think so mechanical and which often proves to be so valuable!). Later it survived the Reformation and the Protestant sack of the monasteries, although it lost its jeweled case and its episcopal covers. Then, like many valuables during a revolution, it came into the possession of an official of the government: Robert Bowyer, Keeper of Records in the Tower of London. From him it was acquired by someone who really knew what it meant: a genuine collector, Sir Robert Cotton. From him, because of a political dispute, it was confiscated by the crown. Now it is in the British Museum among other treasures.

The most moving of all such stories, however, and most encouraging, would be the biography of an ancient book, not as a physical object, but as a work of art and thought. First we should have to describe its author, and the contemporary audience whom he meant to read or hear his work. Then, some time later, the Greek and Roman scholars who accepted it as a valuable achievement and edited it (as Joyce and Eliot are being edited today); and then, as the Dark Age set in, the far-sighted optimists (pagan like Symmachus, or Christian like Cassiodorus) who preserved it from obliteration; and, after them, the monks who saved it at least once more by recopying it in spite of the difficulties presented by its antique script;

later we should meet the fine-scented book hounds like
Petrarch and Boccaccio and Poggio and Aurispa who discovered it forgotten in a recess of an old library, and sometimes copied it out with their own hands; until finally, after
more perils than a displaced person and more sufferings than
a tormented prisoner, it emerged fifteen hundred or two thousand or twenty-five hundred years after its birth, to be copied
on a miraculous machine and multiplied through the work of
scholars and critics and publishers, and—incredibly—to reach
an audience who loved it as dearly as those who were present
at its origin. Even then the life of such a book is not over. It
will be read by Shakespeare. It will inspire a picture by
Rembrandt, a satirical parody by Pope, and a lyric by Keats.
It will be edited by Housman, distorted by Picasso, translated
into music by Ravel, and remain inexhaustibly vital, im-
mortally versatile, today and tomorrow and into a long future,
as long as there are a few men and women who can read, and
understand, and appreciate true greatness.

Index

Important references are shown by bold figures, thus: **123**. A subject not explicitly named, but referred to indirectly, is signalized by a figure in parentheses, thus: (123).

Bletch, Miss Ettie, of Cincinnati, 167
Blood, Sweat, and Tears, 229–30
Bloom, Leopold, 140–41, (142), (285);
  Molly, 285–86, 301
Bluebeard, 317
Boccaccio, 272, **361–62,** 363, 365
Bodleian Library, 358
Bonnie House o' Airlie, The, 275
Boer, 74
boor, 74–75
Boris, 211
Borrow, George, 62
botom, Marjory's, 158, (160)
Bowyer, Robert, 364
Boycott, Charles Cunningham, **102–3**
Boyse, 49
Brahms, 226
Brando, Marlon, 270
Brezhnev Award, 205
Bridge, 87, 88
Britain, *see* England *and* Great
  Britain
British Museum, 363–64
Brittany and the Bretons, 219
Brougham, Henry, 123–24
Brown, 88; John (not the fanatic),
  162
Brutus, M. Iunius, 202, 262, 263
Bryce, James, Viscount, 4
Buchanan, Mrs. Bessie A., **322–24,**
  327; James, 88
Bucknill, Mr. Justice, 340
bulb, 112
Bulgarian language, 75
Bulwer-Lytton, Edward, 294
Burgess, Gelett, 278
Burma, 189
Burns, Robert, 21 n., 26
Burroughs, William, 274
Burton, Sir Richard, 56, 280 n.,
  318 n.
Byron, 76, 166
Byzantium, 347; *and see* Constantinople

Caesar, *see* Augustus *and* Julius;
  Caesarism, 302
Cairo, 10, 11, 12, 15, 17, 39, 208, 346,
  358, 359

Calcutta University, 166
Calder, Alexander, 122
California, 147, 148, 149, 150, 151,
  153, 164, 167, 169, 179; University
  of, 258
Caligula, 198
Callot, Jacques, 277
Calvinism, 24, 46
Cambridge University, 4, 8, 73
Camden, Mrs. Harriet Parker, 325
Campbell, Mrs. Patrick, 106
Campidoglio, 199, (293)
Capistrano, 179
capitalism, 302
Capitol (Rome), (199), 293
Capone, Al, 335
Cardigan, James Thomas Brudenell,
  His Grace the Earl of, **105–7**
Cardozo, Benjamin, 336
Carl, 74
Carnegie, Andrew, 7 n.
Carroll, Lewis, (131), **274–77,** 278
Carthage, 254
Casanova, Giovanni Jacopo, 41, 128
Casca, P. Seruilius, 143 n.
Cassandra, 135
Cassiodorus, 364
Cassius Longinus, Gaius, 262, 263;
  Cassius Severus, 354
Catalans, 171, 176
Cathleen, 91
Catholic church, *see* Roman Catholic church
Cato, M. Porcius, 202
Catullus, 344, 348, 355
Cecil, Henry, 337
Celts, 89–90, 141; Celtic language,
  110; *and see* Gaelic
censorship, **354–55,** 363
Cervantes, 28; *Don Quixote,* 52,
  (130), 142
Champollion, Jean-François, 99
Chaplin, Charlie, 145, 172, 176
charisma, 31, 155
Charlemagne, 90
Charles, 74, 90; Charles I, 72;
  Charles II, 72, 233, (234), 235, 236,
  237, (240), 242
Chaucer, 70